# AMERICA

BRIEF FOURTH EDITION

STUDY GUIDE

Volume 2

# TINDALL and SHI
# AMERICA

## A NARRATIVE HISTORY

## STUDY GUIDE

VOLUME II / BRIEF FOURTH EDITION

**CHARLES W. EAGLES**
UNIVERSITY OF MISSISSIPPI

and

**THOMAS S. MORGAN**
Late of WINTHROP UNIVERSITY

W • W • NORTON & COMPANY • NEW YORK • LONDON

Copyright © 1997, 1993, 1989, 1984 by W. W. Norton & Company, Inc.
All Rights Reserved
Printed in the United States of America.

ISBN 0-393-97068-X

W. W. Norton & Company, Inc.
500 Fifth Avenue, New York, N. Y. 10110
W. W. Norton & Company Ltd.
10 Coptic Street, London WC1A 1PU

1 2 3 4 5 6 7 8 9 0

# CONTENTS

|  | Introduction | vii |
|---|---|---|
|  | Structure of this Study Guide | vii |
|  | Studying History | viii |
|  | How to Read a Textbook | ix |
|  | Acknowledgments | x |
| 17. | Reconstruction: North and South | 131 |
| 18. | New Frontiers: South and West | 144 |
| 19. | Big Business and Organized Labor | 154 |
| 20. | The Emergence of Modern America | 163 |
| 21. | Gilded Age Politics and Agrarian Revolt | 172 |
| 22. | The Course of Empire | 183 |
| 23. | Progressivism: Roosevelt, Taft, and Wilson | 190 |
| 24. | Wilson and the Great War | 198 |
| 25. | Society and Culture Between the Wars | 209 |
| 26. | Republican Resurgence and Decline, 1920–1932 | 217 |
| 27. | Franklin D. Roosevelt and the New Deal | 224 |
| 28. | From Isolation to Global War | 236 |
| 29. | The World at War | 246 |
| 30. | The Fair Deal and Containment | 255 |
| 31. | Through the Picture Window: Society and Culture, 1945–1960 | 265 |
| 32. | Conflict and Deadlock: The Eisenhower Years | 273 |
| 33. | New Frontiers: Kennedy and Johnson | 280 |
| 34. | Rebellion and Reaction in the Seventies | 287 |
| 35. | A New Gilded Age | 298 |
| 36. | Cultural Politics | 307 |

# INTRODUCTION

This *Study Guide* is designed to help you learn the important concepts in *America: A Narrative History,* Brief Fourth Edition, by George B. Tindall and David E. Shi. It is not intended as a replacement for the textbook, but as an aid to be used along with the text. When used conscientiously, this *Study Guide* will help you to understand the major themes in American history and to do well on quizzes based on your reading.

## STRUCTURE OF THIS STUDY GUIDE

Each chapter of the *Study Guide* contains the following sections:
Chapter Objectives
Chapter Outline
Key Items of Chronology
Terms to Master
Vocabulary Building
Exercises for Understanding:
   Multiple-Choice Questions
   True-False Questions
   Essay Questions
Document(s) or Reading(s)

The purpose of each of the sections, along with instructions for its use, is explained below.

## Chapter Objectives

For each chapter you will find about five objectives, or key concepts, on which you should focus your attention as you read. You should read the whole of each chapter, taking in details as well as major themes, but by keeping the chapter objectives in mind you will avoid getting bogged down and missing the key ideas.

## Chapter Outline

Skim this outline carefully before you begin reading a chapter. The outline provides a more detailed overview than do the objectives. Often headings in the outline are worded to suggest questions about the material. For example, "Duties of the King" and "Patterns of Colonization" raise the questions "What were the duties of the king?" and "What were the patterns of colonization?" Look for the answers to such questions as you read the text. This approach will help those of you who are new to reading history.

## Key Items of Chronology

Each chapter of this *Study Guide* will include a list of dates. You need not learn every date you encounter in the chapter, but if you learn the key ones listed here and any other dates emphasized by your instructor, you will have the sound chronological framework so important for understanding historical events.

Keep in mind that dates, while important, are not the sole subject matter of history. Seldom will any of the quizzes in this *Study Guide* ask for recall of dates. On the other hand, term papers and answers to essay questions should include important dates and show that you are familiar with the chronology of your subject.

**Terms to Master**

This section of the *Study Guide* gives you a list of important terms to study. (Remember, of course, that your instructor may emphasize additional terms that you should learn.) After reading each chapter, return to the list of terms and write a brief definition of each. If you cannot recall the term readily, turn to the relevant pages in the textbook and reread the discussion of the term. If you need or want to consult another source, go to the annotated bibliography at the end of the relevant chapter, or ask your instructor for suggestions.

**Vocabulary Building**

This is a section of the *Study Guide* that you may or may not need. If you do not know the meaning of the words or terms listed in Vocabulary Building, look them up in a dictionary before you begin reading a chapter. By looking up such words and then using them yourself, you will increase your vocabulary.

When the terms in Vocabulary Building are not readily found in the standard dictionary or when their use in your text lends them a special meaning, we have defined them for you. We've used the *American Heritage Dictionary*, Second College Edition, as a guide to determine which terms should be defined here for you.

**Exercises for Understanding**

You should reserve these exercises to use as a check on your reading after you study the chapter. The multiple-choice and true-false questions included here will test your recall and understanding of the facts in the chapter. The answers to these questions are found at the end of each *Study Guide* chapter.

**Essay Questions**

The essay questions that come next may be used in several ways. If you are using this *Study Guide* entirely on your own, you should try to outline answers to these questions based on your reading of the chapter. In the early stages of the course you may want to consider writing formal answers to these essay questions just as you would if you encountered them on an exam. The questions will often be quite broad and will lead you to think about material in the chapter in different ways. By reviewing the essay questions in this *Study Guide* before attending class, you will better understand the class lecture or discussion.

**Documents and Readings**

All the chapters in this *Study Guide* contain a section of documents or readings. The documents are sources from the time period of the chapter (primary sources), chosen to illumine some aspect of the period covered in the text. The readings are excerpts from works of historians (secondary sources), chosen either to illustrate the approach of a master historian or to offer varying interpretations of an event. Study the document or reading after you have completed the chapter, and consult the headnotes given in this *Study Guide* before each document. Then attempt to answer the questions that follow the document.

## STUDYING HISTORY

The term *history* has been defined in many ways. One way to define it is "everything that has happened in the past." But there are serious problems with this definition. First, it is simply impossible to recount *everything* that has happened in the past. Any single event is a combination of an infinite number of subevents. Each of these is itself composed of an unlimited number of subevents. The past, which includes everything that has happened, is shapeless; history is a way of lending shape to the past by focusing on significant events and their relationships.

# INTRODUCTION

Second, the historical record is limited. As you will discover, there is much we don't know about everyday life in seventeenth-century America. History must be based on fact and evidence. The historian then, using the evidence available, fashions a story in which certain past events are connected and take on special meaning or significance. If we accept this definition, we will recognize that much history is subjective, or influenced by the perspective and bias of the historian attempting to give meaning to events.

This is why there is so much disagreement about the importance of some past events. You may have been taught in high school that it was important simply to learn dates and facts: that the Declaration of Independence was adopted on July 4, 1776, or that Franklin D. Roosevelt was inaugurated on March 4, 1933. But these facts by themselves are limited in meaning. They gain significance when they become parts of larger stories, such as why the American colonies revolted against England, or how America responded to the Great Depression. When historians construct stories or narratives in which these facts or events take on special significance, room for disagreement creeps in.

Since it is valid for historians to disagree, you should not automatically accept what any one historian writes. You should learn to apply general rules of logic and evidence in assessing the validity of different historical interpretations. This *Study Guide* will at times give you an opportunity to assess different interpretations of events. By doing this you will learn to question what you read and hear, to think critically.

## HOW TO READ A TEXTBOOK

Reading a textbook should be both pleasurable and profitable. The responsibility for this is partly the author's and partly yours, the reader's. George Tindall and David Shi have written a text that should teach and entertain. In order to get the most out of it you must read actively and critically. One way to avoid passive, mindless reading is to write, underline, or highlight material by hand. Simply by highlighting or underlining pertinent passages in the textbook, you will later be better able to recall what you have read, and you will be able to review important material quickly. The key to effective highlighting is to be judicious about what you choose to mark. You should highlight key words and phrases, not whole sentences unless all the words are important. For example, the two paragraphs below show the way we would highlight them:

> Even the Tudors, who acted as autocrats, preserved the forms of constitutional procedure. In the making of laws the king's subjects consented through representatives in the House of Commons. By custom and practice **the principle was established that the king taxed his subjects only with the consent of Parliament.** And by its control of the purse strings Parliament would draw other strands of power into its hands. This structure of habit broadened down from precedent to precedent to form a **constitution that was** not written in one place, or for that matter, **not fully written down at all.** The *Magna Carta* (Great Charter) of 1215, for instance, had been a statement of privileges wrested by certain nobles from the king, but it became part of a broader tradition that the people as a whole had rights which even the king could not violate.
>
> **A further buttress to English liberty** was the **great body of common law** which had developed since the twelfth century in royal courts established to check the arbitrary caprice of local nobles. Without laws to cover every detail, judges had to exercise their own ideas of fairness in settling disputes. **Decisions once made became precedents for later decisions** and over the years a body of judge-made law developed, the outgrowth more of experience than of abstract logic. Through the courts the principle evolved that **a subject could be arrested or his goods seized only upon a warrant issued by a court** and that **he was entitled to a trial by a jury of his peers** (his equals) in accordance with established rules of evidence.

Probably no two persons would agree on exactly what words in the passage should be underlined, but you can readily see that we have emphasized only the major points concerning English justice.

Highlighting like this can be helpful, but even more useful in increasing your retention of the material is to jot down brief notes about what you read. For example, from the passage above you might list some key elements in the development of liberty under the Tudors: the principle that the king could tax his subjects only with the consent of Parliament, the development of an unwritten constitution, the principle that a court order was required for arrest or seizure of property, and the principle of trial by jury.

Taking notes makes it easier to commit important points to memory. This will help especially when you review for a test.

# ACKNOWLEDGMENTS

We wish to thank George B. Tindall and David E. Shi for having written the excellent text around which we developed this *Study Guide*. Our hope is that the text and the *Study Guide* will combine to promote in students a clear understanding of the history of the United States. We have a great debt to Steven Forman, our editor at W. W. Norton & Company, who has again used his considerable skill to fashion the final product. He has created a unified revision from the different parts on which we each worked.

C.W.E.
T.S.M.

# 17

## RECONSTRUCTION: NORTH AND SOUTH

### CHAPTER OBJECTIVES

*After you complete the reading and study of this chapter you should be able to*

1. Describe the impact of the Civil War on both the South and the North and on the status of freed blacks.
2. Explain the circumstances that led to Radical Reconstruction.
3. Describe the nature and extent of Radical Reconstruction.
4. Explain the process that returned control of the South to the conservatives.
5. Evaluate the contributions and failures of the Grant administration.
6. Explain the outcome of the election of 1876, the effects of that election, and the special arrangements made to conclude it.
7. Evaluate the overall impact of Reconstruction.

### CHAPTER OUTLINE

I. The war's aftermath
   A. The South at the end of the war
      1. Slaves freed
      2. Property destroyed
      3. Wealth gone
      4. Rebuilding necessary
      5. Bitter in defeat
        a. Emigration
        b. Opposition to Union forces
   B. Development of a plan of Reconstruction
      1. Military governors in Tennessee, Arkansas, and Louisiana
      2. Lincoln's plan of Reconstruction
        a. Provisions
        b. Implementation in Tennessee, Arkansas, and Louisiana
        c. Congressional reaction
        d. Counterclaims of Lincoln and Congress
        e. Wade-Davis Bill
        f. Lincoln's response to the Wade-Davis Bill
        g. Creation of Freedmen's Bureau
        h. Lincoln's final statement on Reconstruction
II. The assassination of Lincoln
III. Andrew Johnson and Reconstruction
   A. Johnson's background
   B. Radicals' perception of him
   C. Johnson's plan for Reconstruction
IV. Southern state reorganization
   A. Actions taken
   B. Congressional reaction to southern states
   C. Provisions and impact of black codes

V. The Radicals
   A. Joint Committee on Reconstruction
   B. Radical motivation
   C. Constitutional theories of status of southern states
VI. Johnson and Congress in battle
   A. Veto of Freedmen's Bureau extension
   B. Effect of Johnson's Washington's Birthday speech
   C. Congress overrides veto of the Civil Rights Act
   D. The Fourteenth Amendment
   E. Race riots in the South
   F. The congressional elections
VII. Congressional Reconstruction triumphant in 1867
   A. Command of the Army Act
   B. Tenure of Office Act
   C. Military Reconstruction Act
VIII. Constitutional issues and the Supreme Court
IX. The impeachment and trial of Johnson
   A. Failure of early efforts to impeach him
   B. Violation of Tenure of Office Act
   C. The articles of impeachment
   D. The Senate trial
   E. Ramifications of the impeachment
X. Blacks in Reconstruction
   A. Experience in military
   B. Establishment of black churches
   C. Families reaffirmed
   D. Schools started
   E. Politics
      1. Suffrage
      2. Statewide conventions
   F. Black Reconstruction
      1. Divisions in black communities
      2. Black officeholders
      3. Carpetbaggers
      4. Scalawags
      5. Accomplishments
   G. White terror
      1. Response to blacks in politics
      2. Ku Klux Klan
      3. Enforcement Acts
XI. Radical rule in the South
   A. Readmission of southern states
   B. Duration of Radical control
   C. Role of the Union League prior to Reconstruction
XII. The return of conservative control
   A. Reasons for abandonment of the Radical programs
   B. Duration of Radical control
XIII. The Grant years
   A. The election of 1868
      1. Reasons for support of Grant
      2. The Grant ticket and platform
      3. Democratic programs and candidates
      4. Results
   B. The character of Grant's leadership
   C. Proposal to pay the government debt
   D. Scandals
      1. Jay Gould's effort to corner the gold market
      2. The Crédit-Mobilier exposure
      3. Secretary of War and the Indian Bureau
      4. Other scandals
      5. Grant's personal role in the scandals
   E. Reform and the election of 1872
      1. Liberal Republicans nominate Greeley in 1872
      2. Grant's advantages
   F. Economic panic
      1. Causes for the depression
      2. Severity of the depression
   G. Democratic control of the House in 1874
   H. Reissue of greenbacks
   I. Resumption of specie payments approved in 1875
XIV. Election of 1876
   A. Elimination of Grant and Blaine
   B. Republicans nominate Hayes
   C. Democrats nominate Tilden
   D. Views of the parties
   E. Results of the popular vote
   F. The Electoral Commission
   G. Electoral compromise
      1. Promises of each side
      2. Promises filled and unfilled
   H. The end of Reconstruction
      1. A betrayal of the blacks?
      2. An enduring legacy

## KEY ITEMS OF CHRONOLOGY

| | |
|---|---|
| Lincoln's plan for Reconstruction announced | 1863 |
| Thirteenth Amendment ratified | 1865 |
| Creation of Freedmen's Bureau | 1865 |
| Assassination of Lincoln | April 14, 1865 |
| Johnson's plan for Reconstruction announced | May 29, 1865 |
| Veto of Freedmen's Bureau Extension Bill | February 1866 |
| Congress overrode Johnson's veto of Civil Rights Bill | April 1866 |
| Ku Klux Klan organized in the South | 1866 |
| Military Reconstruction Act | March 2, 1867 |
| Johnson replaces Stanton with Grant as secretary of war | August 1867 |
| House votes to impeach Johnson | February 1868 |
| Trial of Johnson in Senate | March 5 to May 26, 1868 |
| Fourteenth Amendment ratified | 1868 |
| All southern states except Mississippi, Texas, and Virginia readmitted to Congress | June 1868 |
| *Texas v. White* decision of Supreme Court | 1869 |
| Grant administrations | 1869–1877 |
| Mississippi, Texas, and Virginia readmitted | 1870 |
| Fifteenth Amendment ratified | 1870 |
| Resumption Act | 1875 |

## TERMS TO MASTER

*Listed below are some important terms or people with which you should be familiar after you complete the study of this chapter. Identify each name or term.*

1. Freedmen's Bureau
2. Wade-Davis Bill
3. "ironclad" oath
4. black codes
5. Radicals
6. Fourteenth Amendment
7. Military Reconstruction
8. Command of the Army Act
9. Tenure of Office Act
10. carpetbaggers and scalawags
11. Ku Klux Klan
12. Liberal Republicans
13. Jay Gould
14. Crédit-Mobilier
15. Samuel J. Tilden
16. Compromise of 1877

## VOCABULARY BUILDING

*Listed below are some words used in this chapter. Look in the dictionary for the meaning of each.*

1. fervent
2. stringent
3. peonage
4. impenitence
5. chiseled
6. petulant
7. perversity
8. foment
9. abridge
10. litigation
11. ludicrous
12. rescind
13. lithograph
14. revile
15. chide
16. mollify
17. chicanery
18. odious

19. clamorous
20. quixotic

## EXERCISES FOR UNDERSTANDING

*When you have completed reading the chapter, answer each of the following questions. If you have difficulty, go back to the text and reread the section of the chapter related to the question.*

### Multiple-Choice Questions

*Select the letter of the response that best completes the statement.*

1. The Reconstruction policies of the Radical Republicans were probably motivated by
   A. a humanitarian concern for the former slaves.
   B. hopes for Republican power in the South.
   C. bitterness over having to fight the costly war.
   D. all of the above
2. Andrew Johnson's plan to restore the Union
   A. closely resembled Lincoln's.
   B. was quite similar to the Radicals' program.
   C. involved total reconstruction of the South.
   D. did not include any black suffrage.
3. The Fourteenth Amendment to the Constitution
   A. outlawed slavery.
   B. guaranteed citizens the equal protection of the law.
   C. specifically gave the former slaves the right to vote.
   D. ended Reconstruction in the South.
4. During "black Reconstruction,"
   A. few whites held office.
   B. five blacks served as state governors.
   C. two blacks served in the U.S. Senate.
   D. blacks controlled most southern state governments.
5. The Radical southern governments during Reconstruction
   A. were unusually honest and moral.
   B. operated frugally and did not go into debt.
   C. refused to aid private corporations such as railroads.
   D. gave unusual attention to education and poor relief.
6. U.S. Grant was guilty of
   A. refusing to turn documents over to Congress for its investigation.
   B. trying to block the implementation of Reconstruction laws.
   C. choosing his appointees unwisely.
   D. taking funds from the federal treasury.
7. Reconstruction came to an end in
   A. 1870.
   B. 1877.
   C. 1888.
   D. 1890.

### True-False Questions

*Indicate whether each statement is true or false.*

1. After the Civil War, many Confederates left the South.
2. The black codes were laws enacted by southern legislatures that were controlled by the former slaves.
3. Congress generally accepted the "forfeited rights theory" in explaining secession.
4. The Military Reconstruction Act did not provide for a radical reconstruction of the South.
5. Scalawags were white, southern-born Republicans.
6. Andrew Johnson was impeached for refusing to obey the Tenure in Office Act.
7. The Crédit-Mobilier was involved in trading greenbacks to France for gold.
8. The Compromise of 1877 included a southerner as Speaker of the House.

### Essay Questions

1. Discuss the impact of the Civil War on the South, the North, and the former slaves.
2. How successful was "black Reconstruction"? What role did southern blacks play in Reconstruction?

3. Radical Reconstruction was not imposed until two years after the end of the Civil War and caused bitter opposition from the whites in the South. Would it have been better accepted if it had been imposed in May 1865 instead of March 1867? Explain why or why not.
4. Assess the achievements and limitations of the Grant administrations.
5. Why was Andrew Johnson impeached? What was the outcome?
6. What were the major provisions of the Fourteenth Amendment?
7. Explain the provisions of the Compromise of 1877 and its effects on the South.

## READINGS

### Reading 1. William A. Dunning Explains the Failure of Reconstruction in Terms of Corruption and Failure of the Governments

Like other significant periods in U.S. history, Reconstruction has gone through cycles of interpretation. Some of the earliest scholarly work on the period was carried out by William A. Dunning and his students, who believed that the Radicals in Congress sought to impose their rule on the South for selfish motives of personal gain. Dunning's synthesis of Reconstruction, written in the early 1900s when he was a professor at Columbia University, presented a southern point of view. Dunning also directed a group of scholars who investigated developments in the southern states from a similar point of view. In the excerpts below from one of his articles, Dunning, while explaining the failure of Reconstruction, reveals his attitude about the corruption and inadequacy of Reconstruction governments and his reservations about the abilities of African Americans.

> The leading motive of the reconstruction had been, at the inception of the process, to insure to the freedmen an effective protection of their civil rights,—of life, liberty, and property. In the course of the process, the chief stress came to be laid on the endowment of the blacks with full political rights,—with the electoral franchise and eligibility to office. And by the time the process was complete, a very important, if not the most important part had been played by the desire and the purpose to secure to the Republican party the permanent control of several Southern states in which hitherto such a political organization had been unknown. This last motive had a plausible and widely accepted justification in the view that the rights of the negro and the "results of the war" in general would be secure only if the national government should remain indefinitely in Republican hands, and that therefore the strengthening of the party was a primary dictate of patriotism.
>
> Through the operation of these various motives successive and simultaneous, the completion of the reconstruction showed the following situation: (1) the negroes were in the enjoyment of the equal political rights with the whites; (2) the Republican party was in vigorous life in all the Southern states, and in firm control of many of them; and (3) the negroes exercised an influence in political affairs out of all relation to their intelligence or property, and, since so many of the whites were defranchised, excessive even in proportion to their numbers. At the present day, in the same states, the negroes

enjoy practically no political rights; the Republican party is but the shadow of a name; and the influence of the negroes in political affairs is nil. This contrast suggests what has been involved in the undoing of reconstruction.

Before the last state was restored to the Union the process was well under way through which the resumption of control by the whites was to be effected. The tendency in this direction was greatly promoted by conditions within the Republican party itself. Two years of supremacy in those states which had been restored in 1868 had revealed unmistakable evidences of moral and political weakness in the governments. The personnel of the party was declining in character through the return to the North of the more substantial of the carpetbaggers, who found Southern conditions, both social and industrial, far from what they had anticipated, and through the very frequent instances in which the "sctalawags" ran to open disgrace. Along with this deterioration in the white element of the party, the negroes who rose to prominence and leadership were very frequently of a type which acquired and practiced the tricks and knavery rather than the useful arts of politics, and the vicious courses of these negroes strongly confirmed the prejudices of the whites. But at the same time that the incapacity of the party in power to administer any government was becoming demonstrable the problems with which it was required to cope were made by its adversaries such as would have taxed the capacity of the most efficient statesmen the world could produce.... No attention was paid to the claim that the manifest inefficiency and viciousness of the Republican governments afforded a partial, if not wholly adequate explanation of their overthrow. Not even the relative quiet and order that followed the triumph of the whites in these states were recognized as justifying the new regime.

[From William A. Dunning, "The Undoing of Reconstruction," *Atlantic Monthly*, October 1901, pp. 437–38.]

## Reading 2. La Wanda Cox Questions Whether Reconstruction Could Have Been Effective

In a strong departure from Dunning's racial arguments, most historians in recent years have come to see the failure of Reconstruction as the refusal to establish a sound basis for black equality. According to this view, Reconstruction as a reform movement aiming to improve the status of former slaves was undermined by events at the end of the nineteenth century. Several key historians have argued that the declining fortunes of blacks in the 1890s stemmed from the political failure to provide land for the freed slaves. In the excerpt below, La Wanda Cox, writing in 1981, takes issue with that view, finding other reasons for the failure of Reconstruction. As you read, carefully identify each of her other arguments.

... Yet there can be no question but that the equality of citizenship embodied in national and state law during the 1860s lay shattered and apparently unmendable as the South entered the twentieth century. Most former slaves and their children still lived in agrarian dependence and poverty, poorly educated, increasingly disfranchised and segregated, with little protection against a new surge of white violence.

All accounts of Reconstruction recognize the intensity of white southern resistance to the new status of blacks imposed by Republicans upon the defeated South. Curiously, in explaining the outcome, generally characterized by modern historians as the failure of Reconstruction (though with qualification and some dissent), they tend to place major responsibility not upon the South but upon "the North." By "the North" they usually mean the Republican party, which held national political power, and sometimes say as much. Their explanation is not free of moral stricture, often patently implicit when not expressly stated. Since the mid-1960s there has seldom been missing from accounts of the "First Reconstruction" the pejorative term "betrayal." . . .

Failure to enforce black civil and political rights in the South is often attributed to a lack of will on the part of Republican leaders and their constituencies due to their racial views. The explanation may not be susceptible of definite disproof, but it has not been proven and probably cannot be. Many factors entered into the abandonment of the cause of the black man in the South, and Republicans gave up neither quickly nor easily. The voting record of regular Republicans in Congress through 1891 remained remarkably consistent and cohesive behind efforts to strengthen federal enforcement of Reconstruction legislation. Democratic party obstruction was equally consistent and created a major roadblock. Republicans enacted a drastic enforcement law in 1870 and another in 1871. For most of the twenty years after the elections of 1870 they did not have the power in Congress to pass additional legislation supportive of black rights but they kept the issue alive. It is true that as early as 1872 some Republicans, notably those who joined the Liberal Republican movement, broke with the policy of national action in tsupport of black rights. But race prejudice was neither a conscious nor a major determinant of their new attitude toward federal intervention in the South. Indeed, the Liberal Republican platform of 1872 tried to reconcile a policy of national retreat with loyalty to the Reconstruction amendments. When Republicans regained control of both houses of Congress in 1890–1891 by only a narrow margin, they passed in the House an enforcement bill to protect black voters but narrowly lost it in the Senate by the perfidy of a few who broke ranks to gain support for silver legislation. On the local front in the northern states, in keeping with party tradition, the Republican record on black rights remained stronger than that of their opponents.

In 1877 when President Hayes withdrew federal troops and acquiesced to "home rule" for the South, racism was not the key to presidential decision. . . . The will to continue the battle was undermined by growing doubt of the wisdom of immediate universal black enfranchisement, increasingly seen as the source of corruption. There was revulsion against the turmoil of disputed elections and the force used to settle them. Many Republicans were discouraged as state after state came under "Redeemer" control, or distracted by the pressure of problems closer at home. There was a general desire in the North for the peace and national reconciliation that Grant had invoked but could not attain as president. Whatever part race prejudice played in weakening Republican support for continuing military intervention, its role was peripheral rather than central.

A critical question needs to be addressed. Could a greater use of force have brought white southerners to accept civil and political rights for blacks? Neither history nor theory can answer this question with certainty. A number of historians have implied that direct coercion could have effected a fundamental change, that Reconstruction was the nation's great missed opportunity. . . . Given the nation's traditional commitment to civilian control and majority rule, "the use of force was self-defeating."

Force *and* consent, how to achieve the one by use of the other, posed a dilemma which by the 1870s strained the bounds of the possible. The outcome would have been only a little less problematic had Reconstruction been formulated in early 1865 and backed by force, i.e., by force alone. Particularly vulnerable is the assumption that by eliminating the power of the landed aristocracy, resistance would have been broken and a new order of equal rights for blacks securely established. There would still have remained for the South as a whole a white majority with prejudices and interests inimicable to the advancement of blacks. . . .

Certainly by the mid-1870s the use of coercion had intensified a deep and bitter reaction. Instead of passive resignation, coercion led to a "negative consensus" that rejected the legitimacy of national authority over the status of blacks, fed resistance and united white southerners to an unprecedented degree. It is well to be reminded that the coercion used had been considerable. . . .

The force employed in the 1870s was grossly insufficient for the task at hand. Too often local officials and courts sidestepped justice for blacks without interference. Troops stationed in the South were woefully inadequate in number to contain violent resistance wherever it erupted. . . .

Nonetheless, the direct coercion mobilized by the national government in the 1860s and 1870s was substantial, far greater than any similar action in support of desegregation and black voting in the 1950s and '60s. It was large enough to give strong support to the contention that a century ago the amount of force necessary to realize equal civil and political rights in the South was impossible to sustain in a nation whose democratic traditional and constitutional structure limited the use of power, exalted the rule of law, and embodied the concept of government by the consent of the governed. Neither national institutions nor public opinion could be expected to have sustained a military intervention of indefinite length and of sufficient strength to crush all local resistance. And by the mid-1870s, the issue at stake no longer appeared clear-cut, even to northern Republicans.

. . . No explanation for the tragic outcome of the postwar decades for black America has been more generally accepted in modern scholarship than that Reconstruction failed because the federal government did not provide land for the freedman. The thesis has been sharply challenged, and the challenge has not been met. The work of historians and economists in exploring afresh the roots of poverty, particularly of black poverty, in the postbellum South afford some relevant perspectives. Between 1974 and 1979 six book-length studies appeared with significant bearing on the problem of black poverty, and others were in progress; conference papers and published articles also reflected the vigor of scholarly interest in the question.

No consensus has developed either as explanation for the continuing dependence and poverty of southern blacks or as an analysis of the potential economic effect of land distribution. However, four of five econometricians who addressed the latter question concluded that grants of land, while desirable and beneficial, would not have solved the predicament of the freedmen and their children. . . .

More than a land program was needed to insure the freedman's economic future. Although areas of land with high fertility prospered, it seems doubtful that income from cotton between the close of the war and the turn of the century, even if equitably distributed, could have sustained much beyond a marginal level of existence for those who worked the cotton fields whether as wage earner, cropper, tenant, or small owner. And the lower South because of its soils and climate, . . . had no viable alternative to cotton as a commercial crop until the scientific and technological advances of the twentieth century. Nor could nonmarket subsistence farming offer much by way of material reward. The "more" that was needed can be envisaged in retrospect, and was glimpsed by contemporaries, but it is not clear how it could have been achieved. . . . Despite scholarship, new and old, there is no certain explanation of why the South failed to catch up with the North. If historians and economists should agree upon a diagnosis, it is unlikely that they will uncover a remedy that could have been recognized and implemented a century ago. . . .

. . . More than a land program, the civil and political rights Republicans established in law, had they been secured in practice, could have mitigated the discrimination that worsened their condition and constricted whatever opportunities might otherwise have existed for escape from poverty. . . .

The priority Republicans gave to civil and political rights in their fight to establish a meaningful new status for ex-slaves had been too readily discounted by historians. Small landholdings could not have protected blacks from intimidation, or even from many forms of economic coercion. They would not have brought economic power. In the face of overwhelming white opposition, they could not have safeguarded the new equality of civil and political status. Where blacks voted freely, on the other hand, there was always the potential for sharing political power and using it as a means to protect and advance their interests. There is considerable evidence that this did happen. Local officials elected by black votes during the years of Republican control upheld blacks against planters, state legislators repealed Black Codes, shifted the burden of taxation from the poor, granted agricultural laborers a first lien on crops, increased expenditures for education. . . . And beyond immediate gains, black votes meant support for educational facilities through which blacks could acquire the literacy and skills essential for advancement.

Security for black civil and political rights required acceptance by white southerners. An acquiescence induced by a judicious combination of force and consent needed for its perpetuation reinforcement by self-interest. The most effective vehicle of self-interest would have been a Union-Republican party able to command substantial continuing support from native whites. The Republican party that gained temporary dominance through the congressional legislation of 1867 enfranchising blacks failed to meet the test of substantial white support. Despite a strong white following in a few states, its scalawag component from the start was too limited to offset the opposition's attack on it as the party of the black man and the Yankee. And white participation diminished as appeals to race prejudice and sectional animosity intensified.

The potential for a major second party among southern whites existed in the aftermath of Confederate defeat. The Democratic party was in disarray, discredited for having led the South out of the Union and having lost the war. Old Whig loyalties subsumed by the slavery issue had nonetheless endured; southern unionism had survived in varying degrees from wartime adherence to the Union to reluctant support of the Confederacy. . . .

Had party recruitment and organization, with full presidential support, begun at the end of hostilities and escaped the period of confusion and bitterness that thinned the ranks of the willing during the conflict between Johnson and Congress, the result could have been promising. . . .

Even under the guidance of a Lincoln, the building of a permanent biracial major party in the South was by no means assured. A broad enduring coalition of disparate elements would face the necessity of reconciling sharply divergent economic interests. Agricultural workers sought maximum autonomy, more than bare necessities, and an opportunity for land ownership while planter-merchants strove to control labor and maximize profit. The burden of increased taxation to meet essential but unaccustomed social services, particularly for blacks, meant an inescapable clash of class and racial interests. Concessions by the more privileged were especially difficult in a South of limited available resources and credit, impoverished by war and enmeshed in inflated costs, crop disasters, and falling cotton prices. By the mid-1870s a nationwide depression intensified regional problems. Efforts to promote a more varied and vigorous economy by state favor, credit, and appropriation became a political liability as the primary effect appeared to be the proliferation of civic corruption and entrepreneurial plunder.

The years of political Reconstruction, to borrow an apt phrase from Thomas B. Alexander's study of Tennessee, offered no "narrowly missed opportunities to leap a century forward in reform." Not even a Lincoln could have wrought such a miracle. To have secured something less, yet something substantially more than blacks had gained by the end of the nineteenth century, did not lie beyond the limits of the possible given a president who at war's end would have joined party in an effort to realize "as nearly as we can" the fullness of freedom for blacks.

[From La Wanda Cox, *Lincoln and Black Freedom: A Study in Presidential Leadership* (Columbia: University of South Carolina Press, 1981), pp. 155–56, 162–64, 165–69, 174–83.]

## Reading 3. Eric Foner Contends That Reconstruction Did Not Go Far Enough

Historical scholarship on the Reconstruction era continues to grow at a remarkable rate. In the following excerpt Eric Foner summarizes some of the most recent scholarship and suggests a new way to view Reconstruction.

Despite the excellence of recent writing and the continual expansion of our knowledge of the period, historians of Reconstruction today face a unique dilemma. An old interpretation has been overthrown, but a coherent new synthesis has yet to take its place. The revisionists of the 1960s effectively established a series of negative points: the Reconstruction governments were not as bad as had been portrayed, black supremacy was a myth, the Radicals were not cynical manipulators of the freedmen. Yet no convincing overall portrait of the quality of political and social life emerged from their writings.

... a new portrait of Reconstruction ought to begin by viewing it not as a specific time period, bounded by the years 1865 and 1877, but as an episode in a prolonged historical process—American society's adjustment to the consequences of the Civil War and emancipation.

... the focal point of Reconstruction was the social revolution known as emancipation. Plantation slavery was simultaneously a system of labor, a form of racial domination, and the foundation upon which arose a distinctive ruling class within the South. Its demise threw open the most fundamental questions of economy, society, and politics. A new system of labor, social, racial, and political relations had to be created to replace slavery.

Few modern scholars believe the Reconstruction governments established in the South in 1867 and 1868 fulfilled the aspirations of their humble constituents. While their achievements in such realms as education, civil rights, and the economic rebuilding of the South are now widely appreciated, historians today believe they failed to affect either the economic plight of the emancipated slave or the ongoing transformation of independent white farmers into cotton tenants. Yet their opponents did perceive the Reconstruction governments in precisely this way—as representatives of a revolution that had put the bottom rail, both racial and economic, on top. This perception helps explain the ferocity of the attacks leveled against them and the pervasiveness of violence in the postemancipation South.

The spectacle of black men voting and holding office was anathema to large numbers of Southern whites. Even more disturbing, at least in the view of those who still controlled the plantation regions of the South, was the emergence of local officials, black and white, who sympathized with the plight of the black laborer.... During presidential Reconstruction, and after "Redemption," with planters and their allies in control of politics, the law emerged as a means of stabilizing and promoting the plantation system. If Radical Reconstruction failed to redistribute the land of the South, the ouster of the planter class from control of politics at least ensured that the sanctions of the criminal law would not be employed to discipline the black labor force.

An understanding of this fundamental conflict over the relation between government and society helps explain the pervasive complaints concerning corruption and "extravagance" during Radical Reconstruction. Corruption there was aplenty; tax rates did rise sharply. More significant than the rate of taxation, however, was the change in its incidence. For the first time, planters and white farmers had to pay a significant portion of their income to the government, while propertyless blacks often escaped scot-free. Several states, moreover, enacted heavy taxes on uncultivated land to discourage land speculation and force land onto the market, benefiting, it was hoped, the freedmen.

As time passed, complaints about the "extravagance" and corruption of Southern governments found a sympathetic audience among influential Northerners. The Democratic charge that universal suffrage in the South was responsible for high taxes and governmental extravagance coincided with a rising conviction among the urban middle classes of the North that city government had to be taken out of the hands of the immigrant poor and returned to the "best men"— the educated, professional, financially independent citizens unable to exert much political influence at a time of mass parties and machine politics. Increasingly the "respectable" middle classes began to retreat from the very notion of universal suffrage. The poor were no longer perceived as honest producers, the backbone of the social order; now they became the "dangerous classes," the "mob." As the historian Francis Parkman put it, too much power rested with "masses of imported ignorance and hereditary ineptitude." To Parkman the Irish of the Northern cities and the blacks of the South were equally incapable of utilizing the ballot: "Witness the municipal corruptions of New York, and the monstrosities of negro rule in South Carolina." Such attitudes helped to justify Northern inaction as, one by one, the Reconstruction regimes of the South were overthrown by political violence.

In the end, then, neither the abolition of slavery nor Reconstruction succeeded in resolving the debate over the meaning of freedom in American life. Twenty years before the American Civil War, writing about the prospect of abolition in France's colonies, Alexis de Tocqueville had written, "If the Negroes have the right to become free, the [planters] have the incontestable right not to be ruined by the Negroes' freedom." And in the United States, as in nearly every plantation society that experienced the end of slavery, a rigid social and political dichotomy between former master and former slave, an ideology of racism, and a dependent labor force with limited economic opportunities all survived abolition. Unless one means by freedom the simple fact of not being a slave, emancipation thrust blacks into a kind of no-man's land, a partial freedom that made a mockery of the American ideal of equal citizenship.

Yet by the same token the ultimate outcome underscores the uniqueness of Reconstruction itself. Alone among the societies that abolished slavery in the nineteenth century, the United States, for a moment, offered the freedmen a measure of political control over their own destinies. However brief its sway, Reconstruction allowed scope for a remarkable political and social mobilization of the black community. It opened doors of opportunity that could never be completely closed. Reconstruction transformed the lives of Southern blacks in ways unmeasurable by statistics and unreachable by law. It raised their expectations and aspirations, redefined their status in relation to the larger society, and allowed space for the creation of institutions that enabled them to survive the repression that followed. And it established constitutional principles of civil and political equality that, while flagrantly violated after Redemption, planted the seeds of future struggle.

[From Eric Foner, "The New View of Reconstruction," *American Heritage* 34, no. 6 (October–November 1983): 13–15.]

## Questions for Reflection

What good, if any, does Dunning seem to imply came from Reconstruction? What appear to be Dunning's views of African Americans? What does Dunning mean by "The failure of Radicalism is thus a part of the wider failure of bourgeois liberalism to solve the problems of the new age which was dawning"?

Explain how Cox's view of the failure of Reconstruction is different from Dunning's. Why does she say that the use of more force would not have solved the problems of Reconstruction? What issue does she contend was more important than the need to provide land for former slaves? What is the basis for her argument? Do you agree with her view? Explain.

Cox seems to imply that if Lincoln had lived, Reconstruction would have developed more effectively. What is her basis for that view? Why does she think that even Lincoln would have had difficulty in making Reconstruction succeed?

According to Eric Foner, how did Reconstruction lead to the ouster of the planter class from control of politics and why was that important? How did attitudes toward blacks in Reconstruction interact with attitudes toward immigrants and other oppressed groups in the North? What reason does Foner give for the failure of Reconstruction governments to give blacks long-term freedom?

All three of these writers assert that Reconstruction failed from one perspective or another. How do *you* think the problems of Reconstruction in the South could have been better solved?

## ANSWERS TO MULTIPLE-CHOICE AND TRUE-FALSE QUESTIONS

### Multiple-Choice Questions

1-D, 2-A, 3-B, 4-C, 5-D, 6-C, 7-B

### True-False Questions

1-F, 2-F, 3-T, 4-T, 5-T, 6-T, 7-F, 8-F

# 18

## NEW FRONTIERS: SOUTH AND WEST

**CHAPTER OBJECTIVES**

*After you complete the reading and study of this chapter you should be able to*

1. Explain the concept of the New South, its development, and how it affected the South after the Civil War.
2. Account for the rise of the Bourbons to power in the South and explain their impact on the region.
3. Explain the causes and process of disenfranchisement of blacks in the South.
4. Compare the views of Washington and Du Bois on the place of blacks in American life.
5. Understand the process of settling the West.
6. Describe the Indian wars and explain the new Indian policy of 1887.
7. Assess the importance of violence in the culture of the West.
8. Appraise the problems of farming and ranching on the western frontier.
9. Explain the importance of Turner's theory of the significance of the frontier in American history.

**CHAPTER OUTLINE**

I. The New South
   A. Concept of the New South
      1. Henry Grady's background
      2. His vision
      3. Other prophets of the New South creed
   B. Economic growth
      1. Growth of cotton textile manufacturing
      2. Development of the tobacco industry
         a. Duke family
         b. Techniques used by Buck Duke for growth
         c. Creation and breakup of the American Tobacco Company
      3. Coal production
      4. Lumbering
      5. Beginnings of petroleum and hydroelectric power
   C. Agriculture in the New South
      1. Limited diversity in agriculture
      2. Features of sharecropping and tenancy
      3. Impact of the crop lien system
   D. Role of the Bourbon Redeemers
      1. Nature of the Bourbons
      2. Bourbon economic policies
         a. Laissez-faire

b. Retrenchment in government spending
   c. Assistance of private philanthropy
   d. Convict lease system
   e. Repudiation of Confederate debts in some states
   f. Positive contributions of the Bourbons
   g. Varied development of color lines in social relations
  E. Disenfranchisement of blacks
   1. Impetus for elimination of the black vote
    a. Fears of retrogression
    b. Impact of Populists
   2. Techniques used to exclude blacks
    a. Mississippi
    b. Louisiana
   3. Spread of segregation
    a. Segregation in railway cars
    b. Impact of *Civil Rights Cases*, 1883
    c. Impact of *Plessy v. Ferguson*, 1896
   4. Spread of violence against blacks
  F. Clash of Booker T. Washington and W. E. B. Du Bois
II. The New West
  A. Nature of the West and its settlement after the war
   1. Manifest Destiny
   2. Colonization
   3. Three frontiers
   4. Change in the Great American Desert
   5. Migration
    a. Native-born whites
    b. Foreigners
    c. Blacks
  B. The mining frontier
   1. Pattern of mining development
   2. Locations of major mineral discoveries
   3. Development of new states
  C. Displacement of the Indians
   1. Conflicts that arose during the Civil War
   2. Establishment of Indian Peace Commission, 1867
    a. Policy of large reservations
    b. Agreements with the Indians in 1867 and 1868
   3. Continued resistance of Indians
    a. Massacre at Little Big Horn
    b. Conquest of Sioux and others
    c. Significance of Chief Joseph and Nez Perce
   4. Impact of annihilation of buffalo herds
   5. Stirrings for reform in Indian policy
    a. Eastern view of Indian slaughter
    b. Role of Helen Hunt Jackson
   6. Dawes Severalty Act, 1887
    a. Concept of new policy
    b. Provisions of Dawes and subsequent acts
    c. Impact of new policy
  D. Range wars
   1. Issues
    a. Land rights
    b. Water rights
   2. Combatants
    a. Ranchers vs. farmers
    b. Cattle ranchers vs. shepherds
    c. Large vs. small ranchers
    d. Ethnic and religious differences
  E. The cattle industry in the West
   1. Development of the open range
   2. Long drives after the Civil War
    a. Joseph McCoy
    b. Features of the cowtown
   3. Codes of the open range
  F. The farming frontier
   1. Land policy after the Civil War
   2. Changed institutions in the West
   3. Efforts at reclamation of arid lands
   4. An assessment of land distribution
   5. Pioneer women
  G. Violent culture
  H. Turner's frontier thesis
   1. Turner's claims for the frontier
   2. Other views

## KEY ITEMS OF CHRONOLOGY

| | |
|---|---|
| Homestead Act | 1862 |
| First of the long drives | 1866 |
| Indian Peace Commission settlements | 1867–1868 |
| *Civil Rights Cases* | 1883 |
| Dawes Severalty Act | 1887 |
| Mississippi Constitution incorporates disenfranchisement of blacks | 1890 |
| Census shows frontier closed | 1890 |
| Turner frontier thesis presented | 1893 |
| B. T. Washington's "Atlanta Compromise" speech | 1895 |
| *Plessy v. Ferguson* | 1896 |
| Disenfranchisement of blacks essentially completed in southern states | 1910 |

## TERMS TO MASTER

*Listed below are some important terms or people with which you should be familiar after you complete the study of this chapter. Explain the significance of each name or term.*

1. Henry W. Grady
2. James Buchanan Duke
3. sharecropping
4. crop lien system
5. Bourbons
6. convict lease system
7. Mississippi Plan for disenfranchisement
8. grandfather clauses
9. segregation
10. *Plessy v. Ferguson*
11. Booker T. Washington
12. W. E. B. Du Bois
13. Great American Desert
14. Exodusters
15. George A. Custer
16. Chief Joseph
17. *A Century of Dishonor*
18. Dawes Severalty Act
19. "dry farming"
20. Code of the West
21. Frederick Jackson Turner

1. wistfully
2. entrepreneurs
3. incentive
4. improvident
5. proliferate
6. scrimp
7. paradox
8. gerrymander
9. finesse
10. venality
11. adversity
12. oblique
13. dubious
14. trucklers
15. decimate
16. polygamy
17. indignation
18. mercenary
19. obsessive
20. prolific

## VOCABULARY BUILDING

*Listed below are some words used in this chapter. Look up each word in your dictionary.*

## EXERCISES FOR UNDERSTANDING

*When you have completed reading the chapter, answer each of the following* questions. *If you have difficulty, go back and reread the section of the chapter related to the question.*

## Multiple-Choice Questions

*Select the letter of the response that best completes the statement.*

1. James B. Duke's greatest contribution to the South's progress was in
   A. development of the cigarette industry.
   B. promotion of education.
   C. inventions for textile manufacturing.
   D. stimulating competition among industries in the South.

2. The most significant impact of the crop lien system in the South was that it
   A. made possible cash payments for goods.
   B. provided a source of labor in the post-Reconstruction South.
   C. made possible low-interest-rate loans for blacks.
   D. encouraged the South to raise only one crop, cotton.

3. Mississippi's techniques for disenfranchising blacks included all of the following *except* a
   A. residency requirement.
   B. poll tax.
   C. grandfather clause.
   D. literacy test.

4. "In all things that are purely social we can be as separate as the five fingers, yet one as the hand in all things essential to mutual progress," said
   A. Henry Grady.
   B. W. E. B. Du Bois.
   C. the Supreme Court in *Plessy v. Ferguson.*
   D. Booker T. Washington.

5. After Reconstruction, black migrants known as Exodusters went to
   A. Kansas.
   B. California.
   C. northern cities.
   D. back to Africa.

6. In the Battle of Little Big Horn, General George A. Custer fought
   A. gold and silver miners in Colorado.
   B. Indians in the Montana territory.
   C. "Calamity Jane" and "Wild Bill Hickok" in South Dakota.
   D. Indians in the Southwest.

7. Range wars in the West often involved
   A. men fighting over women.
   B. access to water.
   C. rival claims to valuable minerals.
   D. political control over local governments.

8. The crucial factor in ending the open, free range was the
   A. coming of the railroad.
   B. irrigation of arid lands.
   C. use of barbed wire.
   D. admission of new states to the Union.

## True-False Questions

*Indicate whether each statement is true or false.*

1. Henry Grady's view of the New South emphasized the development of industry.
2. The Bourbons increased spending for public education in the South.
3. The *Plessy v. Ferguson* decision included a ruling that states could not interfere with the rights of blacks.
4. W. E. B. Du Bois's *A Century of Dishonor* criticized the disenfranchisement of blacks.
5. Most of the migrants to the West were very poor people desperate to buy cheap land.
6. General George Custer was defeated at the battle of Little Big Horn.
7. Landowners in the West usually obtained their land directly from the government.
8. Between 1851 and 1871 the federal government granted railroads about 200 million acres in the West.

## Essay Questions

1. How did race relations in the South change in the late nineteenth century?
2. Explain how the sharecropping and

tenant systems worked in southern agriculture.
3. Contrast the visions of Booker T. Washington and W. E. B. Du Bois for freed blacks.
4. What factors contributed to the settlement of the West? Explain.
5. In what ways was life on the western frontier violent?
6. Did the federal government's Indian policy have more or less effect on the development of the West than its land policy?
7. How did black social and political life change in the South during the 1890s?

## DOCUMENTS

**Document 1. An Act to Secure Homesteads to Actual Settlers on the Public Domain**

Congress passed the Homestead Act in 1862 to provide public lands to settlers.

*Be it enacted,* That any person who is the head of a family, or who has arrived at the age of twenty-one years, and is a citizen of the United States, or who shall have filed his declaration of intention to become such, as required by the naturalization laws of the United States, and who has never borne arms against the United States Government or given aid and comfort to its enemies, shall, from and after the first of January, eighteen hundred and sixty-three, be entitled to enter one quarter-section or a less quantity of unappropriated public lands, upon which said person may have filed a pre-emption claim, or which may, at the time the application is made, be subject to pre-emption at one dollar and twenty-five cents, or less, per acre; or eighty acres or less of such unappropriated lands, at two dollars and fifty cents per acre, to be located in a body, in conformity to the legal subdivisions of the public lands, and after the same shall have been surveyed: *Provided,* That any person owning or residing on land, may, under the provisions of this act, enter other land lying contiguous to his or her said land, which shall not, with the land so already owned and occupied, exceed in the aggregate one hundred and sixty acres.

Sec. 2. That the person applying for the benefit of this act shall, upon application to the register of the land office in which he or she is about to make such entry, make affidavit before the said register or receiver that he or she is the head of a family, or is twenty-one or more years of age, or shall have performed service in the Army or Navy of the United States, and that he has never borne arms against the Government of the United States or given aid and comfort to its enemies, and that such application is made for his or her exclusive use and benefit, and that said entry is made for the purpose of actual settlement and cultivation, and not, either directly or indirectly, for the use or benefit of any other person or persons whomsoever; and upon filing the said affidavit with the register or receiver, and on payment of ten dollars, he or she shall thereupon be permitted to enter the quantity of land specified: *Provided, however,* That no certificate shall be given or patent issued therefor until the expiration of five years from the date of such entry; and if, at the expiration of such time, or at any time within two years thereafter, the person making such entry—or if he be dead, his widow; or in case of her death, his heirs or devisee; or in case of a widow making such entry, her heirs or devisee, in case of her death—shall prove by two credible witnesses that he, she, or they have resided upon or cultivated the same for the term of five years immediately succeeding the time of filing the affidavit aforesaid, and shall make affidavit that no part of said land has been alienated, and that he has borne true allegiance to the Government of the United States; then, in such case, he, she, or they, if at that time a citizen of the United States, shall be entitled to a patent, as in other cases provided for by law: *And provided, further,* That in case of the death of both father and mother, leaving an infant child or children under twenty-one years of age, the right and fee shall inure to the benefit of said infant child or children; and the executor, administrator, or guardian may, at any time within two years after the death of the surviving parent, and in accordance with the laws of the State in which such children for the time being have their domicile, sell said land for the benefit of said infants, but for no other purpose; and the purchaser shall acquire the absolute title by the purchase, and be entitled to a patent from the United States, on payment of the office fees and sum of money herein specified....

[From *U.S. Statutes at Large*, XII, 392ff.]

## Document 2. Life on Prairie Farms

In 1893 E. V. Smalley described the social isolation experienced by many farmers on the plains in the late nineteenth century.

... the life of a poor settler on a homestead claim in one of the Dakotas or Nebraska. Every homesteader must live upon his claim for five years to perfect his title and get his patent; so that if there were not the universal American custom of isolated farm life to stand in the way, no farm villages would be possible in the first occupancy of a new region in the West without a change in our land laws. If the country were so thickly settled that every quarter-section of land (160 acres) had a family upon it, each family would be half a mile from any neighbor, supposing the houses to stand in the centre of the farms, and in any case the average distance between them could not be less. But many settlers own 320 acres, and a few have a square mile of land, 640 acres. Then there are school sections, belonging to the State, and not occupied at all, and everywhere you find vacant tracts owned by Eastern speculators or by mortgage companies, to which former settlers have abandoned their claims, going to newer regions, and leaving their debts and their land behind. Thus the average space separating the farmsteads is, in fact, always more than half a mile, and many settlers must go a mile or two to reach a neighbor's house. This condition obtains not on the frontiers alone, but in fairly well peopled agricultural districts.

If there be any region in the world where the natural gregarious instincts of mankind should assert itself, that region is our Northwestern prairies, where a short hot summer is followed by a long cold winter, and where there is little in the aspect of nature to furnish food for thought. On every hand the treeless plain stretches away to the horizon line. In summer, it is checkered with grain fields or carpeted with grass and flowers, and it is inspiring in its color and vastness; but one mile of it is almost exactly like another, save where some watercourse nurtures a fringe of willows and cottonwoods. When the snow covers the ground the prospect is bleak and dispiriting. No brooks babble under icy armor. There is no bird life after the wild geese and ducks have passed on their way south. The silence of death rests on the vast landscape, save when it is swept by cruel winds that search out every chink and cranny of the buildings, and drive through each unguarded aperture the dry, powdery snow. In such a region, you would expect the dwellings to be of substantial construction, but they are not. The new settler is too poor to build of brick or stone. He hauls a few loads of lumber from the nearest railway station, and puts up a frail little house of two, three or four rooms that looks as though the prairie winds would blow it away. Were it not for the invention of tarred building-paper, the flimsy walls would not keep out the wind and snow. With this paper the walls are sheathed under the weather-boards. The barn is often a nondescript affair of sod walls and straw roof. Lumber is much too dear to be used for dooryard fences, and there is no inclosure about the house. A barbed-wire fence surrounds the barnyard. Rarely are there any trees, for on the prairies trees grow very slowly, and must be nursed with care to get a start. There is a saying that you must first get the Indian out of the soil before a tree will grow at all; which means that some savage quality must be taken from the ground by cultivation.

In this cramped abode, from the windows of which there is nothing more cheerful in sight than the distant houses of other settlers, just as ugly and lonely, and stacks of straw and unthreshed grain, the farmer's family must live. In the summer there is a school for the children, one, two, or three miles away; but in the winter the distances across the snow-covered plains are too great for them to travel in severe weather; the schoolhouse is closed, and there is nothing for them to do but to house themselves and long for spring. Each family must live mainly to itself, and life, shut up in the little wooden farmhouses, cannot well be very cheerful. A drive to the nearest town is almost the only diversion. There the farmers and their wives gather in the stores and manage to enjoy a little sociability. The big coal stove gives out a grateful warmth, and there is a pleasant odor of dried codfish, groceries, and ready-made clothing. The women look at the display of thick cloths and garments, and wish the crop had been better, so that they could buy some of the things of which they are badly in need. The men smoke corncob pipes and talk politics. It is a cold drive home across the wind-swept prairies, but at least they have had a glimpse of a little broader and more comfortable life than that of the isolated farm.

There are few social events in the life of these prairie farmers to enliven the monotony of the long winter evenings; no singing-schools, spelling-schools, debating clubs, or church gatherings. Neighborly calls are infrequent, because of the long distances which separate the farmhouses, and because, too, of the lack of homogeneity of the people. They have no common past to talk about. They were strangers to one another when they arrived in this new land, and their work and ways have not thrown them much together. Often the strangeness is intensified by the differences of national origin. There are Swedes, Norwegians, Germans, French Canadians, and perhaps even such peculiar people as Finns and Icelanders, among the settlers, and the Americans come from many different States. It is hard to establish any social bond in such a mixed population, yet one and all need social intercourse, as the thing most essential to pleasant living, after food, fuel, shelter, and clothing. An alarming amount of insanity occurs in the new prairie States among farmers and their wives. In proportion to their numbers, the Scandinavian settlers furnish the largest contingent to the asylums. The reason is not far to seek. These people came from cheery little farm villages. Life in the fatherland was hard and toilsome, but it was not lonesome. Think for a moment how great the change must be from the white-walled, red-roofed village of a Norway fiord, with its church and schoolhouse, its fishing-boats on the blue inlet, and its green mountain walls towering aloft to snow fields, to an isolated cabin on a Dakota prairie, and say if it is any wonder that so many Scandinavians lose their mental balance.

[From E. V. Smalley, "The Isolation of Life on Prairie Farms," *Atlantic Monthly,* 72 (1893): 378–83.]

## Document 3. Wheat Farming in Iowa

Herbert Quick remembers the economic trials his family experienced as wheat farmers in Iowa.

We grew wonderful wheat at first; the only problem was to get it to market and to live on the proceeds when it was sold. My father hauled his wheat from the Iowa River to Waterloo, and even to Iowa City, when it was the railhead for our part of the country; hauled it slowly over mere trails across the prairie. It took him three days to market a load of wheat in Waterloo. . . .

But the worst, however, was yet to come. A harvest came when we found that something was wrong with the wheat. No longer did the stalks stand clean and green as of old until they went golden in the sun. The broad green blades were spotted red and black with rust. Still it grew tall and rank; but as it matured it showed signs of disease. The heads did not fill well. Some blight was at work on it. However, we thought next year all would be well again. And when it grew worse year by year, it became a blight not only on the life of the grain but on human life as well. Wheat was almost our sole cash crop. If it failed, what should we do? And it was failing!

We were incurring, of course, the penalty for a one-crop system. We ought to have known that it was inevitable. . . .

This . . . gave me my first contact with the phenomenon which puzzles so many city people. If the farmers are losing money on a certain crop, why in the world don't they change to something else? It is not so easy to change as the city man may think. The wheat growers of the Central States at the time of this writing have been losing money on their wheat for years; but if they endeavor to change, they are confronted by a great problem. Such a change means the adoption of an entirely new rotation of crops. They have for years used a three- or four-year rotation—wheat, then corn, then clover. The sowing of the wheat gives them the chance to put in their fertilizer. They are used to this system. Any change from it involves the risking of a new crop on which losses are also probable. . . .

The fields of grain had always been a delight to me. . . . But now all the poetry went out of it. There was no joy for the soul of the boy who was steeped in such poetry as he could stumble upon, in these grain-fields threatened by grasshoppers, eaten by chinchbugs, blackened with molds and rusts, their blades specked as with the shed blood of the husbandman, their gold dulled by disease, their straw crinkling down in dead brittleness instead of rising and falling and swaying with the beautiful resiliency of health and abundance. . . .

All this time, while we were playing the role of the tortured victims in the tragedy of the wheat, we were feeling our way toward some way out. We knew that our fields would grow great crops of maize—it was a good corn country. But if there was more than one person who grew and fed cattle for the market there, I did not know of it. The average small farmer grew into the combination of hogs and corn. Gradually we changed over from wheat farming to big cornfields and populous hog lots. And then the price of both corn and pork went down, down, down, until corn sold for less than ten cents a bushel in our depreciated money and hogs for even less than three cents a pound. We had not found out about the balanced ration and the hog's need of pasture; and after a few generations of a diet of corn, the swine lost vitality and the crop of young pigs failed save where there was milk for them. The villain of misfortune still pursued us. . . .

Gradually we worked out a better *modus vivendi*—worked it out in a welter of debt and a depression which has characterized the rural mind to this day. Corn and hogs came to pay us as little as had wheat; yet for a while they were our only recourse, for the soil refused to grow wheat. For a long time there was plenty of open prairie on which cattle could be grazed freely. . . . Then the expanding acres of wheat land cut us off from any extended range of free grass. We had no fencing until barbed wire came in. So our cows were picketed on the prairie, led to water and cared for much as the Danes handle their cows now.

In spite of these difficulties, however, it gradually dawned upon us that by the sale of butter we were getting a little money from time to time. And though eggs were sometimes as low as eight cents a dozen, they brought in some funds. The skim milk restored our hogs to health. Without conscious planning, we were entering the business of mixed farming. My mother's butter was famed in all the nearby villages. In view of all the pains she took with it, it should have been; for she met the hot weather of our Iowa summers by hanging both cream and butter down the well where it was cool. Finally a creamery was started in Holland, a small town near us; and by this time we had a nice little herd of cows. A tank was made where water could be pumped through it and in this we set our cans of milk; and the cream hauler of the creamery came, skimmed off the cream, gave us tickets for it and hauled it away, thus giving us the cash when we went to town and saving the women the work of making the butter. It was the first contact of the factory system with the Iowa farm.

All this made life easier both as to labor and money. But it was not our only amelioration. We began to have a better food supply.... our strawberries, raspberries, grapes, gooseberries, currants and cherries yielded abundantly. I had a patch of raspberries which I pruned and tended on a system of my own which gave us all we could consume and furnished dividends for our friends. In place of the old regimen of dried fruits and just dry groceries, we were surfeited on jams, jellies, preserves and other delicious viands; and with our supply of milk and cream, found the pioneer epoch definitely past so far as the larder was concerned. The prairie had been tamed. Iowa had been civilized. Our eighty-acre farm was furnishing us a real living for the first time....

The farmer is often accused by the city dweller of being a confirmed calamity howler. He is. He is such because almost every calamity which comes on the land hits him sooner or later. Whenever any other industry shifts from under an economic change it shifts it in part upon the farmer, and the farmer is unable to shift it in his turn; while most other shiftees can, by adding to prices or wages, get from under the load. The farmer is so placed that there is nothing beyond him but the wall. He is crushed against it. There is nothing under him but the earth. He is pressed into it. He is the end of the line in the economic game of crack the whip, and he is cracked off.

[From Herbert Quick, *One Man's Life* (Indianapolis, Ind., 1925), pp. 207–9, 212–17.]

## Questions for Reflection

How did the government promote settlement of the public lands in the West? Do you think that farming in the Midwest and West was as attractive as many of the settlers probably expected? What problems did the new farmers experience? Were there advantages, which Smalley and Quick may not mention, that compensated for the difficulties? How and why has the life of farmers changed in the last hundred years?

## ANSWERS TO MULTIPLE-CHOICE AND TRUE-FALSE QUESTIONS

### Multiple-Choice Questions

1-A, 2-D, 3-C, 4-D, 5-A, 6-B, 7-B, 8-C

### True-False Questions

1-T, 2-F, 3-F, 4-F, 5-F, 6-T, 7-F, 8-T

# 19

# BIG BUSINESS AND ORGANIZED LABOR

**CHAPTER OBJECTIVES**

*After you complete the reading and study of this chapter you should be able to:*

1. Describe the economic impact of the Civil War.
2. Explain the important factors in the growth of the economy in the late nineteenth century.
3. Describe the role of the major entrepreneurs like Rockefeller, Carnegie, and Morgan.
4. Account for the limited growth of unions in this period, and the success of the Knights of Labor and the American Federation of Labor.
5. Describe the major labor confrontations in the period.
6. Account for the limited appeal of socialism for American labor.

**CHAPTER OUTLINE**

I. The post–Civil War economy
   A. Economic changes in the 1869–1899 period
   B. Railroad building
      1. The transcontinental plan
         a. Central Pacific
            i. organizers
            ii. Chinese laborers
         b. Union Pacific
      2. Financing the railroads
         a. Crédit-Mobilier fraud
         b. Jay Gould's work
         c. Cornelius Vanderbilt
      3. Railroads controlled by seven major groups
   C. New products and inventions
      1. Number of patents
      2. Improvements and inventions
      3. Development of the telephone
      4. Edison's work with electricity
   D. Entrepreneurs of the era
      1. Rockefeller and the oil industry
         a. Background
         b. Concentration on refining and transportation
         c. Development of the trust
         d. Evolution of the holding company
      2. Andrew Carnegie and the Gospel of Wealth
         a. Background
         b. Concentration on steel
         c. Philosophy for big business

            d. Other proponents of the Gospel of Wealth
        3. J. P. Morgan and investment banking
            a. Background
            b. Concentration on railroad financing
            c. Control of organizations
            d. Consolidation of the steel industry
    E. Impact of growth on the distribution of wealth
II. Developments in labor
    A. Circumstances for workers
        1. Wages and hours
        2. Living and working conditions
        3. Control by impersonal forces
    B. Obstacles to unions
    C. Molly Maguires
    D. Railroad strike of 1877
        1. Causes
        2. Scope and violence
        3. Effects
    E. Efforts at union building
        1. National Labor Union
        2. Knights of Labor
            a. Early development
            b. Emphasis on the union
            c. Role of Terence Powderly
            d. Victories of the Knights
            e. Anarchism
            f. Haymarket Affair
            g. Lasting influence of the Knights of Labor
        3. Development of the American Federation of Labor
            a. Development of craft unions
            b. Role of Samuel Gompers
            c. Growth of the union
    F. Violence in the 1890s
        1. Homestead Strike, 1892
        2. Pullman Strike, 1894
            a. Causes
            b. Role of the government
            c. Impact on Eugene V. Debs
    G. Socialism and American labor
        1. Daniel DeLeon and Eugene Debs
        2. Social Democratic party
            a. Early work
            b. Height of influence
    H. Rise of the IWW
        1. Sources of strength
        2. Revolutionary goals
        3. Causes for decline


## KEY ITEMS OF CHRONOLOGY

| | |
|---|---|
| National Labor Union formed | 1866 |
| Completion of the first transcontinental railroad | 1869 |
| Standard Oil of Ohio incorporated | 1870 |
| Telephone patented | 1876 |
| Incandescent light bulb invented | 1879 |
| Terence Powderly becomes president of the Knights of Labor | 1879 |
| First electric current supplied to eighty-five customers in New York City | 1882 |
| Creation of the Standard Oil Trust | 1882 |
| Haymarket Affair | 1886 |
| Founding of the American Federation of Labor | 1886 |
| Pullman Strike | 1894 |
| U.S. Steel Corporation formed | 1901 |
| IWW founded | 1905 |

## TERMS TO MASTER

*Listed below are some important terms or people with which you should be familiar after you complete the study of this chapter. Explain the significance of each name or term.*

1. Union Pacific
2. transcontinental railroads
3. Crédit-Mobilier
4. Cornelius Vanderbilt
5. Alexander Graham Bell
6. Thomas Alva Edison
7. George Westinghouse
8. John D. Rockefeller
9. Gospel of Wealth
10. Horatio Alger
11. J. Pierpont Morgan
12. United States Steel Corporation
13. holding company
14. Molly Maguires
15. industrial and craft unions
16. Knights of Labor
17. American Federation of Labor
18. Haymarket Affair
19. Samuel Gompers
20. Pullman Strike
21. Eugene V. Debs
22. Wobblies

## VOCABULARY BUILDING

*Listed below are some words used in this chapter. Look up each word in your dictionary.*

1. treble (v.)
2. machination
3. indelible
4. judicious
5. connive
6. inscrutable
7. dissuade
8. alms
9. pauper
10. leper
11. revulsion
12. anarchism
13. reprieve
14. leverage
15. tedium
16. proviso
17. charismatic
18. embellish
19. petulant
20. ardent

## EXERCISES FOR UNDERSTANDING

*When you have completed reading the chapter, answer each of the following questions. If you have difficulty, go back and reread the section of the chapter related to the question.*

### Multiple-Choice Questions

*Select the letter of the response that best completes the statement.*

1. The first transcontinental railroad was built by
   A. private companies with government subsidies.
   B. private companies granted a monopoly by the government.
   C. private companies with no federal assistance.
   D. the federal government.

2. The Central Pacific construction crews were largely
   A. Indians.
   B. Chinese.
   C. failed miners and farmers.
   D. Irish and Italian immigrants.

3. Andrew Carnegie's Gospel of Wealth called on the rich to
   A. support overseas missionaries.
   B. get richer.
   C. provide for the public good.
   D. help others gain wealth by turning their businesses over to the workers.

4. J. P. Morgan was actively engaged in
   A. investment banking.
   B. the steel industry.
   C. railroading.
   D. all of the above.

5. The social costs of industrialization included
   A. closer relationships between workers and factory owners.
   B. numerous job-related injuries and deaths.
   C. rising wages for workers.
   D. healthier working conditions for most workers.
6. The Homestead Strike of 1892 involved
   A. workers on the transcontinental railroad.
   B. settlers on the western frontier.
   C. steelworkers.
   D. anarchists in the oil industry.
7. American workers tended to reject unions because
   A. they believed they would only be workers for a short time until they could own their own farms or move up otherwise.
   B. they were so strongly committed to a system of equality and uniform wages for all.
   C. they did not like the association with immigrants in unions.
   D. they thought all unions were corrupt.
8. "Recognition of the irrepressible conflict between the capitalist class and the working class" was a key belief of the
   A. Knights of Labor.
   B. American Federation of Labor.
   C. Industrial Workers of the World.
   D. all of the above.

## True-False Questions

*Indicate whether each statement is true or false.*

1. The first big business with large-scale bureaucracies was the steel industry.
2. The Bessemer process was used to make steel.
3. John D. Rockefeller made his fortune in the oil industry.
4. Horatio Alger's novels portrayed the lives of robber barons in the late nineteenth century.
5. In 1900 the average worker in manufacturing worked only about 45 hours per week.
6. The first major interstate strike was led by the Molly Maguires in the coal industry.
7. The American Federation of Labor was an organization of national craft unions.
8. Anarchists advocated a stateless society.

## Essay Questions

1. List and explain the factors that promoted the growth of industry in the United States in the late nineteenth century.
2. What was the relationship among inventors, entrepreneurs, and great wealth in the late–nineteenth-century United States? Give several examples.
3. Compare and contrast the business practices of John D. Rockefeller and Andrew Carnegie.
4. What were the major conflicts between labor and capitalists in the late nineteenth century? What effects did they have?
5. How did the goals and tactics of the Knights of Labor differ from those of the Wobblies? Which were more effective?

# DOCUMENTS

## Document 1. Andrew Carnegie Provides Rules for Disposing of Wealth

As the textbook indicates, Andrew Carnegie developed the concept of the Gospel of Wealth in an essay originally entitled "Wealth." Excerpted below are sections dealing with the best method for a person to use in disposing of his or her fortune.

It will be understood that *fortunes* are here spoken of, not moderate sums saved by many years of effort, the returns from which are required for the comfortable maintenance and education of families. This is not *wealth,* but only *competence,* which it should be the aim of all to acquire.

There are but three modes in which surplus wealth can be disposed of. It can be left to the families of the decedents; or it can be bequeathed for public purposes; or, finally, it can be administered during their lives by its possessors. Under the first and second modes most of the wealth of the world that has reached the few has hitherto been applied. Let us in turn consider each of these modes. The first is the most injudicious. In monarchical countries, the estates and the greatest portion of the wealth are left to the first son, that the vanity of the parent may be gratified by the thought that his name and title are to descend to succeeding generations unimpaired. The condition of this class in Europe to-day teaches the futility of such hopes or ambitions. The successors have become impoverished through their follies or from the fall in the value of land. . . . Under republican institutions the division of property among the children is much fairer, but the question which forces itself upon thoughtful men in all lands is: Why should men leave great fortunes to their children? If this is done from affection, is it not misguided affection? Observation teaches that, generally speaking, it is not well for the children that they should be so burdened. Neither is it well for the State. Beyond providing for the wife and daughters moderate sources of income, and very moderate allowances indeed, if any, for the sons, men may well hesitate, for it is no longer questionable that great sums bequeathed oftener work more for the injury than for the good of the recipients. Wise men will soon conclude that, for the best interests of the members of their families and of the State, such bequests are an improper use of their means.

It is not suggested that men who have failed to educate their sons to earn a livelihood cast them adrift in poverty. If any man has seen fit to rear his sons with a view to their living idle lives, or, what is highly commendable, has instilled in them the sentiment that they are in a position to labor for public ends without reference to pecuniary considerations, then, of course, the duty of the parent is to see that such are provided for *in moderation.* There are instances of millionaires' sons unspoiled by wealth, who, being rich, still perform great services in the community. Such are the very salt of the earth, as valuable as, unfortunately, they are rare; still it is not the exception, but the rule, that men must regard, and, looking at the usual result of enormous sums conferred upon legatees, the thoughtful man must shortly say, "I would as soon leave to my son a curse as the almighty dollar," and admit to himself that it is not the welfare of the children, but family pride, which inspires these enormous legacies.

As to the second mode, that of leaving wealth at death for public uses, it may be said that this is only a means for the disposal of wealth, provided a man is content to wait until he is dead before he becomes of much good in the world. Knowledge of the results of legacies bequeathed is not calculated to inspire the brightest hopes of much posthumous good being accomplished. The cases are not few in which the real object sought by the testator is not attained, nor are they few in which his real wishes are thwarted. In many cases the bequests are so used as to become only monuments of his folly. It is well to remember that it requires the exercise of no less ability than that which acquired the wealth to use it so as to be really beneficial to the community. Besides this, it may fairly be said that no man is to be extolled for doing what he cannot help doing, nor is he to be thanked by the community to which he only leaves wealth at death. Men who leave vast sums in this way may fairly be thought men who would not have left it at all, had they been able to take it with them. The memories of such cannot be held in grateful remembrance, for there is no grace in their gifts. It is not to be wondered at that such bequests seem so generally to lack the blessing.

The growing disposition to tax more and more heavily large estates left at death is a cheering indication of the growth of a salutary change in public opinion. The State of Pennsylvania now takes—subject to some exceptions—one-tenth of the property left by its citizens.... Of all forms of taxation, this seems the wisest. Men who continue hoarding great sums all their lives, the proper use of which for public ends would work good to the community, should be made to feel that the community, in the form of the State, cannot thus be deprived of its proper share. By taxing estates heavily at death the State marks its condemnation of the selfish millionaire's unworthy life.

It is desirable that nations should go much further in this direction. Indeed, it is difficult to set bounds to the share of a rich man's estate which should go at his death to the public through the agency of the State, and by all means such taxes should be graduated, beginning at nothing upon moderate sums to dependents, and increasing rapidly as the amounts swell, until of the millionaire's hoard, as of Shylock's, at least

> The other half
> Comes to the privy coffer of the state.

This policy would work powerfully to induce the rich man to attend to the administration of wealth during his life, which is the end that society should always have in view, as being that by far the most fruitful for the people. Nor need it be feared that this policy would sap the root of enterprise and render men less anxious to accumulate, for to the class whose ambition it is to leave great fortunes and be talked about after their death, it will attract even more attention, and, indeed, be a somewhat nobler ambition to have enormous sums paid over to the state from their fortunes.

There remains, then, only one mode of using great fortunes; but in this we have the true antidote for the temporary unequal distribution of wealth, the reconciliation of the rich and the poor—a reign of harmony—another ideal, differing, indeed, from that of the Communist in requiring only the further evolution of existing conditions, not the total overthrow of our civilization. It is founded upon the present most intense individualism, and the race is prepared to put it in practice by degrees whenever it pleases....

This, then, is held to be the duty of the man of Wealth: First, to set an example of modest, unostentatious living, shunning display or extravagance; to provide moderately for the legitimate wants of those dependent upon him; and after doing so to consider all surplus revenues which come to him simply as trust funds, which he is called upon to administer, and strictly bound as a matter of duty to administer in the manner which, in his judgment, is best calculated to produce the most beneficial results for the community—the man of wealth thus becoming the mere agent and trustee for his poorer brethen, bringing to their service his superior wisdom, experience, and ability to administer, doing for them better than they would or could do for themselves.

. . . It were better for mankind that the millions of the rich were thrown into the sea than so spent as to encourage the slothful, the drunken, the unworthy. Of every thousand dollars spent in so called charity to-day, it is probable that $950 is unwisely spent, so spent, indeed, as to produce the very evils which it proposes to mitigate or cure. A well-known writer of philosophic books admitted the other day that he had given a quarter of a dollar to a man who approached him as he was coming to visit the house of his friend. He knew nothing of the habits of this beggar, knew not the use that would be made of this money, although he had every reason to suspect that it would be spent improperly. This man professed to be a disciple of Herbert Spencer; yet the quarter-dollar given that night will probably work more injury than all the money which its thoughtless donor will ever be able to give in true charity will do good. He only gratified his own feelings, saved himself from annoyance—and this was probably one of the most selfish and very worst actions of his life, for in all respects he is most worthy.

In bestowing charity, the main consideration should be to help those who will help themselves; to provide part of the means by which those who desire to improve may do so; to give those who desire to rise the aids by which they may rise; to assist, but rarely or never to do all. Neither the individual nor the race is improved by alms-giving. Those worthy of assistance, except in rare cases, seldom require assistance. The really valuable men of the race never do, except in cases of accident or sudden change. Every one has, of course, cases of individuals brought to his own knowledge where temporary assistance can do genuine good, and these he will not overlook. But the amount which can be wisely given by the individual for individuals is necessarily limited by his lack of knowledge of the circumstances connected with each. He is the only true reformer who is as careful and as anxious not to aid the unworthy as he is to aid the worthy, and, perhaps, even more so, for in alms-giving more injury is probably done by rewarding vice than by relieving virtue.

[Andrew Carnegie, "Wealth," *North American Review* 148, no. 391 (June 1889): 657–663]

## Document 2. Russell Conwell Encourages Christians to Obtain Wealth

In the sermon "Acres of Diamonds," which Russell Conwell delivered more than 6,000 times, he advised Christians to use their talent and energy to obtain wealth.

. . . I say you ought to be rich; you have no right to be poor. . . . You ought to be rich. But persons with certain religious prejudice will ask, "How can you spend your time advising the rising generation to give their time to getting money—dollars and cents—the commercial spirit?"

Yet I must say that you ought to spend time getting rich. You and I know there are some things more valuable than money; of course, we do. Ah, yes! By a heart made unspeakably sad by a grave on which the autumn leaves now fall, I know there are some things higher and grander and sublimer than money. Well does the man know, who has suffered, that there are some things sweeter and holier and more sacred than gold. Nevertheless, the man of common sense also knows that there is not one of those things that is not greatly enhanced by the use of money. Money is power.... Money is power; money has powers; and for a man to say, "I do not want money," is to say, "I do not wish to do any good to my fellowmen." It is absurd thus to talk. It is absurd to disconnect them. This is a wonderfully great life, and you ought to spend your time getting money, because of the power there is in money. And yet this religious prejudice is so great that some people think it is a great honor to be one of God's poor.... We ought to get rich if we can by honorable and Christian methods, and these are the only methods that sweep us quickly toward the goal of riches.

I remember, not many years ago a young theological student who came into my office and said to me that he thought it was his duty to come in and "labor with me." I asked what had happened, and he said: "I feel it is my duty to come in and speak to you, sir, and say that the Holy Scriptures declare that money is the root of all evil." I asked him where he found that saying, and he said he found it in the Bible. ... So he took the Bible and read it: "The *love* of money is the root of all evil." ... Oh, that is it. It is the worship of the means instead of the end, though you cannot reach the end without the means. When a man makes an idol of the money instead of the purposes for which it may be used, when he squeezes the dollar until the eagle squeals, then it is made the root of all evil. Think, if you only had the money, what you could do for your wife, your child, and for your home and your city.

[Agnes Rush Burr, *Russell H. Conwell, Founder of the Institutional Church in America: The Work and the Man* (Philadelphia: The John C. Winston Co., 1905), pp. 324–326]

## Questions for Reflection

Has Carnegie listed all the methods for the disposal of fortunes? Would most wealthy people today agree with his notions of how to treat members of the family? How do you react to his notion of using the inheritance tax? Does it appear to you that most very wealthy people today follow his dictates for modest living? Is Carnegie right about the harm of almsgiving? What appear to be the sources for Carnegie's ideas? Are his concepts valid today or were they appropriate only for the nineteenth century, if that?

How does Russell Conwell's sermon reflect attitudes similar to Carnegie's? Is Conwell providing an appropriate reflection of the ethic of modern Christianity? How would Conwell's ideas have been received by the wealthy people of his era? Why? Based on a reading of this portion of Conwell's sermon, how would you define the "Gospel of Wealth"?

## ANSWERS TO MULTIPLE-CHOICE AND TRUE-FALSE QUESTIONS

### Multiple-Choice Questions

1-A, 2-B, 3-C, 4-D, 5-B, 6-C, 7-A, 8-C

### True-False Questions

1-F, 2-T, 3-T, 4-F, 5-F, 6-F, 7-T, 8-T

# 20

## THE EMERGENCE OF MODERN AMERICA

## CHAPTER OBJECTIVES

*After you complete the reading and study of this chapter you should be able to*

1. Discuss the important intellectual trends in the period 1877–1890.
2. Describe city growth in the late nineteenth century.
3. Account for the new immigration and the reaction that it engendered.
4. Trace major developments in higher education after the Civil War.
5. Explain the concepts of Social Darwinism and Reform Darwinism.
6. Describe the local color, realist, and naturalist movements in literature.
7. Explain the social gospel and describe its manifestations.

## CHAPTER OUTLINE

I. Urbanization
   A. Urbanization reflected in westward migration
   B. Factors important to urban growth
   C. Characteristics of the new urban scene
   D. Vertical and horizontal growth of cities
      1. Development of elevators
      2. Introduction of cast-iron and steel-frame construction
      3. Development of electric streetcars
   E. City problems
      1. Tenements
      2. Health
      3. City services
   F. Role of city boss
   G. Lure of the city

II. The new immigration
   A. Reasons for emigration to America
   B. Nature of the new immigrants
   C. Ellis Island
      1. scale of operation
      2. reception of immigrants
   D. The immigrants' experiences
   E. The nativist response
      1. Reasons for objection to new immigrants
      2. Rise of American Protective Association
   F. Efforts at immigration restriction
      1. Legislation
      2. Treatment of Chinese on West Coast

III. Growth of education
   A. Indication of the spread of schooling
   B. Developments in higher education
      1. Growth of colleges

2. Growth of the elective system
3. Expansion of opportunities for women
4. Development of graduate schools
C. The rise of professionalism
 1. Nature of the movement
 2. Fields developed
IV. Theories of social change
 A. Darwinism
  1. Darwin's ideas and their implications
  2. Social Darwinism
   a. Herbert Spencer's contributions
   b. William Graham Sumner's contributions
  3. Lester Frank Ward and Reform Darwinism
 B. Developments in other fields of learning
  1. Developments in history
  2. Pragmatism
   a. Ideas of William James
   b. John Dewey and instrumentalism
V. Realism in American literature
 A. The local colorists
  1. Sarah Orne Jewett
  2. George Washington Cable
  3. Joel Chandler Harris
 B. Mark Twain
 C. William Dean Howells
 D. Henry James
 E. Literary naturalism
  1. Frank Norris
  2. Stephen Crane
  3. Jack London
  4. Theodore Dreiser
VI. Social critics
 A. Henry George and the single tax
 B. Henry Demarest Lloyd and cooperation
 C. Thorstein Veblen and conspicuous consumption
VII. The religious response: social gospel
 A. Abandonment of inner-city churches
 B. Development of the institutional church
  1. YMCA and the Salvation Army
  2. Other facilities
 C. Washington Gladden
 D. Catholic responses to modernity
VIII. Early efforts at urban reform
 A. The settlement house movement
 B. Women's rights
  1. Growth of the female labor force
  2. Women's suffrage
   a. Conflicts in the movement
   b. Gains in the states
  3. Other women's efforts
 C. The status of laissez-faire government at the end of the century

## KEY ITEMS OF CHRONOLOGY

| | |
|---|---|
| Founding of The Johns Hopkins University | 1876 |
| Henry George's *Progress and Poverty* | 1879 |
| Publication of *Dynamic Sociology* | 1883 |
| Publication of *Huckleberry Finn* | 1883 |
| First electric elevator | 1889 |
| Electric streetcar systems in cities | 1890s |
| Publication of *Maggie: A Girl of the Streets* | 1893 |
| Veblen's *Theory of the Leisure Class* | 1899 |

## TERMS TO MASTER

*Listed below are some important terms or people with which you should be familiar after you complete the study of this chapter. Explain the significance of each name or term.*

1. Frederick Law Olmstead
2. "streetcar suburbs"
3. the "new" immigration
4. American Protective Association
5. The Johns Hopkins University
6. professionalism
7. Social Darwinism
8. William Graham Sumner
9. Lester Frank Ward
10. "scientific" history
11. pragmatism
12. John Dewey
13. local color movement
14. Henry James
15. naturalism
16. Henry George
17. social gospel
18. settlement houses
19. Susan B. Anthony

## VOCABULARY BUILDING

*Listed below are some words used in this chapter. Look up each in your dictionary.*

1. tenor
2. cumbersome
3. patronage
4. vaudeville
5. fraught
6. cavernous
7. steerage
8. debilitating
9. noxious
10. decry
11. impede
12. pseudonym
13. expatriate
14. illicit
15. increment
16. freelance
17. flaunt
18. encyclical
19. blandishment
20. rudimentary

## EXERCISES FOR UNDERSTANDING

*When you have completed the reading of the chapter, answer each of the following questions. If you have difficulty, go back and reread the section of the chapter related to the question.*

## Multiple-Choice Questions

*Select the letter of the response that best completes the statement.*

1. Most Americans lived in urban areas by
   A. 1890.
   B. 1900.
   C. 1910.
   D. 1920.

2. Urban problems included
   A. tenements.
   B. streetcar suburbs.
   C. vaudeville shows.
   D. high-rise apartments.

3. Most immigrants probably came to the United States because of
   A. famine and poverty in Europe.
   B. religious and ethnic persecution in their home countries.
   C. wars in Europe.
   D. the chance for jobs and land in America.

4. An important new trend in higher education after the Civil War was
   A. coeducation.
   B. the development of a varied curriculum.
   C. the rise of graduate schools.
   D. the creation of land-grant colleges.

5. Lester Frank Ward stressed
   A. the power of folkways in determining social conditions.
   B. the potential of human intelligence in planning change.
   C. the importance of heredity in human progress.
   D. the similarity of social evolution and biological evolution.

6. "Theory of the leisure class" and "conspicuous consumption" were ideas of
   A. Henry George.
   B. Thorstein Veblen.
   C. Henry Ward Beecher.
   D. Walter Rauchenbusch.

7. The social gospel of Washington Gladden encouraged
   A. assistance to middle-class Christians.

B. a focus on personal sins and saving souls.
   C. community services and helping the poor.
   D. the laissez-faire business philosophy.
8. A leader in the settlement house movement was
   A. Thorstein Veblen.
   B. William Dean Howells.
   C. Jane Addams.
   D. Susan B. Anthony.

**True-False Questions**

*Indicate whether each statement is true or false.*

1. After the Civil War, more people moved to the frontier than to cities.
2. After 1890, most immigrants came from southern and eastern Europe.
3. From 1870 to 1890, the American college student population tripled.
4. William James said the "life of the law has not been logic, it has been experience."
5. Stephen Crane was the first major writer born and raised west of the Appalachians.
6. Women's suffrage was achieved first in the urban states of the Northwest.
7. Railroads in the late-nineteenth century were effectively regulated by state laws strongly enforced by judges.

**Essay Questions**

1. What factors fueled the growth of cities in the late 1800s?
2. Who were the immigrants to America around 1900 and what was their experience in their new country?
3. Compare and contrast the implications of social Darwinism and reform Darwinism regarding such public issues as public education and regulation of business.
4. How did realism affect American literature?
5. Explain the critiques of modern American society offered by Veblen, Gladden, and others.

## DOCUMENT

### Circumstances of Typical Illinois Working Families

In 1884 the Illinois Bureau of Labor Statistics conducted a survey of typical laboring families. The survey included over 2,000 families, of whom 167 were selected for detailed accounts. Excerpted here are the accounts of eight families diverse in occupation, income, and circumstances.

In order to present a closer view of the manner of living, the surroundings, habits, tastes and daily diet of the Illinois workingman of to-day, under various circumstances and conditions, and to afford a more definite impression as to the details of his environment than can be obtained from the mere contemplation of columns of figures, we transcribe, for a limited number of representative families, their entire record, as procured by our agents, together with the notes of observation, made at the time of the visit. . . .

This minute catalogue of the details governing the life of each family portrays more vividly than any mere array of figures can the common current of daily life among the people. The extremes of condition and the average types are alike presented, and it may be seen, not only what manner of life ordinarily prevails with a given income, but also how some families, by thrift, temperance and prudence, save money and increase their store, upon earnings which other families find insufficient for their support. . . .

### No. 1     **Baker**                    **Scandinavian**

*Earnings*—Of father                           $375
           Of daughter, aged eighteen          150
           Of son, aged fifteen                 48
           Total                              $573

*Condition*—Family numbers 7—father, mother and five children, three girls and two boys. The girls aged eight, eleven and eighteen; boys, six and fifteen. The children attend school regularly. The house they occupy contains four rooms, and they pay $9 per month rent. The house is in an unhealthy and dirty locality, furnished very poorly, and kept in poor condition. The children, when out of school, pick fuel from the railroad tracks and accompanying lumber yards. The family are very ignorant, and live as the generality of the Swede race. Life insurance and trades unions are ignored.

*Food*—Breakfast—Coffee, bread, syrup.
       Dinner—Lunches, always.
       Supper—Meat, soup and bread.

*Cost of Living*—
    Rent                                        $108
    Fuel                                          12
    Meat and groceries                           200
    Clothing, boots and shoes, and dry goods     150
    Books, papers, etc.                            3
    Sundries [miscellaneous items]                50
    Total                                       $523

### No. 23    **Cigar Maker**                **French**

*Earnings*—Of father          $790

*Condition*—Family numbers 4—parents and two children, girl aged seven years and boy five. Live in house containing 6 rooms and pay for same rent at the rate of $10 per month. Both children attend school. Father carries some life insurance and belongs to trades union, and claims his wages this year are increased thereby about $200 over his wages of previous years, enabling them to live more comfortably, dress the children better, and eat more substantial and healthy food. Children healthy, bright and intelligent, and attend Sunday school. House is well furnished and has a small library. Live well and seem to be well satisfied, although their expenses equal their earnings.

*Food*—Breakfast—Coffee, bread, butter, milk, sugar
           and potatoes.
       Dinner—Tea, bread, butter, ham and eggs,
           poultry and dessert.
       Supper—Coffee, bread, butter, cheese,
           potatoes.

*Cost of Living*—
    Rent                                        $120
    Fuel                                          35

|   |   |
|---|---:|
| Meat | 100 |
| Groceries | 300 |
| Clothing | 75 |
| Boots and shoes | 15 |
| Dry goods | 20 |
| Books, papers, etc. | 8 |
| Life insurance | 17 |
| Trades union | 11 |
| Sickness | 80 |
| Sundries | 9 |
| Total | $790 |

### No. 65  Plumber                              Scotch-American

*Earnings*—Of father         $1,050

*Condition*—Family numbers 3—parents and one girl seven years old, who attends school. Occupy 3 rooms, for which they pay $13 per month rent; situation not very pleasant, but healthy; have had very little sickness. Rooms comfortably furnished. Family dress plainly, are below the average in intelligence, do not attend church or better class of public entertainments. The head of the family has employment fifty weeks during the year, and earns more than the average of wage-workers, which would indicate sobriety and industry, notwithstanding much of his leisure time is spent in beer-gardens and like places of amusement.

*Food*—Breakfast—Bread, butter, meat, potatoes, eggs, fruit.
Dinner—Lunch.
Supper—About the same as breakfast.

*Cost of Living*—

|   |   |
|---|---:|
| Rent | $156 |
| Fuel | 36 |
| Meat | 100 |
| Groceries | 200 |
| Clothing | 60 |
| Boots and shoes | 27 |
| Dry goods | 15 |
| Books, papers, etc. | 7 |
| Sickness | 10 |
| Sundries | 150 |
| Total | $761 |

### No. 77  Street-Car Conductor                       American

*Earnings*—Of father         $691

*Condition*—Family numbers 4—parents and two boys, aged two and four years. Father works 38 weeks in the year and 12 hours per day, and receives for his services an average of $2.60 per day. Occupies house containing 4 comfortable rooms. Husband belongs to trades union, but does not carry any life insurance. Father does not have steady employment the entire year, and has very unpleasant hours to work. Goes to work at 5 o'clock A.M., works about six hours, then lays off until 4 P.M., from which time he works until 11 P.M.

*Food*—Breakfast—Bread, steak, and coffee.
　　　　Dinner—Bread, vegetables, meat and fish.
　　　　Supper—Same as breakfast.

*Cost of Living*—
| | |
|---|---:|
| Rent | $120 |
| Fuel | 60 |
| Meat and groceries | 280 |
| Clothing, boots and shoes and dry goods | 150 |
| Books, papers, etc. | 15 |
| Trades union | 5 |
| Sickness | 20 |
| Sundries | 40 |
| Total | $690 |

## No. 100　Upholsterer　　　　　　　　　　Bohemian

*Earnings*—Of father　　$420

*Condition*—Family numbers 8—husband, wife and six children, four girls and two boys, the former aged, respectively, one month, one and a half, three and nine years, the latter five and seven. One of the children attends school; the rest of them, that are old enough, pick up coal, and go to the fruit warehouses and collect decayed fruit and other spoiled food. The family eat poor and spoiled meats, and live miserably, but seem to grow fat on it, and have but very little sickness. House contains three rooms, into which the eight persons are huddled. They pay $6 per month for the house. Family is dirty and ignorant in the extreme. The stench from the rooms is as bad as that from the stock yards.

*Food*—Breakfast—Coffee and bread.
　　　　Dinner—Soup and potatoes.
　　　　Supper—Coffee and bread.

*Cost of Living*—
| | |
|---|---:|
| Rent | $72 |
| Fuel | 8 |
| Meat and groceries | 240 |
| Clothing, boots and shoes | 80 |
| Dry goods | 10 |
| Sickness | 10 |
| Total | $420 |

## No. 129　Coal Miner　　　　　　　　　　Irish

*Earnings*—
| | |
|---|---:|
| Of father | $368 |
| Of son, 17 years of age | 368 |
| Of son, 14 years of age | 172 |
| Total | $908 |

*Condition*—Family numbers 9—parents and seven children, five boys and two girls, their ages ranging from two to seventeen years. Three of these attend school, and the two oldest boys work in the mines. Family occupy a house containing 3 rooms, with an addition of a shanty, for which they pay $5 per month rent. Father is an industrious and hard-working man, but only had thirty weeks work during the year. He is a leader among his class, is a great reader, belongs to temperance society, life insurance society, and trades union. Family healthy, and members of a church. They work half an acre of land, and raise vegetables enough for family use. They are making payments on a lot, sewing machine and back debts.

*Food*—Breakfast—Bread, butter, meat and coffee.
        Dinner—Bread, butter, cheese or meat and tea.
        Supper—Meat, potatoes, vegetables, bread, butter, pie and tea.

*Cost of Living*—

| | |
|---|---:|
| Rent | $60 |
| Fuel | 15 |
| Meat | 120 |
| Groceries | 360 |
| Clothing | 170 |
| Boots, shoes and dry goods | 63 |
| Books, papers, etc. | 8 |
| Life insurance | 30 |
| Trades union | 5 |
| Sickness | 4 |
| Sundries | 63 |
| Total | $898 |

### No. 142    Laborer               American

*Earnings*— Of father              $324

*Condition*—Family numbers 5—parents and three children, all boys, aged two, five and nine years respectively. Family occupy a house containing 3 rooms, situated in a very unhealthy locality, miserable surroundings, in the vicinity of a slough. Have a few chairs, bedstead, two poor stoves, but no carpets. Family poorly dressed; father works in saw mill; one cent per hour is retained by his employers on condition that he loses it if he leaves their service before the season closes. Father claims to have lost this 11 cts per day for the year 1881, as he had three of his fingers cut off, and could not work the season out.

*Food*—Breakfast—Bread, butter and coffee.
        Dinner—Bread, meat and coffee.
        Supper—Bread, butter, coffee and potatoes.

*Cost of Living*—

| | |
|---|---:|
| Rent | $48 |
| Fuel | 22 |
| Meat and groceries | 220 |
| Clothing, boots, shoes and dry goods | 30 |
| Sickness | 35 |
| Total | $355 |

### No. 165    Superintendent, Glass Works    American

*Earnings*—

| | |
|---|---:|
| Of father | $1,010 |
| Of son, 17 years old | 612 |
| Of son, 15 years old | 180 |
| Total | $1,802 |

*Condition*—Family numbers 8—parents and six children, three boys, aged eight, sixteen and eighteen years, and three girls, aged one, five and eleven years. Two of the children attend school. Family occupy a comfortable house, containing 7 rooms, for which they pay a rental of $25 per month. Floors are all carpeted. Have piano and sewing machine. Family intelligent, and attend church regularly. They manage to save but little of their earnings. Father receives $125 per month, but only worked thirty-six weeks of the past year. He carries no life insurance.

*Food*—Breakfast—Bread, meat, coffee, and potatoes.
Dinner—Meats, vegetables, coffee and fruits.
Supper—Meat, potatoes, tea and fruits.

*Cost of Living*—

| | |
|---|---:|
| Rent | $300 |
| Fuel | 40 |
| Meat | 200 |
| Groceries | 300 |
| Clothing | 125 |
| Boots and shoes | 75 |
| Dry goods | 100 |
| Books, papers, etc. | 20 |
| Sickness | 100 |
| Sundries | 150 |
| Total | $1,410 |

[From *Third Biennial Report of the Bureau of Labor Statistics of Illinois* (Springfield, Ill.: State Printer and Binder, 1884), pp. 357–358, 361, 365, 379, 383, 391, 401, 405, 413]

## Questions for Reflection

Analyze carefully the different amounts spent by each family on the major categories. What factors seem to affect family income? Which categories seem to increase most as families become more affluent? After examining this information, how much would you estimate to be the minimum amount required for a family to live comfortably?

The comments about family lifestyles were made by investigators who visited the families. What evidence can you cite to show the basic assumptions or attitudes about family life which were likely held by these investigators?

From all this information, what conclusions can you draw about family life among the working class in Illinois in the 1880s?

## ANSWERS TO MULTIPLE-CHOICE AND TRUE-FALSE QUESTIONS

### Multiple-Choice Questions

1-D, 2-A, 3-D, 4-C, 5-B, 6-B, 7-C, 8-C

### True-False Questions

1-F, 2-T, 3-T, 4-F, 5-F, 6-F, 7-F

# 21

## GILDED AGE POLITICS AND AGRARIAN REVOLT

## CHAPTER OBJECTIVES

*After you complete the reading and study of this chapter you should be able to*

1. Describe the major features of politics in the late-nineteenth century.
2. Describe the political alignments and issues in the "third political system."
3. Explain the major issues in the presidential elections of 1888, 1892, and 1896.
4. Account for the rise of the farmers' protest movement of the 1890s.
5. Explain the impact of populism on the American scene.

## CHAPTER OUTLINE

I. Nature of Gilded Age politics
   A. National political parties
      1. Evasion of issues
      2. Some disagreement on tariff
      3. Even division between parties in popular vote (1868–1912)
      4. No strong president
      5. Importance of patronage
   B. The voters
      1. High voter participation
      2. Belief in reality of issues
      3. Intense cultural conflicts
   C. Ethnic and religious divisions
      1. Republicans
      2. Democrats
      3. Issues
         a. Nativism
         b. Prohibition

II. The Hayes administration
   A. Hayes's background
   B. Divided Republicans
      1. Stalwarts and Conkling
      2. Half-Breeds and Blaine
   C. Support for civil service reform
   D. Hayes's limited version of government

III. The election of 1880
   A. Republican nomination
      1. The Grant candidacy
      2. Garfield's nomination as a dark horse
   B. Democratic nomination of Winfield Scott Hancock
   C. Closest election results of the century

IV. The Garfield-Arthur administration

A. Garfield's background and his assassination
B. Arthur's background
C. His strong actions as president
   1. Support of Pendleton Civil Service Act, 1883
   2. Support for tariff reduction
      a. Effects of treasury surplus
      b. Nature of the "Mongrel Tariff" of 1883
D. Scurrilous campaign of 1884
   1. Reasons Arthur was not a candidate
   2. Republican nomination of Blaine and Logan
      a. Blaine's background
      b. Effect of Mulligan letters
      c. Emergence of Mugwumps
   3. Democratic nomination of Cleveland
      a. Cleveland's political background
      b. His illegitimate child
      c. Concept of "rum, Romanism, and rebellion"
   4. Election results

V. Cleveland's presidency
   A. Cleveland's view of the role of government
   B. Special interests
      1. Civil service reform
      2. Union veterans
      3. Railroads
         a. *Wabash* case
         b. Interstate Commerce Commission
      4. Tariff reform
   C. Election of 1888
      1. Cleveland renominated
      2. Republican nomination of Benjamin Harrison
      3. Campaign focuses on the tariff
      4. Personal attacks
      5. Results

VI. Republican reform under Harrison
   A. Treatment of veterans
   B. Republican control of Congress, 1889–1891
      1. Passage of Sherman Antitrust Act, 1890
      2. Sherman Silver Purchase Act, 1890
      3. Effect of McKinley Tariff, 1890
   C. Democratic congressional victories of 1890
      1. Ostensible reaction to heavy spending of Republicans
      2. Impact on the election of prohibition and social issues

VII. Problems of farmers
   A. Worsening economic and social conditions
      1. Causes for declining agricultural prices
         a. Overproduction
         b. Worldwide competition
      2. The railroads as villains
      3. Effects of the tariff on farmers
      4. Problems of currency deflation
      5. Problems of geography and climate
      6. Isolation of farmers
   B. Development of Patrons of Husbandry
      1. Development of the Grange
      2. Effects of Granger political activity
   C. Rise of the Greenback Party
   D. Farm politics
      1. Texas Alliance
         a. Membership
         b. Political activism
         c. Colored Alliance
         d. Charles W. Macune
         e. Cooperative scheme
      2. Northwestern Alliance
      3. Southern Alliance
      4. People's party
         a. Early spokespeople
            i. Mary Elizabeth Lease
            ii. Jerry Simpson
         b. Platform
         c. Candidates in 1892

VIII. Depression of 1893
   A. Nature of the depression
   B. Reactions to the depression
   C. Results of the 1894 elections

IX. Focus on silver
   A. The gold drain
   B. Agitation for free silver
   C. Effect on nominations of 1896

1. Republican actions
2. Democratic candidate
3. Populist position

D. Campaign of 1896 and its results
E. The postelection shift to gold

## KEY ITEMS OF CHRONOLOGY

| | |
|---|---|
| Patrons of Husbandry founded | 1867 |
| Hayes administration | 1877–1881 |
| *Munn v. Illinois* | 1877 |
| Garfield administration | March–September 1881 |
| Arthur administration | September 1881–1885 |
| Pendleton Civil Service Act | 1883 |
| Mongrel Tariff Act | 1883 |
| Cleveland administrations | 1885–1889; 1893–1897 |
| Interstate Commerce Act | 1887 |
| Benjamin Harrison administration | 1889–1893 |
| Sherman Anti-Trust Act | 1890 |
| Sherman Silver Purchase Act | 1890 |
| McKinley Tariff Act | 1890 |
| Populist party founded | 1892 |
| Economic depression | 1893 |
| McKinley administrations | 1897–1901 |

## TERMS TO MASTER

*Listed below are some important terms or people with which you should be familiar after you complete the study of this chapter. Explain the significance of each name or term.*

1. Stalwarts and Half-Breeds
2. Bland-Allison Act
3. Pendleton Civil Service Act (1883)
4. "Mongrel Tariff" of 1883
5. James G. Blaine
6. Mugwumps
7. *Wabash Railroad v. Illinois*
8. Sherman Anti-Trust Act
9. Sherman Silver Purchase Act
10. McKinley Tariff
11. "free and unlimited coinage of silver"
12. Patrons of Husbandry
13. Farmers' Alliances
14. Populist party
15. Jacob S. Coxey
16. William Jennings Bryan

## VOCABULARY BUILDING

*Listed below are some words used in this chapter. Look up each word in your dictionary.*

1. paradoxical
2. muddled
3. deferential
4. snide
5. murky
6. facade
7. jobbery
8. billowing
9. maligner
10. knave
11. insolently
12. inequity
13. plurality
14. rebate
15. hardihood
16. chronic
17. apocalyptic

18. crescendo
19. countenance (v.)
20. vapid

## EXERCISES FOR UNDERSTANDING

*When you have completed reading the chapter, answer each of the following questions. If you have difficulty, go back and reread the section of the chapter related to the question.*

### Multiple-Choice Questions

*Select the letter of the response that best completes the statement.*

1. The political parties from 1870 to 1896 generally
   A. disagreed about the issue of civil service reform.
   B. pursued a policy of evasion on all issues.
   C. most closely agreed with each other on the issue of the tariff.
   D. disagreed most strongly over the regulation of business.
2. The Stalwarts and the Half-Breeds were
   A. names for Democrats and Republicans.
   B. characters in the novel *The Gilded Age*.
   C. the supporters and opponents of Grover Cleveland.
   D. factions in the Republican party.
3. The Pendleton Civil Service Act provided that
   A. most government jobs would be filled on merit.
   B. presidents could increase the jobs covered by civil service.
   C. Congress had to approve all civil service appointees.
   D. presidents could not appoint any political friends to office.
4. "Rum, Romanism, and rebellion" referred to
   A. Democrats.
   B. Mugwumps.
   C. Republicans.
   D. Populists.
5. The Sherman Silver Purchase Act of 1890
   A. reduced the government's purchases of silver.
   B. led to the inflation desired by farmers.
   C. worried eastern business and financial groups.
   D. did all of the above
6. The basic problem of farmers in the late nineteenth century was
   A. high rates charged by railroads.
   B. overproduction of agricultural products.
   C. inflation.
   D. high prices for manufactured goods caused by high tariffs.
7. The Populist party demanded
   A. government ownership of railroads.
   B. coinage of silver.
   C. an income tax.
   D. all of the above
8. "Burn down your cities and leave our farms, and your cities will spring up again as if by magic; but destroy our farms and the grass will grow in the streets of every city in the country," declared
   A. William Jennings Bryan.
   B. William McKinley.
   C. Grover Cleveland.
   D. the Republican platform in 1896.

### True-False Questions

*Indicate whether each statement is true or false.*

1. The Republican party clearly dominated American politics in the Gilded Age.
2. Voter turnout in the Gilded Age was unusually high.
3. President Arthur supported *both* civil service reform and tariff reform.
4. Grover Cleveland advocated raising the tariff.
5. Republicans suffered severe losses in the 1890 elections.
6. The "crime of '73" refers to the assassination of President Garfield.
7. In the 1870s the Grangers primarily sought inflation of the currency.

8. Jacob S. Coxey and his army demanded relief for the unemployed.

**Essay Questions**

1. What was distinctive about the Gilded Age political system?
2. What which issues were important in Gilded Age politics? Explain the relative importance of cultural and ethnic questions.
3. Was Grover Cleveland a successful President? Explain.
4. Explain why the coinage of silver was an important issue in the late nineteenth century.
5. What caused the farmers' problems in the Gilded Age? Explain.
6. Describe the programs advocated by the Populist party in the 1890s. How would you judge their success?

## DOCUMENTS

### Documents 1 and 2. The Farmers' Situation

Some of the grievances of the United States's farmers in the 1890s are discussed in the first two sections. F. B. Tracy described the conditions in Iowa, and W. A. Peffer (later a Populist senator) assessed the plight of Kansas farmers.

> Nothing has done more to injure the [western] region than these freight rates. The railroads have retarded its growth as much as they first hastened it. The rates are often four times as large as Eastern rates.... The extortionate character of the freight rates has been recognized by all parties, and all have pledged themselves to lower them, but no state west of the Missouri has been able to do so.
>
> In the early days, people were so anxious to secure railways that they would grant any sort of concession which the companies asked. There were counties in Iowa and other Western states struggling under heavy loads of bond-taxes, levied twenty-five years ago, to aid railways of which not one foot has been built. Perhaps a little grading would be done, and then the project would be abandoned, the bonds transferred, and the county called upon by the "innocent purchaser" to pay the debt incurred by blind credulity. I have known men to sacrifice fortunes, brains, and lives in fighting vainly this iniquitous bond-swindle.
>
> Railways have often acquired mines and other properties by placing such high freight rates upon their products that the owner was compelled to sell at the railroad company's own terms. These freight rates have been especially burdensome to the farmers, who are far from their selling and buying markets, thus robbing them in both directions.
>
> Another fact which has incited the farmer against corporations is the bold and unblushing participation of the railways in politics. At every political convention their emissaries are present with blandishments and passes and other practical arguments to secure the nomination of their friends. The sessions of these legislatures are dis-

gusting scenes of bribery and debauchery. There is not an attorney of prominence in Western towns who does not carry a pass or has not had the opportunity to do so. The passes, of course, compass the end sought. By these means, the railroads have secured an iron grip upon legislatures and officers, while no redress has been given to the farmer.

The land question, also, is a source of righteous complaint. Much of the land of the West, instead of being held for actual settlers, has been bought up by speculators and Eastern syndicates in large tracts. They have done nothing to improve the land and have simply waited for the inevitable settler who bought cheaply a small "patch" and proceeded to cultivate it. When he had prospered so that he needed more land, he found that his own labor had increased tremendously the value of the adjacent land. . . .

Closely connected with the land abuse are the money grievances. As his pecuniary condition grew more serious, the farmer could not make payments on his land. Or he found that, with the ruling prices, he could not sell his produce at a profit. In either case he needed money, to make the payment or maintain himself until prices should rise. When he went to the moneylenders, these men, often dishonest usurers, told him that money was very scarce, that the rate of interest was rapidly rising, etc., so that in the end the farmer paid as much interest a month as the moneylender was paying a year for the same money. In this transaction, the farmer obtained his first glimpse of the idea of "the contraction of the currency at the hands of Eastern money sharks."

Disaster always follows the exaction of such exorbitant rates of interest, and want or eviction quickly came. Consequently, when demagogues went among the farmers to utter their calamitous cries, the scales seemed to drop from the farmer's eyes, and he saw gold bugs, Shylocks, conspiracies, and criminal legislation *ad infinitum.* Like a lightning flash, the idea of political action ran through the Alliances. A few farmers' victories in county campaigns the previous year became a promise of broader conquest, and with one bound the Farmers' Alliance went into politics all over the West.

[From F. B. Tracy, "Why the Farmers Revolted," *Forum*, 16 (October 1893): 242–43.]

Farmers are passing through the "valley and shadow of death"; farming as a business is profitless; values of farm products have fallen 50 per cent since the great war, and farm values have depreciated 25 to 50 per cent during the last ten years; farmers are overwhelmed with debts secured by mortgages on their homes, unable in many instances to pay even the interest as it falls due, and unable to renew the loans because securities are weakening by reason of the general depression; many farmers are losing their homes under this dreadful blight, and the mortgage mill still grinds. We are in the hands of a merciless power; the people's homes are at stake. . . .

The American farmer of today is altogether a different sort of a man from his ancestor of fifty or a hundred years ago. . . . All over the West, . . . the farmer thrashes his wheat all at one time, he disposes of it all at one time, and in a great many instances the straw is wasted. He sells his hogs, and buys bacon and pork; he sells his cattle, and buys fresh beef and canned beef or corned beef, as the case may be; he sells his fruit, and buys it back in cans. . . . Not more than one farmer in fifty now keeps sheep at all; he relies upon the large sheep farmer for the wool, which is put into cloth or clothing ready for his use. Instead of having clothing made up on the farm in his own house or by a neighbor woman or country tailor a mile away, he either purchases his clothing ready made at the nearest town, or he buys the cloth and has a city tailor make it up for him. Instead of making implements which he uses about the farm—forks, rakes, etc., he goes to town to purchase even a handle for his axe or his mallet; . . . indeed, he buys nearly everything now that he produced at one time himself, and these things all cost money.

Besides all this, and what seems stranger than anything else, whereas in the earlier time the American home was a free home, unencumbered, . . . and whereas but a small amount of money was then needed for actual use in conducting the business of farming, there was always enough of it among the farmers to supply the demand, now, when at least ten times as much is needed, there is little or none to be obtained. . . .

The railroad builder, the banker, the money changer, and the manufacturer undermined the farmer. . . . The manufacturer came with his woolen mill, his carding mill, his broom factory, his rope factory, his wooden-ware factory, his cotton factory, his pork-packing establishment, his canning factory and fruit-preserving houses; the little shop on the farm has given place to the large shop in town; the wagon-maker's shop in the neighborhood has given way to the large establishment in the city where men by the thousand work and where a hundred or two hundred wagons are made in a week; the shoemaker's shop has given way to large establishments in the cities where most of the work is done by machines; the old smoke house has given way to the packing house, and the fruit cellars have been displaced by preserving factories. The farmer now is compelled to go to town for nearly everything that he wants. . . . And what is worse than all, if he needs a little more money than he has about him, he is compelled to go to town to borrow it. But he does not find the money there; in place of it he finds an agent who will "negotiate" a loan for him. The money is in the East . . . five thousand miles away. He pays the agent his commission, pays all the expenses of looking through the records and furnishing abstracts, pays for every postage stamp used in the transaction, and finally receives a draft for the amount of money required, minus these expenses. In this way the farmers of the country today are maintaining an army of middlemen, loan agents, bankers, and others, who are absolutely worthless for all good purposes in the community. . . .

These things, however, are on only the mechanical side of the farmer. His domain has been invaded by men of his own calling, who have taken up large tracts of land and farmed upon the plan of the manufacturers who employ a great many persons to perform the work under one management. This is "bonanza" farming. . . . The aim of some of the great "bonanza farms" of Dakota has been to apply machinery so effectually that the cultivation of one full section, or six hundred and forty acres, shall represent one year's work of only one man. This has not yet been reached, but so far as the production of the grain of wheat is concerned, one man's work will now give to each of one thousand persons enough for a barrel of flour a year, which is the average ration. . . .

The manufacture of oleomargarine came into active competition with farm butter. And about the same time a process was discovered by which a substitute for lard was produced—an article so very like the genuine lard taken from the fat of swine that the farmer himself was deceived by it. . . .

From this array of testimony the reader need have no difficulty in determining for himself "how we got here." The hand of the money changer is upon us. Money dictates our financial policy; money controls the business of the country; money is despoiling the people. . . . These men of Wall Street . . . hold the bonds of nearly every state, county, city and township in the Union; every railroad owes them more than it is worth. Corners in grain and other products of toil are the legitimate fruits of Wall Street methods. Every trust and combine made to rob the people had its origin in the example of Wall Street dealers. . . . This dangerous power which money gives is fast undermining the liberties of the people. It now has control of nearly half their homes, and is reaching out its clutching hands for the rest. This is the power we have to deal with.

[From W. A. Peffer, *The Farmer's Side* (New York, 1891), pp. 42, 56, 58–63, 121–23.]

## Document 3. A Response to the Farmers' Protests

William Allen White, editor of the Emporia, Kansas, *Gazette,* wrote "What's the Matter with Kansas?" as he observed the 1896 presidential campaign. He ridiculed the agrarian challenge of the Populist Party and helped elect William McKinley.

Today the Kansas Department of Agriculture sent out a statement which indicates that Kansas has gained less than two thousand people in the past year. There are about two hundred and twenty-five thousand families in this state, and there were ten thousand babies born in Kansas, and yet so many people have left the state that the natural increase is cut down to less than two thousand net.

This has been going on for eight years.

If there had been a high brick wall around the state eight years ago, and not a soul had been admitted or permitted to leave, Kansas would be a half million souls better off than she is today. And yet the nation has increased in population. In five years ten million people have been added to the national population, yet instead of gaining a share of this—say, half a million—Kansas has apparently been a plague spot and, in the very garden of the world, has lost population by ten thousands every year.

Not only has she lost population, but she has lost money. Every moneyed man in the state who could get out without loss has gone. Every month in every community sees someone who has a little money pack up and leave the state. This has been going on for eight years. Money has been drained out all the time. In towns where ten years ago there were three or four or half a dozen money-lending concerns, stimulating industry by furnishing capital, there is now none, or one or two that are looking after the interests and principal already outstanding.

No one brings any money into Kansas any more. What community knows over one or two men who have moved in with more than $5,000 in the past three years? And what community cannot count half a score of men in that time who have left, taking all the money they could scrape together?

Yet the nation has grown rich; other states have increased in population and wealth—other neighboring states. Missouri has gained over two million, while Kansas has been losing half a million. Nebraska has gained in wealth and population while Kansas has gone downhill. Colorado has gained every way, while Kansas has lost every way since 1888.

What's the matter with Kansas?

There is no substantial city in the state. Every big town save one has lost in population. Yet Kansas City, Omaha, Lincoln, St. Louis, Denver, Colorado Springs, Sedalia, the cities of the Dakotas, St. Paul and Minneapolis and Des Moines—all cities and towns in the West— have steadily grown.

Take up the government blue book and you will see that Kansas is virtually off the map. Two or three little scrubby consular places in yellow-fever-stricken communities that do not aggregate ten thousand dollars a year is all the recognition that Kansas has. Nebraska draws about one hundred thousand dollars; little old North Dakota draws about fifty thousand dollars; Oklahoma doubles Kansas; Missouri leaves her a thousand miles behind; Colorado is almost seven times greater than Kansas—the whole west is ahead of Kansas.

Take it by any standard you please, Kansas is not in it.

Go east and you hear them laugh at Kansas; go west and they sneer at her; go south and they "cuss" her; go north and they have forgotten her. Go into any crowd of intelligent people gathered anywhere on the globe, and you will find the Kansas man on the defensive. The newspaper columns and magazines once devoted to praise of her, to boastful facts and startling figures concerning her resources, are now filled with cartoons, jibes and Pefferian speeches. Kansas just naturally isn't in it. She has traded places with Arkansas and Timbuctoo.

What's the matter with Kansas?

We all know; yet here we are at it again. We have an old mossback Jacksonian who snorts and howls because there is a bathtub in the State House; we are running that old jay for Governor. We have another shabby, wild-eyed, rattlebrained fanatic who has said openly in a dozen speeches that "the rights of the user are paramount to the rights of the owner": we are running him for Chief Justice, so that capital will come tumbling over itself to get into the state. We have raked the old ash heap of failure in the state and found an old human hoop skirt who has failed as a businessman, who has failed as an editor, who has failed as a preacher, and we are going to run him for Congressman-at-Large. He will help the looks of the Kansas delegation at Washington. Then we have discovered a kid without a law practice and have decided to run him for Attorney General. Then, for fear some hint that the state had become respectable might percolate through the civilized portions of the nation, we have decided to send three or four harpies out lecturing, telling the people that Kansas is raising hell and letting the corn go to weed.

Oh, this is a state to be proud of! We are a people who can hold up our heads! What we need is not more money, but less capital, fewer white shirts and brains, fewer men with business judgment, and more of those fellows who boast that they are "just ordinary clodhoppers, but they know more in a minute about finance than John Sherman"; we need more men who are "posted," who can bellow about the crime of '73, who hate prosperity, and who think, because a man believes in national honor, he is a tool of Wall Street. We have had a few of them—some hundred fifty thousand—but we need more.

We need several thousand gibbering idiots to scream about the "Great Red Dragon" of Lombard Street. We don't need population, we don't need wealth, we don't need well-dressed men on the streets, we don't need cities on the fertile prairies; you bet we don't! What we are after is the money power. Because we have become poorer and ornerier and meaner than a spavined, distempered mule, we, the people of Kansas, propose to kick; we don't care to build up, we wish to tear down.

"There are two ideas of government," said our noble Bryan at Chicago. "There are those who believe that if you legislate to make the well-to-do prosperous, this prosperity will leak through on those below. The Democratic idea has been that if you legislate to make the masses prosperous their prosperity will find its way up and through every class and rest upon them."

That's the stuff! Give the prosperous man the dickens! Legislate the thriftless man into ease, whack the stuffing out of the creditors and tell the debtors who borrowed the money five years ago when money "per capita" was greater than it is now, that the contraction of currency gives him a right to repudiate.

Whoop it up for the ragged trousers; put the lazy, greasy fizzle, who can't pay his debts, on the altar, and bow down and worship him. Let the state ideal be high. What we need is not the respect of our fellow men, but the chance to get something for nothing.

Oh, yes, Kansas is a great state. Here are people fleeing from it by the score every day, capital going out of the state by the hundreds of dollars; and every industry but farming paralyzed, and that crippled, because its products have to go across the ocean before they can find a laboring man at work who can afford to buy them. Let's don't stop this year. Let's drive all the decent, self-respecting men out of the state. Let's keep the old clodhoppers who know it all. Let's encourage the man who is "posted." He can talk, and what we need is not mill hands to eat our meat, nor factory hands to eat our wheat, nor cities to oppress the farmer by consuming his butter and eggs and chickens and produce. What Kansas needs is men who can talk, who have large leisure to argue the currency question while their wives wait at home for the nickel's worth of bluing.

What's the matter with Kansas?

Nothing under the shining sun. She is losing her wealth, population and standing. She has got her statesmen, and the money power is afraid of her. Kansas is all right. She has started in to raise hell, as Mrs. Lease advised, and she seems to have an overproduction. But that doesn't matter. Kansas never did believe in diversified crops. Kansas is all right. There is absolutely nothing wrong with Kansas. "Every prospect pleases and only man is vile."

[From William Allen White, *The Autobiography of William Allen White* (New York: Macmillan Co., 1946), pp. 280–83.]

## QUESTIONS FOR REFLECTION

What problems faced farmers in the 1890s? Explain the causes of their predicament according to the farmers and their advocates. Did they have an accurate perception of their situation? How does William Allen White answer their arguments? Was there any validity to White's derisive comments? How has the role of the farmer changed since the 1890s?

## ANSWERS TO MULTIPLE-CHOICE AND TRUE-FALSE QUESTIONS

### Multiple-Choice Questions

1-B, 2-D, 3-B, 4-A, 5-C, 6-B, 7-D, 8-A

### True-False Questions

1-F, 2-T, 3-T, 4-F, 5-T, 6-F, 7-F, 8-T

# 22

## THE COURSE OF EMPIRE

## CHAPTER OBJECTIVES

*After you complete the reading and study of this chapter you should be able to*

1. Explain why the United States entered upon a policy of imperialism.
2. Account for the outbreak of the Spanish-American War.
3. Explain the course of United States relations with Latin America during the late nineteenth century and its impact on later relations with Latin America.
4. Contrast the arguments in 1899 for and against imperialism.
5. Explain the development of America's policy for dealing with its imperial possessions.
6. Account for the acquisition of the Panama Canal.
7. Assess the foreign policies of Theodore Roosevelt and William Howard Taft.

## CHAPTER OUTLINE

I. Stirrings of imperialism
   A. Isolationism prior to the Civil War
   B. Seward's diplomacy
      1. Purchase of Alaska (1867)
   C. Expansionist visions in the Pacific
      1. Early whaling and missionary interests
      2. Treaty with Samoa
      3. Relations with Hawaii
         a. Early American settlements
         b. Reciprocal trade agreement of 1875
         c. Constitutional government
         d. Desire for annexation (1893)
         e. Hawaii proclaimed a republic (1894)
II. Motivation for imperialism
   A. Economic motivations
   B. Mahan's concept of sea power
   C. Social Darwinian justifications
      1. Concept of Social Darwinism
      2. Racial corollaries
   D. Religious justification
III. Development of the Spanish-American War
   A. Effects of American investments and tariffs
   B. Guerrilla warfare by revolutionaries
   C. Weyler's detention policy
   D. Role of the press in the war
      1. Competition between Hearst's *Journal* and Pulitzer's *World*
      2. Examples of yellow journalism
   E. Cleveland's efforts for compromise
   F. Spanish response to McKinley's stance
   G. Arousal of public opinion
      1. de Lôme letter (February 9, 1898)
      2. Sinking of the *Maine* (February 15, 1898)

H. The final moves to war
　　I. Motives for war
IV. Fighting the "splendid little war"
　　A. Naval victory at Manila Bay
　　B. Cuban blockade
　　　　1. Problems of the army
　　　　2. The Rough Riders
　　　　3. Siege of Santiago
　　C. Puerto Rican campaign
　　D. Terms of the armistice
V. Developing and debating imperialism
　　A. Negotiations for the Treaty of Paris (December 10)
　　　　1. Cuban debt question
　　　　2. Annexation of the Philippines
　　B. Motives for annexation
　　C. Terms of the treaty
　　D. Other territorial acquisitions
　　E. Debate over the treaty
　　　　1. Anti-imperialist arguments
　　　　2. Bryan's support
　　　　3. Ratification (February 1899)
　　F. Filipino insurrection
　　G. Emergence of the Anti-Imperialist League (October 1899)
VI. Organizing the new acquisitions
　　A. The Philippines under Taft
　　B. Civil government for Puerto Rico
　　C. Problems in Cuba
　　D. Imperial rivalries and the Open Door Policy in the Far East
　　　　1. The scramble for spheres of influence in China
　　　　2. The Open Door Policy
　　　　　　a. British initiatives
　　　　　　b. Unilateral action
　　　　　　c. Policies of the Open Door Note
　　　　　　d. Reactions of other nations
　　　　3. The Boxer Rebellion
　　　　4. Success of Hay's policy
VII. Rise of Theodore Roosevelt
　　A. Election of 1900
　　　　1. Democrats and imperialism
　　　　2. Republican nominees
　　　　3. Outcome of election
　　B. McKinley's assassination
　　C. TR's background and character
　　　　1. Strenuous life
　　　　2. Life in the West
　　　　3. New York politics
VIII. TR's foreign policies
　　A. The Panama Canal
　　　　1. Negotiations with British and French
　　　　2. Difficulties with Colombia
　　　　3. Revolution in Panama
　　　　4. Treaty with Panama
　　　　5. Opening of Canal
　　B. The Roosevelt Corollary
　　　　1. Problems of debt collection
　　　　2. Principles in new policy
　　C. TR's role in the Russo-Japanese War
　　D. American relations with Japan
　　　　1. Agreements on Korea, China, and Philippines
　　　　2. Racism
　　　　3. "Gentlemen's Agreement" of 1907
　　E. The United States and Europe
　　　　1. Conference at Algeciras
　　　　2. Tour of the "Great White Fleet"

## KEY ITEMS OF CHRONOLOGY

| | |
|---|---|
| Purchase of Alaska | 1867 |
| Mahan's *Influence of Seapower upon History* | 1890 |
| de Lôme letter revealed | February 9, 1898 |
| *Maine* sunk | February 15, 1898 |
| War formally declared between Spain and the United States | April 1898 |
| Hawaii annexed | July 1898 |
| Armistice | August 1898 |
| Treaty of Paris | December 1898 |
| Anti-Imperialist League formed | 1899 |
| Open Door Note | 1899 |
| Assassination of McKinley | 1901 |
| Panama Canal acquired | 1903 |

THE COURSE OF EMPIRE

       Roosevelt Corollary announced               1904
       "Gentlemen's Agreement" with Japan        1907

## TERMS TO MASTER

*Listed below are some important terms or people with which you should be familiar after you complete the study of this chapter. Explain the significance of each name or term.*

1. William H. Seward
2. Alfred Thayer Mahan
3. John Fiske
4. Josiah Strong
5. yellow journalism
6. de Lôme letter
7. Teller Amendment
8. Platt Amendment
9. Open Door Policy
10. Boxer Rebellion
11. Panama Canal
12. Roosevelt Corollary
13. Portsmouth conference
14. "Gentlemen's Agreement"
15. "Great White fleet"

16. tutelary
17. don (v.)
18. collusion
19. perpetuity
20. bellicosity

## VOCABULARY BUILDING

*Listed below are some words used in this chapter. Look up each word in your dictionary.*

1. languid
2. reciprocal
3. dormant
4. garrisoned
5. impale
6. grouse
7. jingoistic
8. begrudgingly
9. autonomous
10. arbitration
11. abate
12. loom (v.)
13. transpire
14. revel
15. sordid

## EXERCISES FOR UNDERSTANDING

*When you have completed reading the chapter, answer each of the following questions. If you have difficulty, go back and reread the section of the chapter related to the question.*

### Multiple-Choice Questions

*Select the letter of the response that best completes the statement.*

1. The "new imperialism" of the 1890s especially stressed
   A. access to new markets.
   B. converting heathens to Christianity.
   C. annexing territory to the United States.
   D. military conquests of other nations.

2. Josiah Strong and John Fiske justified American imperialism by stressing
   A. the need for new markets in Asia.
   B. Anglo-Saxon superiority.
   C. the importance of naval power in world affairs.
   D. competition with European powers for influence.

3. According to the text, a key factor propelling the United States into the Spanish-American War was
   A. the desire of businessmen to control trade and manufacturing in Cuba.
   B. the hope of missionaries to convert the Cuban people.
   C. McKinley's desire to gain political support from his acquisitions.
   D. the frenzy of public opinion for war.
4. The United States entered the war with Spain largely because of
   A. President McKinley's bellicosity.
   B. the aggressive actions of Spain.
   C. a public aroused by the yellow press.
   D. all of the above
5. An early and major American victory in the Spanish-American War occurred at
   A. Algeciras.
   B. Santiago.
   C. Hawaii.
   D. Manila Bay.
6. The Platt Amendment
   A. gave women the right to vote in national elections.
   B. annexed Puerto Rico.
   C. limited the independence of the new Cuban government.
   D. gave the president expanded power in foreign affairs.
7. The proposal that each nation should have equal access to trade with China was known as the
   A. "Gentlemen's Agreement."
   B. Open Door Policy.
   C. Teller Amendment.
   D. white man's burden.
8. In the 1890s, anti-imperialists included
   A. McKinley, Taft, and William Jennings Bryan.
   B. Roosevelt, Mahan, and Marc Hanna.
   C. Gompers, Carnegie, and William James.
   D. Taft, Mahan, and Albert Beveridge.

## True-False Questions

*Indicate whether each statement is true or false.*

1. In the 1880s the major field of United States overseas activity was the Pacific Ocean.
2. In 1887 the United States bought Alaska from Britain for $7.2 million.
3. Henry Cabot Lodge wrote *The Influence of Sea Power upon History*.
4. The toughest question in American foreign policy in the 1890s involved the Philippines.
5. The Spanish-American War lasted four months.
6. By 1920 both Puerto Rico and the Philippines had gained complete independence from the United States.
7. In the Russo-Japanese War the United States fought with the Japanese.
8. The Roosevelt Corollary applied the Monroe Doctrine to Hawaii.

## Essay Questions

1. What arguments did Americans use to justify imperialism, and how did the anti-imperialists rebut them?
2. Trace the key events leading up to the outbreak of the Spanish-American War.
3. Discuss the arguments for and against acquisition of the Philippines.
4. Explain the Open Door Policy and its effects.
5. How did United States policy in Latin America change between 1890 and 1912?
6. How did the United States acquire the Panama Canal? Was it an example of imperialism?

## DOCUMENT

### McKinley's War Message to Congress

McKinley's message of April 11, 1898, attempted to summarize American relations with Cuba. Read it carefully to gain an understanding of his perception of events.

Obedient to that precept of the Constitution which commands the President to give from time to time to the Congress information of the state of the Union and to recommend to their consideration such measures as he shall judge necessary and expedient, it becomes my duty now to address your body with regard to the grave crisis that has arisen in the relations of the United States to Spain by reason of the warfare that for more than three years has raged in the neighboring island of Cuba. . . .

Since the present revolution began, in February, 1895, this country has seen the fertile domain at our threshold ravaged by fire and sword in the course of a struggle unequaled in the history of the island and rarely paralleled as to the numbers of the combatants and the bitterness of the contest by any revolution of modern times where a dependent people striving to be free have been opposed by the power of the sovereign state. . . .

Our trade has suffered, the capital invested by our citizens in Cuba has been largely lost, and the temper and forbearance of our people have been so sorely tried as to beget a perilous unrest among our own citizens. . . .

The agricultural population to the estimated number of 300,000 or more was herded within the towns and their immediate vicinage, deprived of the means of support, rendered destitute of shelter, left poorly clad, and exposed to the most unsanitary conditions. As the scarcity of food increased with the devastation of the depopulated areas of production, destitution and want became misery and starvation. Month by month the death rate increased in an alarming ratio. By March, 1897, according to conservative estimates from official Spanish sources, the mortality among the reconcentrados from starvation and diseases thereto incident exceeded 50 per cent of their total number. . . .

The war in Cuba is of such a nature that short of subjugation or extermination, a final military victory for either side seems impracticable. The alternative lies in the physical exhaustion of the one or the other party, or perhaps of both. . . . The prospect of such a protraction and conclusion of the present strife is a contingency hardly to be contemplated with equanimity by the civilized world, and least of all by the United States, affected and injured as we are, deeply and intimately, by its very existence. . . .

The forcible intervention of the United States as a neutral to stop the war, according to the large dictates of humanity and following many historical precedents where neighboring States have interfered to check the hopeless sacrifices of life by internecine conflicts beyond their borders, is justifiable on rational grounds. It involves, however, hostile constraint upon both the parties to the contest as well to enforce a truce as to guide the eventual settlement.

. . . The present condition of affairs in Cuba is a constant menace to our peace and entails upon this Government an enormous expense. With such a conflict waged for years in an island so near us and with which our people have such trade and business relations; when the lives and liberty of our citizens are in constant danger and their property destroyed and themselves ruined; where our trading vessels are liable to seizure and are seized at our very door by war ships of a foreign nation, the expeditions of filibustering that we are powerless to prevent altogether, and the irritating questions and entanglements thus arising—all these and others that I need not mention, with the resulting strained relations, are a constant menace to our peace and compel us to keep on a semi-war footing with a nation with which we are at peace.

These elements of danger and disorder already pointed out have been strikingly illustrated by a tragic event which has deeply and justly moved the American people. I have already transmitted to Congress the report of the naval court of inquiry on the destruction of the battle ship *Maine* in the harbor of Havana during the night of the 15th of February. The destruction of that noble vessel has filled the national heart with inexpressible horror. Two hundred and fifty-eight brave sailors and marines and two officers of our Navy, reposing in the fancied security of a friendly harbor, have been hurled to death, grief and want brought to their homes and sorrow to the nation.

The naval court of inquiry, which, it is needless to say, commands the unqualified confidence of the Government, was unanimous in its conclusion that the destruction of the *Maine* was caused by an exterior explosion—that of a submarine mine. It did not assume to place the responsibility. That remains to be fixed.

In any event the destruction of the *Maine*, by whatever exterior cause, is a patent and impressive proof of a state of things in Cuba that is intolerable. That condition is thus shown to be such that the Spanish Government can not assure safety and security to a vessel of the American Navy in the harbor of Havana on a mission of peace, and rightfully there.

In view of these facts and of these considerations I ask the Congress to authorize and empower the President to take measures to secure a full and final termination of hostilities between the Government of Spain and the people of Cuba, and to secure in the island the establishment of a stable government, capable of maintaining order and observing its international obligations, insuring peace and tranquillity and the security of its citizens as well as our own, and to use the military and naval forces of the United States as may be necessary for these purposes. . . .

The issue is now with the Congress. It is a solemn responsibility. I have exhausted every effort to relieve the intolerable condition of affairs which is at our doors. . . .

Yesterday, and since the preparation of the foregoing message, official information was received by me that the latest decree of the Queen Regent of Spain directs General Blanco, in order to prepare and facilitate peace, to proclaim a suspension of hostilities, the duration and details of which have not yet been communicated to me.

This fact with every other pertinent consideration will, I am sure, have your just and careful attention in the solemn deliberations upon which you are about to enter. If this measure attains a successful result, then our aspirations as a Christian, peace-loving people will be realized. If it fails, it will be only another justification for our contemplated action.

[James D. Richardson (ed.), *A Compilation of the Messages and Papers of the Presidents, 1789–1897* (Washington, D.C.: U.S. Government Printing Office, 1899), 10: 139–150]

## Questions for Reflection

Does McKinley anywhere in the message ask Congress to declare war on Spain? How could a declaration of war be justified in light of his request? How accurate was McKinley's description of developments between Cuba and the United States? Can you see any reason why Congress might have been skeptical of McKinley's claim that Spain had offered to cease hostilities in Cuba? Does this document suggest that the United States was justified in becoming involved in the Cuban matter and ultimately in the Spanish-American War?

## ANSWERS TO MULTIPLE-CHOICE AND TRUE-FALSE QUESTIONS

### Multiple-Choice Questions

1-A, 2-B, 3-D, 4-C, 5-D, 6-C, 7-B, 8-C

### True-False Questions

1-T, 2-T, 3-F, 4-F, 5-T, 6-F, 7-F, 8-F

# 23

## PROGRESSIVISM: ROOSEVELT, TAFT, AND WILSON

**CHAPTER OBJECTIVES**

*After you complete the reading and study of this chapter you should be able to*

1. Explain the nature and the goals of the progressive movement.
2. Compare the progressive movement with the populist movement.
3. Describe Roosevelt's brand of progressivism.
4. Account for Taft's mixed record as a progressive.
5. Describe Wilson's efforts for progressive reform.
6. Assess the impact of progressivism on American politics, society, and economy.

**CHAPTER OUTLINE**

I. The nature of progressivism
   A. General features
     1. Aimed against the abuses of the Gilded Age bosses
     2. More businesslike and efficient than populism
     3. A paradox of regulation of business by businessmen
     4. A diverse movement
   B. Antecedents
     1. Populism
     2. Mugwumps
     3. Socialist critiques of living and working conditions
     4. Role of the muckrakers
       a. Henry Demarest Lloyd and Lincoln Steffens
       b. Bringing about popular support for reform
       c. Stronger on diagnosis than remedy
   C. The themes of progressivism
     1. Efforts to democratize government
       a. Direct primaries
       b. Initiative, referendum, recall, and other local actions
       c. Direct election of senators
     2. A focus on efficiency and good government
       a. Role of Frederick W. Taylor and scientific management
       b. Commission and city-manager forms of city government
       c. Use of specialists in government and business
         i. Robert M. LaFollette
         ii. "Wisconsin Idea"
     3. Regulation of giant corporations

a. Acceptance and regulation of big business
   b. Problem of regulating the regulators
 4. Impulse toward social justice
   a. Use of private charities and state power
   b. Outlawing child labor
   c. Erratic course of the Supreme Court
   d. Restricting working hours and dangerous occupations
   e. Stricter building codes and factory inspection acts
   f. Pressure for prohibition
II. Roosevelt's progressivism
  A. Need for his cautious role
  B. Focus on trust regulation
    1. Opposition to wholesale trust-busting
    2. Northern Securities case (1904) used to promote the issue
  C. Coal strike of 1902
    1. Basis for the UMW strike
    2. Recalcitrant attitude of management
    3. Roosevelt's efforts to force arbitration
    4. Effects of the incident
  D. Congressional action
    1. Department of Commerce and Labor
    2. Elkins Act
  E. Other antitrust suits
III. TR's second term
  A. Election of 1904
    1. Republican nomination
    2. Democratic positions and candidate
    3. Campaign and results
  B. Roosevelt's legislative leadership
    1. Hepburn Act
    2. Roosevelt's support of regulation of food and drugs
      a. Role of muckrakers: Upton Sinclair and others
      b. Legislation achieved
  C. Efforts for conservation
    1. Earlier movements for conservation
    2. Roosevelt's actions
IV. Taft's administration

  A. Selection of a successor in 1908
    1. TR's choice
    2. Democrats and Bryan
    3. Election results
  B. Taft's background and character
  C. Campaign for tariff reform
    1. Problems in the Senate
    2. Taft's clash with the Progressive Republicans
  D. Ballinger-Pinchot controversy
  E. Roosevelt's response upon his return to the United States
    1. Initial silence
    2. Development of the New Nationalism
    3. TR enters the race
  F. Taft's achievements
V. The election of 1912
  A. The Republican nomination of 1912
  B. Creation of the Progressive party
  C. Wilson's rise to power
    1. His background
    2. His actions in New Jersey
    3. His nomination
  D. Focus of the campaign on the New Nationalism and the New Freedom
  E. Wilson's election
  F. Significance of the election of 1912
    1. High-water mark for progressivism
    2. Brought Democrats back into office
    3. Brought southerners into control
VI. Wilsonian reform
  A. Wilson's style
  B. Tariff reform
    1. Personal appearance before Congress
    2. Tariff changes in the Underwood-Simmons Act
    3. Income tax provisions
  C. The Federal Reserve Act
    1. Compromises required
    2. Description of the Federal Reserve System
  D. Efforts for new antitrust laws
    1. Wilson's approach in 1912
    2. Federal Trade Commission Act (September 1914)
    3. Clayton Antitrust Act (October 1914)
      a. Practices outlawed

       b. Provisions for labor and farm organizations
   4. Disappointments with administration of the new laws
 E. The shortcomings of Wilson's progressivism
   1. Women's suffrage
   2. Child labor
   3. Racist attitudes
 F. Wilson's return to reform
   1. Plight of the Progressive party
   2. Appointment of Brandeis to the Supreme Court
   3. Support for land banks and long-term farm loans
   4. Farm demonstration agents and agricultural education
   5. Labor reform legislation
VII. The paradoxes of progressivism
 A. Disenfranchisement of southern blacks
 B. Manipulation of democratic reforms
 C. Decision making by faceless bureaucratic experts
 D. Decline of voter participation
 E. From optimism to war

## KEY ITEMS OF CHRONOLOGY

| | |
|---|---|
| Roosevelt administrations | 1901–1909 |
| Anthracite coal strike | 1902 |
| Northern Securities Case | 1904 |
| Elkins Act | 1903 |
| Hepburn Act | 1906 |
| Pure Food and Drug Act | 1906 |
| Wilson administrations | 1913–1921 |
| Sixteenth Amendment (income tax) ratified | 1913 |
| Seventeenth Amendment (direct Senate election) ratified | 1913 |
| Underwood-Simmons Tariff Act | 1913 |
| Federal Reserve Act | 1913 |
| Federal Trade Commission Act | 1914 |
| Clayton Antitrust Act | 1914 |
| Adamson Act | 1916 |

## TERMS TO MASTER

*Listed below are some important terms or people with which you should be familiar after you complete the study of this chapter. Explain the significance of each name or term.*

1. muckrakers
2. initiative and referendum
3. Frederick W. Taylor
4. Northern Securities case
5. anthracite coal strike
6. Robert M. La Follette
7. Elkins Act
8. Hepburn Act
9. Upton Sinclair's *Jungle*
10. Ballinger-Pinchot controversy
11. New Nationalism
12. New Freedom

13. Federal Reserve System
14. Federal Trade Commission
15. Clayton Antitrust Act

## VOCABULARY BUILDING

*Listed below are some words used in this chapter. Look up each word in your dictionary.*

1. resonant
2. prevalence
3. invincible
4. solicitor
5. adroit
6. syndicate
7. unsavory
8. rebuke
9. implicit
10. irreparably
11. demise
12. tenacious
13. lament
14. schism
15. insidious
16. dissolution
17. plaudit
18. fruition
19. mandate
20. amalgam

## EXERCISES FOR UNDERSTANDING

*When you have completed reading the chapter, answer each of the following questions. If you have difficulty, go back and reread the section of the chapter related to the question.*

### Multiple-Choice Questions

*Select the letter of the response that best completes the statement.*

1. In the Progressive Era, muckraking journalists
    A. opposed reform of the meat-packing industry.
    B. supported large corporations.
    C. included Lincoln Steffens.
    D. played on the public's emotions without facts.

2. Social justice reforms included
    A. laws restricting child labor.
    B. the Sherman Antitrust Act.
    C. the initiative and the referendum.
    D. the Seventeenth Amendment to the Constitution.

3. Robert M. La Follette was a leading reformer as
    A. a muckraking journalist.
    B. governor of Wisconsin.
    C. senator from California.
    D. mayor of Toledo, Ohio.

4. Under President Roosevelt, Gifford Pinchot directed programs related to the
    A. breaking up of trusts.
    B. conservation of natural resources.
    C. protection of consumers of foods and drugs.
    D. regulation of the major railroads.

5. As president, Theodore Roosevelt favored
    A. business exploitation of natural resources.
    B. control of the environment by the states.
    C. no government involvement in conservation.
    D. scientific management of resources.

6. The phrase "Hamiltonian means to achieve Jeffersonian ends" summarizes the 1912 views of
    A. Woodrow Wilson.
    B. William Howard Taft.
    C. Theodore Roosevelt.
    D. Eugene V. Debs.

7. The Clayton Antitrust Act attempted to regulate trusts by
    A. defining actions of unfair competition.
    B. placing control in the hands of a small group of regulators.
    C. taking control of trusts from the courts.
    D. repealing the Sherman Antitrust Act.

8. About 1916, Wilson renewed his support for progressive reforms because
    A. he needed to build a coalition for reelection.

B. World War I gave the president unlimited powers to act.
C. he was about to leave office and wanted to create an enduring legacy.
D. all of the above

**True-False Questions**

*Indicate whether each statement is true or false.*

1. Populism was completely different from progressivism.
2. Muckraker Henry Demarest Lloyd exposed the evils of the Standard Oil Company.
3. In the anthracite coal strike of 1902 President Roosevelt used troops to keep the mines open.
4. Taft brought more antitrust suits in four years than TR did in eight years.
5. The 1912 election was significant because it brought southerners back into influential positions in national affairs.
6. Before entering politics Woodrow Wilson was the president of a large industrial corporation.
7. The Underwood-Simmons Tariff of 1913 sought to restore competition by lowering import duties.
8. Progressives treated African Americans fairly.

**Essay Questions**

1. Discuss the major antecedents of progressivism and explain their effects on progressive reform.
2. Describe the presidential election of 1912 and explain its significance in national politics.
3. Compare and contrast the policies of presidents Roosevelt and Wilson regarding big business.
4. What were the issues in the Ballinger-Pinchot controversy? How did the disagreement over conservation demonstrate larger differences between Taft and Roosevelt?
5. Was Theodore Roosevelt or Woodrow Wilson the more successful progressive president? Explain your answer.
6. What were the limitations of progressivism? What lasting contributions did it make?

## DOCUMENTS

### Document 1. "The Treason of the Senate"

In 1906, the muckraker David Graham Phillips wrote an attack on Senator Nelson W. Aldrich (Republican, Rhode Island), which was part of his exposé "The Treason of the Senate." The following is an excerpt from Phillips's essay on Aldrich in *Cosmopolitan* magazine.

> Rhode Island is the smallest of our states in area and thirty-fourth in population—twelve hundred and fifty square miles, less than half a million people, barely seventy thousand voters with the rolls padded by the Aldrich machine. But size and numbers are nothing; it contains as many sturdy Americans proportionately as any other state. Its bad distinction of supplying the enemy with a bold leader is due to its ancient and aristocratic constitution, changed once, away back before the middle of the last century, but still an archaic document for class rule. The apportionment of legislators is such that one-

eleventh of the population, and they the most ignorant and most venal, elect a majority of the legislature—which means that they elect the two United States senators. Each city and township counts as a political unit; thus, the five cities that together have two-thirds of the population are in an overwhelming minority before twenty almost vacant rural townships—their total population is not thirty-seven thousand—where the ignorance is even illiterate, where the superstition is mediaeval, where tradition and custom have made the vote an article of legitimate merchandising.

The combination of bribery and party prejudice is potent everywhere; but there come crises when these fail "the interests" for the moment. No storm of popular rage, however, could unseat the senators from Rhode Island. The people of Rhode Island might, as a people and voting almost unanimously, elect a governor; but not a legislature. Bribery is a weapon forbidden those who stand for right and justice—who "fights the devil with fire" gives him choice of weapons, and must lose to him, though seeming to win. A few thousand dollars put in the experienced hands of the heelers, and the senatorial general agent of "the interests" is secure for another six years.

The Aldrich machine controls the legislature, the election boards, the courts—the entire machinery of the "republican form of government." In 1904, when Aldrich needed a legislature to reëlect him for his fifth consecutive term, it is estimated that carrying the state cost about two hundred thousand dollars—a small sum, easily to be got back by a few minutes of industrious pocket-picking in Wall Street....

And the leader, the boss of the Senate for the past twenty years has been—Aldrich!...

The greatest single hold of "the interests" is the fact that they are the "campaign contributors"—the men who supply the money for "keeping the party together," and for "getting out the vote." Did you ever think where the millions for watchers, spellbinders, halls, processions, posters, pamphlets, that are spent in national, state and local campaigns come from? Who pays the big election expenses of your congressman, of the men you send to the legislature to elect senators? Do you imagine those who foot those huge bills are fools? Don't you know that they make sure of getting their money back, with interest, compound upon compound? Your candidates get most of the money for their campaigns from the party committees; and the central party committee is the national committee with which congressional and state and local committees are affiliated. The bulk of the money for the "political trust" comes from "the interests." "The interests" will give only to the "political trust." And that means Aldrich and his Democratic (!) lieutenant, Gorman of Maryland, leader of the minority in the Senate. Aldrich, then, is the head of the "political trust" and Gorman is his right-hand man. When you speak of the Republican party, of the Democratic party, of the "good of the party," of the "best interests of the party," of "wise party policy," you mean what Aldrich and Gorman, acting for their clients, deem wise and proper and "Republican" or "Democratic."...

No railway legislation that was not either helpful to or harmless against "the interests"; no legislation on the subject of corporations that would interfere with "the interests," which use the corporate form to simplify and systematize their stealing; no legislation on the tariff question unless it secured to "the interests" full and free license to loot; no investigations of wholesale robbery or of any of the evils resulting from it—there you have in a few words the whole story of the Senate's treason under Aldrich's leadership, and of why property is concentrating in the hands of the few and the little children of the masses are being sent to toil in the darkness of mines, in the dreariness and unhealthfulness of factories instead of being sent to school; and why the great middle class—the old-fashioned Americans, the people with the incomes of from two thousand to fifteen thousand a year—is being swiftly crushed into dependence and the repulsive miseries of "genteel poverty."

[From David Graham Phillips, "The Treason of the Senate," *Cosmopolitan,* April 1906, pp. 628–38.]

## Document 2. "Wall Street and the House of Dollars"

Also appearing in *Cosmopolitan* was the following by Ernest Crosby.

This is the situation. Here we are, a great and vigorous people, generating power enough to run a dozen governments and our government has got away from us, and switched us off, and our nominal representatives are getting their motive power elsewhere. There in the Senate Chamber is the center of the conspiracy which has defrauded us of our rights. It will soon be with us as it was with the Roman oligarchy. "*Senatus Populusque Romanus,*" they used to say, when they spoke of the state. "S.P.Q.R."—"The Senate and the Roman People," and the Senate came first. It is "The Senate and the American People" to-day, and we may soon improve on the Roman legend and drop the "People" altogether, and then, politically speaking, the Senate will be the Whole Thing. But they tempered the asperities of oligarchy in Rome by naming tribunes of the people who had the courage to call a halt when the Senate went too far, and to maintain the rights of the people against their rulers. We need such tribunes in this country, and their aim should be to bring the senators back to their allegiance. Legislative elections have proved to be almost invariably corrupt and the sure means of handing over the selection to the money power. The senators as a rule are either direct representatives of the trusts or political bosses by the grace of the trusts. The problem before us is to select our own bosses for ourselves and make the senators *our* representatives, and to cut off the connection which binds them to interests which are diametrically opposed to ours. Popular election seems to be the obvious reform. The electors of a whole state cannot be handled as a legislature can be. The people should rise in their wrath and demand this change. The world of finance has its own proper functions to accomplish, but it should have no place in the management of our government. Let the people once more become the Real Thing.

[From Ernest Crosby, "Wall Street and the House of Dollars," *Cosmopolitan,* April 1906, p. 610.]

## Document 3. The Seventeenth Amendment

In May 1912 Congress adopted and submitted to the states for ratification what became the Seventeenth Amendment to the Constitution. It provided for the popular election of U.S. senators and was declared ratified on May 31, 1913.

> Amendment XVII.
>
> The Senate of the United States shall be composed of two senators from each State, elected by the people thereof, for six years; and each Senator shall have one vote. The electors in each State shall have the qualifications requisite for electors of the most numerous branch of the State legislature.
>
> When vacancies happen in the representation of any State in the Senate, the executive authority of such State shall issue writs of election to fill such vacancies: *Provided,* That the legislature of any State may empower the executive thereof to make temporary appointments until the people fill the vacancies by election as the legislature may direct.
>
> This amendment shall not be so construed as to affect the election or term of any senator chosen before it becomes valid as part of the Constitution.

### Questions for Reflection

Would David Graham Phillips have supported the Seventeenth Amendment? How did reformers think direct election of U.S. Senators would change the way government functioned? In what ways did the Seventeenth Amendment reflect the general values of progressives?

Three-quarters of a century later, what has been the effect of the Seventeenth Amendment on U.S. politics? Has the Senate been dramatically changed and improved? Do wealthy business leaders and industrialists continue to exert undue influence?

## ANSWERS TO MULTIPLE-CHOICE AND TRUE-FALSE QUESTIONS

### Multiple-Choice Questions

1-C, 2-A, 3-B, 4-B, 5-D, 6-C, 7-A, 8-A

### True-False Questions

1-F, 2-T, 3-F, 4-T, 5-T, 6-F, 7-T, 8-F

# 24

## WILSON AND THE GREAT WAR

### CHAPTER OBJECTIVES

*After you complete the reading and study of this chapter you should be able to*

1. Describe Wilson's idealistic diplomacy and show the clash of ideals and reality in Mexico.
2. Explain early United States reaction to the World War.
3. Account for the entry of the United States into World War I.
4. Explain the status of civil liberties during World War I and during the Red Scare afterward.
5. Explain the process and product of peacemaking after World War I.
6. Account for the failure of the United States to ratify the peace treaty after World War I.
7. Describe the problems of reconversion from World War I to civilian life.

### CHAPTER OUTLINE

I. Wilson and foreign affairs
  A. Inexperience and idealism
  B. Intervention in Mexico
    1. Díaz overthrown in revolution
    2. Nonrecognition of the Huerta government
    3. Invasion at Veracruz
    4. Carranza's government
    5. The pursuit of Pancho Villa
  C. Problems in the Caribbean
II. World War I and the early American response
  A. Outbreak of the war
  B. Initial American response
    1. Declaration of neutrality
    2. Attitudes of hyphenated Americans
    3. Views of other American groups
    4. Effect of propaganda on Americans
  C. Extension of economic credit to the Allies
  D. Problems of neutrality
    1. Conflicts over neutral rights at sea
    2. British declaration of the North Sea war zone and other restrictions
    3. German use of submarines
    4. Sinking of the *Lusitania*
      a. American protests
      b. Bryan's resignation
      c. *Arabic* pledge
  E. Debate over preparedness
    1. Demands for stronger army and navy
    2. Antiwar advocates
    3. National Defense Act of 1916
    4. Move for a stronger navy
    5. Efforts to obtain revenue for preparedness

III. Election of 1916
   A. Republicans nominated
   B. Democratic program
   C. Issues of the campaign
   D. Results of the election

IV. Steps toward war
   A. Wilson's effort to mediate
   B. Wilson's assertion of terms of peace
   C. German decision for unrestricted submarine warfare
   D. Diplomatic break with Germany
   E. The Zimmerman Telegram
   F. The Russian Revolution

V. United States entry into the war
   A. The sinking of American vessels
   B. Wilson's call for war
   C. An assessment of reasons for United States entry into the war
   D. Limited expectations from the U.S.
   E. Financial assistance to the Allies
   F. First contingents of troops

VI. Mobilizing a nation
   A. Raising the armed forces
   B. Regulation of the economy
   C. War Industries Board
   D. Changes in labor
      1. Blacks
      2. Mexican-Americans
      3. Women
      4. Unions
   E. Committee on Public Information
   F. Civil liberties in the war
      1. Popular disdain for all things German
      2. Espionage and Sedition Acts
         a. Terms of the acts
         b. Prosecutions
         c. Impact of the acts
         d. *Schenck v. United States*

VII. The American role in war
   A. Little action through 1917
   B. American offensives in 1918
   C. The Fourteen Points
      1. Origins
      2. Content
      3. Purposes
      4. Responses
   D. Terms of the armistice
   E. Intervention in Russia

VIII. The fight for the peace
   A. Wilson's role
      1. Decision to attend the peace conference
      2. Effects of congressional elections of 1918
      3. Wilson's reception in Europe
      4. Structure of the conference
   B. Emphasis on the League of Nations
      1. Article X of the charter
      2. Machinery of the League
   C. Early warning from Lodge
   D. Amendments made to respond to critics at home
   E. Compromises on national self-determination
   F. The agreement for reparations
   G. Obtaining the German signature

IX. Wilson's loss at home
   A. Support for the peace
   B. Lodge's reaction
   C. Opponents of the treaty
   D. Wilson's speaking tour
   E. Wilson's stroke
   F. Failure of the Senate votes
   G. Formal ending of the war

X. Conversion to peace
   A. Spanish flu epidemic
   B. Lack of leadership and planning
   C. Postwar boom and slump
   D. Labor unrest
   E. Race riots
   F. The Red Scare
      1. Fear of radicals
      2. Bombs in the mail
      3. Deportation of aliens
      4. Evaporation of the Red Scare
      5. Legacy of the Red Scare

# KEY ITEMS OF CHRONOLOGY

| | |
|---|---|
| Huerta in power in Mexico | February 1913 |
| Invasion of Veracruz | April 1914 |
| Outbreak of World War I | August 1914 |

| | |
|---|---|
| *Lusitania* sunk | May 1915 |
| *Arabic* pledge from Germany | September 1915 |
| Germany resumes unrestricted submarine warfare | February 1917 |
| United States declares war | April 1917 |
| Creation of War Industries Board | July 1917 |
| Armistice | November 1918 |
| Paris Peace Conference | January–May 1919 |
| Senate votes on treaty | November 1919 and March 1920 |
| Red Scare | 1919–1920 |

## TERMS TO MASTER

*Listed below are some important terms or people with which you should be familiar after you complete the study of this chapter. Explain the significance of each name or term.*

1. Victoriano Huerta
2. hyphenated Americans
3. Central Powers
4. *Lusitania*
5. *Arabic* pledge
6. Revenue Act of 1916
7. Zimmerman Telegram
8. War Industries Board
9. Committee on Public Information
10. Espionage and Sedition Acts
11. *Schenck v. United States*
12. Fourteen Points
13. Big Four
14. Henry Cabot Lodge
15. reparations
16. irreconcilables
17. Boston police strike
18. A. Mitchell Palmer
19. Red Scare

10. sedition
11. imminent
12. overture
13. chafe
14. affront
15. sanction
16. liable
17. relish (v.)
18. lambaste
19. adamant
20. pandemic

## VOCABULARY BUILDING

*Listed below are some words used in this chapter. Look up each word in your dictionary.*

1. incendiary
2. renegade
3. consortium
4. belligerent
5. illusion
6. munitions
7. bolster
8. rampage
9. sycophant

## EXERCISES FOR UNDERSTANDING

*When you have completed the reading of the chapter, answer each of the following questions. If you have difficulty, go back and reread the section of the chapter related to the question.*

### Multiple-Choice Questions

*Select the letter of the response that best completes the statement.*

1. American foreign policy in China and later the Caribbean was called
   A. gunboat diplomacy.
   B. "dollar diplomacy."
   C. good neighbor diplomacy.
   D. renegade intervention diplomacy.

2. After the sinking of the *Lusitania*, William Jennings Bryan

A. urged Wilson to declare war.
B. resigned in protest over American demands on Germany.
C. called for arming all passenger ships.
D. campaigned for strengthening the military preparation for war.

3. The Revenue Act of 1916 placed most of the financial burden of preparedness on
A. farmers.
B. munitions manufacturers.
C. banks that lent money to foreign nations.
D. wealthy persons.

4. The Zimmerman Telegram
A. asked Theodore Roosevelt to raise an army battalion to go to war.
B. revealed Germany's policy of unrestricted submarine warfare.
C. warned Germany not to sink unarmed passenger ships.
D. suggested a wartime alliance between Mexico and Germany.

5. The wartime Espionage and Sedition Acts
A. were upheld by the Supreme Court.
B. led to the persecution of more than 1,500 people.
C. hit hard at Socialists and radicals.
D. did all the above

6. In 1917, United States forces in Europe
A. played a crucial part in fighting the Germans at sea.
B. concentrated on the eastern front.
C. played only a token role.
D. saved France from German defeat.

7. For Wilson the most important part of the peace negotiations involved
A. the League of Nations.
B. Germany's admission of "war guilt."
C. war debts and reparations.
D. the principle of self-determination.

8. The major opponent of the Treaty of Versailles was
A. Theodore Roosevelt.
B. Warren Harding.
C. William Jennings Bryan.
D. Henry Cabot Lodge.

**True-False Questions**

*Indicate whether each statement is true or false.*

1. Under President Wilson, United States military forces never intervened in Mexico.
2. Wilson strongly advocated "dollar diplomacy."
3. "He kept us out of war" was the 1916 Republican campaign cry against Wilson.
4. The War Industries Board was the most important agency mobilizing the nation for war.
5. The Committee on Public Information enforced censorship of newspapers and magazines.
6. With the Fourteen Points, Wilson sought to keep Russia in the war and to create disunity among the Central Powers.
7. The influenza epidemic in 1919 killed more Americans than did World War I.
8. The Red Scare was directed against racist and conservative groups like the KKK.

**Essay Questions**

1. How did idealism influence Wilson's diplomacy? Was its effect beneficial?
2. Describe the debate over the United States's role in World War I. How did it resemble the later debate over the League of Nations?
3. Trace the major developments in American policy on intervention from the start of World War I in 1914 to the United States entry into the war in 1917.
4. Describe how the United States mobilized men, arms, and money for World War I.
5. What factors led to the defeat of Wilson's plans for the postwar peace? Assess Wilson's success as a leader in foreign policy.
6. Assess the American contribution to the Allied victory in World War I.
7. Wars are sometimes followed by conservative reactions. Was that true for the United States immediately after World War I? Why or why not?

# DOCUMENTS

### Document 1. Woodrow Wilson's Speech to Congress on Mexico

On April 20, 1914, in an address to Congress on the crisis developing in Mexico, President Wilson asked for authority to act against Mexico.

Gentlemen of the Congress: It is my duty to call your attention to a situation which has arisen in our dealings with General Victoriano Huerta at Mexico City which calls for action, and to ask your advice and cooperation in acting upon it. On the 9th of April a paymaster of the U.S.S. Dolphin landed at the Iturbide Bridge landing at Tampico with a whaleboat and boat's crew to take off certain supplies needed by his ship, and while engaged in loading the boat was arrested by an officer and squad of men of the army of General Huerta. . . . Admiral Mayo regarded the arrest as so serious an affront that he was not satisfied with the apologies offered, but demanded that the flag of the United States be saluted with special ceremony by the military commander of the port.

The incident cannot be regarded as a trivial one, especially as two of the men arrested were taken from the boat itself—that is to say, from the territory of the United States—but had it stood by itself it might have been attributed to the ignorance or arrogance of a single officer. Unfortunately, it was not an isolated case. A series of incidents have recently occurred which cannot but create the impression that the representatives of General Huerta were willing to go out of their way to show disregard for the dignity and rights of this Government and felt perfectly safe in doing what they pleased, making free to show in many ways their irritation and contempt. . . .

The manifest danger of such a situation was that such offenses might grow from bad to worse until something happened of so gross and intolerable a sort as to lead directly and inevitably to armed conflict. It was necessary that the apologies of General Huerta and his representatives should go much further, that they should be such as to attract the attention of the whole population to their significance, and such as to impress upon General Huerta himself the necessity of seeing to it that no further occasion for explanations and professed regrets should arise. I, therefore, felt it my duty to sustain Admiral Mayo in the whole of his demand and to insist that the flag of the United States should be saluted in such a way as to indicate a new spirit and attitude on the part of the Huertistas.

Such a salute, General Huerta has refused, and I have come to ask your approval and support in the course I now propose to pursue.

This Government can, I earnestly hope, in no circumstances be forced into war with the people of Mexico. Mexico is torn by civil strife. If we are to accept the tests of its own constitution, it has no government. General Huerta has set his power up in the City of Mexico, such as it is, without right and by methods for which there can be no justification. Only part of the country is under his control. If armed conflict should unhappily come as a result of his attitude of personal resentment toward this Government, we should be fighting only General Huerta and those who adhere to him and give him their support, and our object would be only to restore to the people of the distracted Republic the opportunity to set up again their own laws and their own government.

But I earnestly hope that war is not now in question. I believe I speak for the American people when I say that we do not desire to control in any degree the affairs of our sister Republic. Our feeling for the people of Mexico is one of deep and genuine friendship, and everything that we have so far done or refrained from doing has proceeded from our desire to help them, not to hinder or embarrass them. We would not wish even to exercise the good offices of friendship without their welcome and consent. The people of Mexico are entitled to settle their own domestic affairs in their own way, and we sincerely desire to respect their right. The present situation need have none of the grave implications of interference if we deal with it promptly, firmly, and wisely.

No doubt I could do what is necessary in the circumstances to enforce respect for our Government without recourse to the Congress, and yet not exceed my constitutional powers as President; but I do not wish to act in a manner possibly of so grave consequence except in close conference and cooperation with both the Senate and House. I, therefore, come to ask your approval that I should use the armed forces of the United States in such ways and to such an extent as may be necessary to obtain from General Huerta and his adherents the fullest recognition of the rights and dignity of the United States, even amidst the distressing conditions now unhappily obtaining in Mexico.

There can in what we do be no thought of aggression or of selfish aggrandizement. We seek to maintain the dignity and authority of the United States only because we wish always to keep our great influence unimpaired for the uses of liberty, both in the United States and wherever else it may be employed for the benefit of mankind.

[From *Congressional Record*, 63rd Cong., 2d sess., April 20, 1914, vol. 51, pt. 4, p. 6925.]

## Document 2. *The Nation* on Mexico

An editorial in The Nation questioned whether intervention in Mexico was justified.

The plain facts of the case are these: that the Administration has undertaken hostile operations against a man whom it has refused to recognize as *de-facto* President of Mexico, because he temporized about making reparation to this country for an insult to the flag in the precise form prescribed by international usage. It was not even that an apology had been refused, for it had not. Huerta had made an apology; more, he had undertaken to salute the flag in the manner demanded, the only stipulation being that the salute should be returned and that a protocol to this effect should be put into writing. That was the occasion for the undertaking of an enterprise the end of which no man can foresee, but which has already exacted its price in the lives of Americans and Mexicans. And the reason for the refusal of the protocol? Because it was not in accord with diplomatic usage? But what has diplomatic usage to do with a private individual whose official existence we do not recognize? Or because the mere signing of it might involve that recognition which we have so studiously avoided? So, we may talk to a man through our accredited diplomatic agent in Mexico, but rather than correspond with him we will go to war. It is straining at a gnat and swallowing a camel.

These are the official reasons advanced for our action in Mexico. Nobody pretends that they are the sole reasons. If they were, our justification for the extreme measures that have been taken would appear even more miserably inadequate than it does. Huerta has pursued a policy of pinpricks exceedingly trying to the patience of the Administration, galling to the pride of any but a nation that is truly great and secure in the consciousness of its national honor. The lives and property of American citizens have been in danger in Mexico, and to protect their lives is one of the first duties of a government; but in the part of Mexico controlled by Huerta Americans have enjoyed heretofore a greater security than in those districts which are in the hands of Villa and the rebels. Yet, be it remembered, it is against Huerta, and Huerta alone, not against Villa, not against the Mexican people, Federals or rebels, that all the armed resources of the United States have been arrayed.

These, we think, are the kind of reflections that have been in the minds of many thoughtful Americans during the past week. It is because the majority of the American people realize, perhaps vaguely, the inconsistency which has marked the policy of the Administration, the inadequacy of the grounds on which war has been threatened, that there has been a notable absence of the jingoistic spirit.

[From *The Nation*, 98, no. 2548 (April 30, 1914): 487.]

## Document 3. "The President's War"

An essay in The Independent sharply attacked President Wilson for starting a war with Mexico.

> The war in Mexico is the war of Woodrow Wilson, President of the United States. He was responsible for the policy pursued in dealing with Huerta and Carranza. He was responsible for the diplomacy which failed to assure peace. It was his ultimatum which paved the way to the conflict. It was his seizure of Vera Cruz that brought war.
>
> Granting the President has been actuated by the loftiest sense of patriotism, it must be admitted that his conduct of the war in its first vital stages has been reprehensible in the highest degree. Incredible as it may seem, he ordered American marines and bluejackets to take the custom house at the most important port of the torn republic, believing that General Huerta would not dare to offer resistance....
>
> [T]he President rejected expert advice and planned, in its initial stages, his own war. The result will be a heavy toll in American lives and American treasure.
>
> What justification had the President for the war he has made? In his address to Congress, he based it upon the refusal of General Huerta to salute the Stars and Stripes for the arrest of the American bluejackets by a Mexican Federal officer at Tampico. He spoke also of the arrest of an American mail orderly at Vera Cruz and of the holding up by the official censor of a dispatch addrest by the Secretary of State to the American chargé d'affaires in Mexico City.

He made no reference to the Americans slain and outraged, to others harassed and insulted, to vast property interests destroyed. He based his action, the action of war, upon the mere matter of ceremony.

The truth of the matter is that the President probably saw that his policy of "watchful waiting" was a failure. It was inspired unquestionably by a purpose to refrain from intervention at all hazards. But he learned almost simultaneously with the occurrence of the Tampico incident that Huerta had negotiated a loan of $60,000,000, which would be sufficient to keep him in office another twelve months. He probably realized that if Huerta should be able to retain power that length of time he (the President) would be made ridiculous. Obsessed as he was by an apparently keen personal hatred of the dictator, he determined upon a step which he believed would assure the elimination of the latter without war.

It is extraordinary that the President from the very beginning has failed to grasp the true situation in Mexico. When he came into office, he issued a declaration that he would not recognize a government founded on force. Idealistic as was this policy it was in flat contravention of the attitude of non-intervention in the domestic concerns of other and particularly pan-American states which the United States has observed with one or two exceptions from the time of its foundation.

[From John Callan O'Laughlin, "The President's War," *The Independent,* 78, no. 3413 (May 4, 1914): 194.]

## Document 4. The Fourteen Points: Wilson's Address to Congress, January 8, 1918

In his famous address to Congress of January 8, 1918, Wilson explained the war aims of the United States. His Fourteen Points formed the basis for the peace negotiations.

Gentlemen of the Congress:

. . . It will be our wish and purpose that the processes of peace, when they are begun, shall be absolutely open and that they shall involve and permit henceforth no secret understandings of any kind. The day of conquest and aggrandizement is gone by; so is also the day of secret covenants entered into in the interest of particular governments and likely at some unlooked-for moment to upset the peace of the world. It is this happy fact, now clear to the view of every public man whose thoughts do not still linger in an age that is dead and gone, which makes it possible for every nation whose purposes are consistent with justice and the peace of the world to avow now or at any other time the objects it has in view.

We entered this war because violations of right had occurred which touched us to the quick and made the life of our own people impossible unless they were corrected and the world secured once for all against their recurrence. What we demand in this war, therefore, is nothing peculiar to ourselves. It is that the world be made fit and safe to live in; and particularly that it be made safe for every peace-loving nation which, like our own, wishes to live its own life, determine its own institutions, be assured of justice and fair dealing by the other peoples of the world as against force and selfish aggression. All the peoples of the world are in effect partners in this interest, and for our own part we see very clearly that unless justice be done to others it will not be done to us. The program of the world's peace, therefore, is our program; and that program, the only possible program, as we see it, is this:

I. Open covenants of peace, openly arrived at, after which there shall be no private international understandings of any kind but diplomacy shall proceed always frankly and in the public view.

II. Absolute freedom of navigation upon the seas, outside territorial waters, alike in peace and in war, except as the seas may be closed in whole or in part by international action for the enforcement of international covenants.

III. The removal, so far as possible, of all economic barriers and the establishment of an equality of trade conditions among all the nations consenting to the peace and associating themselves for its maintenance.

IV. Adequate guarantees given and taken that national armaments will be reduced to the lowest point consistent with domestic safety.

V. A free, open-minded, and absolutely impartial adjustment of all colonial claims, based upon a strict observance of the principle that in determining all such questions of sovereignty the interests of the populations concerned must have equal weight with the equitable claims of the government whose title is to be determined.

VI. The evacuation of all Russian territory and such a settlement of all questions affecting Russia as will secure the best and freest coöperation of the other nations of the world in obtaining for her an unhampered and unembarrassed opportunity for the independent determination of her own political development and national policy and assure her of a sincere welcome into the society of free nations under institutions of her own choosing; and, more than a welcome, assistance also of every kind that she may need and may herself desire. The treatment accorded Russia by her sister nations in the months to come will be the acid test of their good will, of their comprehension of her needs as distinguished from their own interests, and of their intelligent and unselfish sympathy.

VII. Belgium, the whole world will agree, must be evacuated and restored, without any attempt to limit the sovereignty which she enjoys in common with all other free nations. No other single act will serve as this will serve to restore confidence among the nations in the laws which they have themselves set and determined for the government of their relations with one another. Without this healing act the whole structure and validity of international law is forever impaired.

VIII. All French territory should be freed and the invaded portions restored, and the wrong done to France by Prussia in 1871 in the matter of Alsace-Lorraine, which has unsettled the peace of the world for nearly fifty years, should be righted, in order that peace may once more be made secure in the interest of all.

IX. A readjustment of the frontiers of Italy should be effected along clearly recognizable lines of nationality.

X. The peoples of Austria-Hungary, whose place among the nations we wish to see safeguarded and assured, should be accorded the freest opportunity of autonomous development.

XI. Rumania, Serbia, and Montenegro should be evacuated; occupied territories restored; Serbia accorded free and secure access to the sea; and the relations of the several Balkan states to one another determined by friendly counsel along historically established lines of allegiance and nationality; and international guarantees of the political and economic independence and territorial integrity of the several Balkan states should be entered into.

XII. The Turkish portions of the present Ottoman Empire should be assured a secure sovereignty, but the other nationalities which are now under Turkish rule should be assured an undoubted security of life and an absolutely unmolested opportunity of autonomous development, and the Dardanelles should be permanently opened as a free passage to the ships and commerce of all nations under international guarantees.

XIII. An independent Polish state should be erected which should include the territories inhabited by indisputably Polish populations, which should be assured a free and secure access to the sea, and whose political and economic independence and territorial integrity should be guaranteed by international covenant.

XIV. A general association of nations must be formed under specific covenants for the purpose of affording mutual guarantees of political independence and territorial integrity to great and small states alike.

In regard to these essential rectifications of wrong and assertions of right we feel ourselves to be intimate partners of all the governments and peoples associated together against the Imperialists. We cannot be separated in interest or divided in purpose. We stand together until the end.

For such arrangements and covenants we are willing to fight and to continue to fight until they are achieved; but only because we wish the right to prevail and desire a just and stable peace such as can be secured only by removing the chief provocations to war, which this program does not remove. We have no jealousy of German greatness, and there is nothing in this program that impairs it. We grudge her no achievement or distinction of learning or of pacific enterprise such as have made her record very bright and very enviable. We do not wish to injure her or to block in any way her legitimate influence or power. We do not wish to fight her either with arms or with hostile arrangements of trade if she is willing to associate herself with us and the other peace-loving nations of the world in covenants of justice and law and fair dealing. We wish her only to accept a place of equality among the peoples of the world,—the new world in which we now live,—instead of a place of mastery.

Neither do we presume to suggest to her any alteration or modification of her institutions. But it is necessary, we must frankly say, and necessary as a preliminary to any intelligent dealings with her on our part, that we should know whom her spokesmen speak for when they speak to us, whether for the Reichstag majority or for the military party and the men whose creed is imperial domination.

We have spoken now, surely, in terms too concrete to admit of any further doubt or question. An evident principle runs through the whole program I have outlined. It is the principle of justice to all peoples and nationalities, and their right to live on equal terms of liberty and safety with one another, whether they be strong or weak. Unless this principle be made its foundation no part of the structure of international justice can stand. The people of the United States could act upon no other principle; and to the vindication of this principle they are ready to devote their lives, their honor, and everything that they possess. The moral climax of this the culminating and final war for human liberty has come, and they are ready to put their own strength, their own highest purpose, their own integrity and devotion to the test.

[From *A Compilation of the Messages and Papers of the Presidents*, Supplement, 1917–1921, vol. 2 (New York: Bureau of National Literature, 1921), pp. 8421ff.]

## Questions for Reflection

How did President Wilson rationalize U.S. military involvement in Mexico? What criticisms of the presidential decision came from *The Nation* and *The Independent*? What were the other reasons for U.S. intervention hinted at by *The Nation*? In your opinion, was U.S. action in Mexico justified?

Compare Wilson's difficulty explaining U.S. action in 1914 against Mexico with his enunciation of the United States position on entering World War I. On what grounds should the United States intervene militarily in another country? Were Wilson's Fourteen Points a practical program for peace? Explain. Describe the controversy sparked by Point XIV. How would you assess Wilson's role in this controversy? Is the "principle of justice to all peoples and nationalities" a useful basis for foreign policy? Why or why not?

## ANSWERS TO MULTIPLE-CHOICE AND TRUE-FALSE QUESTIONS

### Multiple-Choice Questions

1-B, 2-B, 3-D, 4-D, 5-D, 6-C, 7-A, 8-D

### True-False Questions

1-F, 2-F, 3-F, 4-T, 5-F, 6-T, 7-T, 8-F

# 25

## SOCIETY AND CULTURE BETWEEN THE WARS

## CHAPTER OBJECTIVES

*After you complete the reading and study of this chapter you should be able to*

1. Describe and account for the mood of the 1920s.
2. Describe the nativist reaction in the twenties and the revival of the Ku Klux Klan, along with the consequences of these developments.
3. Trace the emergence of fundamentalism and its effects.
4. Account for the experiment in prohibition and its persistence in the face of widespread evasion of the law.
5. Describe and compare the political and social position of women and blacks in the twenties.
6. Explain the scientific basis of the moral relativism of the decade.
7. Describe the literary flowering of the 1920s and the contributions of major American novelists and poets of the era.

## CHAPTER OUTLINE

I. Reaction in the 1920s
  A. Changing moods
    1. Disillusionment
    2. Defiance against change
  B. Nativism
    1. Sacco and Vanzetti case
    2. Efforts to restrict immigration
  C. Revival of the Ku Klux Klan
  D. Fundamentalism
    1. Emergence of fundamentalism
    2. William Jennings Bryan
    3. Scopes trial
  E. Prohibition
    1. An expression of reforming zeal
    2. Organization for the cause
    3. Crusade for a constitutional amendment
    4. Effectiveness of prohibition
    5. Its link with organized crime
    6. Al Capone

II. Social tensions
  A. A time of cultural conflict
    1. Urban disdain for rural small-town values
    2. Rural fears of cities
  B. The new morality
    1. Emphasis on youth

        2. Obsession with sex
        3. Impact of Freud
        4. Jazz
    C. The women's movement
        1. The work for women's suffrage
            a. Alice Paul and new tactics
            b. Contributions of Carrie Chapman Catt
            c. Passage and ratification of the amendment
            d. Effects of women's suffrage
        2. Push for an Equal Rights Amendment
        3. Women in the work force
    D. The "New Negro"
        1. The Great Migration north
            a. Demographics
            b. Impact of the move
        2. The Harlem Renaissance
        3. Marcus Garvey and Negro Nationalism
        4. Development of the NAACP
            a. Emergence of the organization
            b. Role of Du Bois
            c. Strategy
            d. The campaign against lynching
            e. The Scottsboro case
III. The culture of modernism
    A. Loss of faith in progress
    B. Einstein and the Theory of Relativity
    C. Impact of relativity and uncertainty
        1. Denial of absolute values
        2. Assertion of relativism in cultures
    D. Modernist literature
        1. Chief features
            a. Exploration of the irrational
            b. Uncertainty seen as desirable
            c. Positive view of conflict
            d. Formal manners discounted for contact with "reality"
        2. Development of artistic bohemias
        3. The Armory Show
        4. Emphasis on the "new" in many facets of life
        5. Role of Harriet Monroe
        6. Chief American prophets of modernism
            a. Ezra Pound
            b. T. S. Eliot
            c. Gertrude Stein
        7. Expatriates
            a. F. Scott Fitzgerald
            b. Ernest Hemingway
                i. Cult of masculinity
                ii. Terse literary style

## KEY ITEMS OF CHRONOLOGY

| | |
|---|---|
| Einstein's paper on the Theory of Relativity | 1905 |
| Organization of the NAACP | 1910 |
| Ratification of the Eighteenth Amendment (Prohibition) | 1919 |
| Ratification of the Nineteenth Amendment (women's suffrage) | 1920 |
| Sinclair Lewis's *Babbitt* | 1922 |
| Scopes trial | 1924 |
| Hemingway's *Sun Also Rises* | 1926 |
| Execution of Sacco and Vanzetti | 1927 |
| Heisenberg's Principle of Uncertainty stated | 1927 |
| Scottsboro case | 1931 |

## TERMS TO MASTER

*Listed below are some important terms or people with which you should be familiar after you complete the study of this chapter. Explain the significance of each name or term.*

1. Sacco and Vanzetti
2. KKK
3. "monkey trial"
4. Sigmund Freud
5. Eighteenth Amendment
6. Great Migration
7. Harlem Renaissance
8. Marcus Garvey
9. NAACP
10. Theory of Relativity
11. modernist movement
12. F. Scott Fitzgerald
13. Ernest Hemingway

## VOCABULARY BUILDING

*Listed below are some words used in this chapter. Look up each word in your dictionary.*

1. carnage
2. visceral
3. recurrent
4. literal
5. modernism
6. miscellany
7. prescience
8. entourage
9. repressive
10. inane
11. banality
12. sublimation
13. ephemeral
14. milliner
15. conduit
16. verbosity
17. ineffectual
18. allusion
19. juxtaposition
20. emasculate

## EXERCISES FOR UNDERSTANDING

*When you have completed reading the chapter, answer each of the following questions. If you have difficulty, go back and reread the section of the chapter related to the question.*

## Multiple-Choice Questions

*Select the letter of the response that best completes the statement.*

1. The Sacco-Vanzetti case was an example of
   A. the new morality.
   B. modernism.
   C. the "New Negro."
   D. nativism.

2. A leading proponent of fundamentalism was
   A. Sigmund Freud.
   B. Carrie Chapman Catt.
   C. William Jennings Bryan.
   D. Werner Heisenberg.

3. Obstacles to prohibition included
   A. profits from bootlegging.
   B. inadequate congressional support for enforcement.
   C. public demand for alcohol.
   D. all of the above.

4. In the 1920s after women got the vote, they
   A. voted as men did.
   B. brought dramatic political change.
   C. spurred the women's movement to greater achievements.
   D. all of the above.

5. The Harlem Renaissance, an artistic and literary blossoming, featured the works of
   A. Claude McKay, Langston Hughes, and Countee Cullen.
   B. H. L. Mencken, Eugene O'Neill, and Sinclair Lewis.
   C. Thomas Wolfe, Ernest Hemingway, and the Fugitives.
   D. Albert Einstein, Sigmund Freud, and Marcus Garvey.

6. The scientific work of Einstein, Heisenberg, and others
   A. reinforced the traditional faith in reason and order.
   B. increased confidence in our ability to fully understand the world.
   C. was incompatible with the disillusionment and despair of the postwar period.
   D. suggested that there is a limit to our understanding of the universe.

7. The features of modernist literature included *all but which one* of the following:
   A. Exploration of the irrational as an essential part of human nature.

B. The view of the universe as operating on unchanging and stable principles.
C. The view that conflict was more fundamental than harmony.
D. The view that freedom from convention was more important than following tradition.

8. "All of you young people who served in the war, you are a lost generation," said
A. F. Scott Fitzgerald.
B. T. S. Eliot.
C. Gertrude Stein.
D. Ernest Hemingway.

**True-False Questions**

*Indicate whether each statement is true or false.*

1. The end of World War I brought a greater appreciation for diversity and change in American life.
2. The Ku Klux Klan was directed against blacks, Jews, and Catholics.
3. John T. Scopes's conviction for a payroll robbery and murder in Indiana led to the downfall of the KKK.
4. Organized crime began during the depression of the 1930s.
5. The Nineteenth Amendment to the Constitution gave women the right to vote.
6. The NAACP's strategy stressed working through the legal system to achieve changes in race relations.
7. Countee Cullen and James Weldon Johnson were part of the Harlem Renaissance.
8. The modernists had a deep faith in progress and reform.

**Essay Questions**

1. What did nativism, fundamentalism, and prohibition have in common? How did they differ? Which had the greatest impact on American life?
2. Describe the "new morality" of the 1920s.
3. What was the idea of the "New Negro" and what effects did the spirit of the New Negro have on black life?
4. Explain the contributions of Freud, Marx, Einstein, and Heisenberg to the new mood of the twenties.
5. What were the chief features of modernist literature? Show how those features were exhibited in the works of one of the authors mentioned in the text.

## DOCUMENTS

### Document 1. John Dewey on William Jennings Bryan and "The American Intellectual Frontier"

In 1922 the influential philosopher and educator at Columbia University John Dewey commented on William Jennings Bryan's fundamentalist campaign against evolution and found its sources in the powerful forces common in the American past.

> The campaign of William Jennings Bryan against science and in favor of obscurantism and intolerance is worthy of serious study. It demands more than the mingled amusement and irritation which it directly evokes. In its success (and it is meeting with success) it raises fundamental questions about the quality of our democracy. It helps us understand the absence of intellectual radicalism in the United States and the present eclipse of social and political liberalism. It aids, abets and gives comfort to the thoroughgoing critics of any democracy. It gives point to the assertion of our Menckens that democracy by nature puts a premium on mediocrity, the very thing in human nature that least stands in need of any extraneous assistance.
> 
> For Mr. Bryan is a typical democratic figure. There is no gainsaying that proposition. Economically and politically he has stood for and

with the masses, not radically but "progressively." The most ordinary justice to him demands that his usefulness in revolt against privilege and his rôle as a leader in the late progressive movement—late in every sense of the word, including deceased—be recognized. His leadership in antagonism to free scientific research and to popular dissemination of its results cannot therefore be laughed away as a personal idiosyncracy. There is a genuine and effective connection between the political and the doctrinal directions of his activity, and between the popular responses they call out.

What we call the middle classes are for the most part the church-going classes, those who have come under the influence of evangelical Christianity. These persons form the backbone of philanthropic social interest, of social reform through political action, of pacifism, of popular education. They embody and express the spirit of kindly goodwill toward classes which are at an economic disadvantage and toward other nations, especially when the latter show any disposition toward a republican form of government. The "Middle West," the prairie country, has been the centre of active social philanthropies and political progressivism because it is the chief home of this folk. Fairly well to do, enough so at least to be ambitious and to be sensitive to restrictions imposed by railway and financial corporations, believing in education and better opportunities for its own children, mildly interested in "culture," it has formed the solid element in our diffuse national life and heterogeneous populations. It has been the element responsive to appeals for the square deal and more nearly equal opportunities for all, as it has understood equality of opportunity. It followed Lincoln in the abolition of slavery, and it followed Roosevelt in his denunciation of "bad" corporations and aggregations of wealth. It also followed Roosevelt or led him in its distinctions between "on the one hand and on the other hand." It has been the middle in every sense of the word and in every movement. Like every mean it has held things together and given unity and stability of movement.

It has never had an interest in ideas as ideas, nor in science and art for what they may do in liberating and elevating the human spirit. Science and art as far as they refine and polish life, afford "culture," mark stations on an upward social road, and have direct useful social applications, yes: but as emancipations, as radical guides to life, no. There is nothing recondite or mysterious or sinister or adverse to a reputable estimate of human nature in the causes of this state of mind. Historians of thought point out the difference between the fortunes of the new ideas of science and philosophy in the eighteenth century in England and France. In the former, they were accommodated, partially absorbed; they permeated far enough to lose their own inherent quality. Institutions were more or less liberalized, but the ideas were lost in the process. In France, the opposition was entrenched in powerful and inelastic institutions. The ideas were clarified and stripped to fighting weight. They had to fight to live, and they became weapons. What happened in England happened in America only on a larger scale and to greater depths. The net result is social and political liberalism combined with intellectual illiberality. Of the result Mr. Bryan is an outstanding symbol.

Mr. Bryan can have at best only a temporary triumph, a succès d'estime, in his efforts to hold back biological inquiry and teaching. It is not in this particular field that he is significant. But his appeals and his endeavors are a symptom and a symbol of the forces which are most powerful in holding down the intellectual level of American life. He does not represent the frontier democracy of Jackson's day. But he represents it toned down and cultivated as it exists in fairly prosperous villages and small towns that have inherited the fear of whatever threatens the security and order of a precariously attained civilization, along with pioneer impulses to neighborliness and decency. Attachment to stability and homogeneity of thought and belief seem essential in the midst of practical heterogeneity, rush and unsettlement. We are not Puritans in our intellectual heritage, but we are evangelical because of our fear of ourselves and of our latent frontier disorderliness. The depressing effect upon the free life of inquiry and criticism is the greater because of the element of soundness in frontier fear, and because of the impulses of goodwill and social aspiration which have become entangled with its creeds. The forces which are embodied in the present crusade would not be so dangerous were they not bound up with so much that is necessary and good. We have been so taught to respect the beliefs of our neighbors that few will respect the beliefs of a neighbor when they depart from forms which have become associated with aspiration for a decent neighborly life. This is the illiberalism which is deep-rooted in our liberalism. No account of the decay of the idealism of the progressive movement in politics or of the failure to develop an intelligent and enduring idealism out of the emotional fervor of the war, is adequate unless it reckons with this fixed limit to thought. No future liberal movement, when active liberalism revives, will be permanent unless it goes deep enough to affect it. Otherwise we shall have in the future what we have had in the past, revivalists like Bryan, Roosevelt and Wilson, movements which embody moral emotions rather than the insight and policy of intelligence.

[John Dewey, "The American Intellectual Frontier," *New Republic* 30, no. 388 (May 10, 1922): 303–5.]

## Document 2. Walter Lippmann on the Controversial Issues of the Day

An editorialist with the New York World in 1927, Walter Lippmann later became a prize-winning columnist and commentator. Below he explains the issues that really stirred Americans' interests in the 1920s.

The questions which really engage the emotions of the masses of the people are of a quite different order. They manifest themselves in the controversies over prohibition, the Ku Klux Klan, Romanism, Fundamentalism, immigration. These, rather than the tariff, taxation, credit, and corporate control, are the issues which divide the American people. These are the issues men care about. They are just beneath the surface of political discussion. In theory they are not supposed to be issues. The party platforms and the official pronouncements deal with them obliquely, if at all. But they are the issues men talk about privately, and they are, above all, the issues about which men have deep personal feelings.

These questions are diverse, but they all arise out of the same general circumstances. They arise out of the great migration of the last fifty years, out of the growth of cities, and out of the spread of that rationalism and the deepening of that breach with tradition which invariably accompany the development of a metropolitan civilization. Prohibition, the Ku Klux Klan, Fundamentalism, and xenophobia are an extreme but authentic expression of the politics, the social outlook, and the religion of the older American village civilization making its last stand against what looks to it like an alien invasion. The alien invasion is in fact the new America produced by the growth and the prosperity of America.

The evil which the old-fashioned preachers ascribe to the Pope, to Babylon, to atheists, and to the Devil is simply the new urban civilization, with its irresistible economic and scientific and mass power. The Pope, the Devil, jazz, the bootleggers, are a mythology which expresses symbolically the impact of a vast and dreaded social change. The change is real enough. The language in which it is discussed is preposterous only as all mythology is preposterous if you accept it literally. The mythology of the Ku Klux Klan is a kind of primitive science, an animistic and dramatized projection of the fears of a large section of our people who have yet to accommodate themselves to the strange new social order which has arisen in their midst.

This new social order is dominated by metropolitan cities of which New York is the largest and most highly developed. Therefore New York has become the symbol of all that is most wicked and of all that is most alluring in modern America. But New York to-day is only what Chicago, St. Louis, Detroit, Cleveland, Jacksonville, and Miami expect to be to-morrow. It is the seat of a vast population, mixed in its origins, uncertain of its social status, rather vague about the moral code. In these metropolitan centres the ancient social bonds are loosened. The patriarchal family, the well-established social hierarchy, the old roots of belief, and the grooves of custom are all obscured by new human relationships based on a certain kind of personal independence, on individual experiment and adventure, which are yet somehow deeply controlled by fads and fashions and great mass movements.

The campaign in certain localities to forbid the teaching of 'Darwinism' is an attempt to stem the tide of the metropolitan spirit, to erect a spiritual tariff against an alien rationalism which threatens to dissolve the mores of the village civilization. To many of us the effort seems quixotic, as indeed it is, judged by the intellectual standards of metropolitan life. But if we look at the matter objectively, disregarding the petty mannerisms of the movement, there is a pathos about it which always adheres to the last struggle of an authentic type of human living. The anti-evolutionists are usually less charming than Don Quixote. Perhaps that is because they have not been transfigured by an artist. They are at any rate fighting for the memory of a civilization which in its own heyday, and by its own criteria, was as valid as any other.

The anti-evolution bills are, of course, a comparatively trivial symptom of this profound maladjustment. The overt struggle turns politically on two questions: on the Eighteenth Amendment and on the nomination of Governor Alfred E. Smith. The struggle over these two issues implicates all the antagonisms between the older America and the new. The Eighteenth Amendment is a piece of legislation embodied in the Constitution which attempts to impose the moral ideals of the villages upon the whole nation. The force behind the Eighteenth Amendment is the Anti-Saloon League, which is the political arm of the evangelical churches in the small communities. The financial and political strength of the Anti-Saloon League is derived from the members of these churches, chiefly Methodist and Baptist, with other denominations divided but following these militant sects. And the strength of these sects in the last analysis arises from the spiritual isolation of communities which have not yet been radically invaded by the metropolitan spirit.

The defense of the Eighteenth Amendment has, therefore, become much more than a mere question of regulating the liquor traffic. It involves a test of strength between social orders, and when that test is concluded, and if, as seems probable, the Amendment breaks down, the fall will bring down with it the dominion of the older civilization. The Eighteenth Amendment is the rock on which the evangelical church militant is founded, and with it are involved a whole way of life and an ancient tradition. The overcoming of the Eighteenth Amendment would mean the emergence of the cities as the dominant force in America, dominant politically and socially as they are already dominant economically.

[Walter Lippmann, "The Causes of Political Indifference Today," *Atlantic Monthly*, 139, no. 2 (February 1927): 265–67.]

## Questions for Reflection

How did Dewey and Lippmann each explain the appeal of fundamentalism, the KKK, and prohibition? Did they agree entirely? How did they differ in emphasis? Are they persuasive for the 1920s? Are there other explanations that occur to you? Do their analyses have any pertinence today?

## ANSWERS TO MULTIPLE-CHOICE AND TRUE-FALSE QUESTIONS

### Multiple-Choice Questions

1-D, 2-C, 3-D, 4-A, 5-A, 6-D, 7-B, 8-C

### True-False Questions

1-F, 2-T, 3-F, 4-F, 5-T, 6-T, 7-T, 8-F

# 26

## REPUBLICAN RESURGENCE AND DECLINE, 1920–1932

## CHAPTER OBJECTIVES

*After you complete the reading and study of this chapter you should be able to*

1. Describe the effects of the Harding presidency on the nation.
2. Explain the new prosperity of the 1920s.
3. Describe the features of the economy in the New Era decade.
4. Explain Hoover's policies for the nation and indicate their effects.
5. Account for the stock market crash of 1929.
6. Describe the status of farmers during the twenties.
7. Describe the status of labor unions during the 1920s.

## CHAPTER OUTLINE

I. The fate of progressivism in the twenties
   A. Causes for the dissolution of the progressive coalition in Congress
      1. Disaffection with the war and the war's aftermath
      2. Administration and labor
      3. Farmers' concerns
      4. Intellectuals' disillusionment
      5. Middle-class preoccupation with business
   B. Survivals of progressivism in the twenties
      1. Domination of Congress
      2. Strong pressure at local levels for "good government" and public services
      3. Reform impulse transformed into the drive for moral righteousness

II. The election of 1920
   A. Mood of the country
   B. Republican shift to the right
   C. Democratic nomination
   D. Results

III. The Harding administration
   A. The Harding appointments
   B. Nature of the Harding presidency
   C. Efforts for economy
      1. Tax cuts
      2. Spending cuts
      3. Tariffs
   D. Deemphasis on regulating agencies
   E. Corruption in the administration
      1. Veterans Bureau
      2. Harry Daugherty
      3. Teapot Dome
      4. Role of Harding
   F. Harding's death
   G. Assessment

IV. The Coolidge years
   A. Character of the man
   B. The election of 1924
      1. Coolidge's control of the Republican party

2. Dissension among the Democrats
3. Emergence of the Progressive party
4. Results of the election
C. Aspects of the New Era
    1. The consumption ethic
    2. Growth of advertising
    3. Development of the movies
    4. Growth of radio
    5. Aviation
        a. Growth of industry
        b. Charles A. Lindbergh, Jr.
        c. Amelia Earhart
    6. Impact of the automobile
D. Hoover's role in the economy
    1. His concept of voluntary cooperation
    2. Growth of the Commerce Department
    3. Promotion of trade associations
    4. The acquiescence of the Supreme Court
E. Problems in agriculture
    1. Reasons for the agricultural slump
    2. Mechanization of farms
    3. New farm organizations
        a. Marketing associations
        b. Formation of the Farm Bloc in Congress
    4. Legislation favorable to agriculture
        a. Early acts
        b. The McNary-Haugen scheme
F. Setbacks for unions
    1. Earnings in industry
    2. Efforts to forestall unions

V. The Hoover presidency
A. The election of 1928
    1. The Republican position
    2. The Democratic choice
    3. Issues of the election
    4. Results
B. The prospects for success
C. Hoover's general policies
D. His support for agriculture
    1. Aids for cooperative marketing
    2. Tariff increases
E. The speculative mania
    1. The Florida real estate bubble
    2. Development of the Great Bull Market
    3. Efforts to curb the market
F. The crash
    1. Description of the crash
    2. Immediate effects
    3. Causes of the crash
G. Efforts for recovery
    1. Advocates of laissez-faire
    2. Hoover's exhortations
    3. Public works and credit
    4. Democratic victory in 1930
    5. International complications
H. Congressional initiatives
    1. The Reconstruction Finance Corporation and its role
    2. Help for financial institutions
    3. Plans for relief
I. Plight of the farmers and veterans
    1. Means of farmer protest
    2. The Bonus Expeditionary Force
J. Mood of the nation

## KEY ITEMS OF CHRONOLOGY

| | |
|---|---|
| First radio commercial | 1922 |
| Death of Harding | 1923 |
| Florida real estate collapse | 1926 |
| Lindbergh flight | May 1927 |
| McNary-Haugen bills passed Congress | 1927, 1928 |
| Stock market crash | October 1929 |
| Smoot-Hawley Tariff | 1930 |
| Hoover's moratorium on war-debt payments | 1931 |
| Creation of Reconstruction Finance Corporation | 1932 |
| Attack on the Bonus Expeditionary Force | July 1932 |

# REPUBLICAN RESURGENCE AND DECLINE, 1920–1932

## TERMS TO MASTER

*Listed below are some important terms or people with which you should be familiar after you complete the study of this chapter. Explain the significance of each name or term.*

1. "normalcy"
2. Andrew Mellon
3. Teapot Dome affair
4. Robert M. La Follette
5. Calvin Coolidge
6. Amelia Earhart
7. Herbert Hoover
8. associationalism
9. marketing cooperatives
10. McNary-Haugen scheme
11. "yellow dog" contract
12. Alfred E. Smith
13. Agricultural Marketing Act
14. margin buying
15. Reconstruction Finance Corporation
16. Federal Home Loan Bank Act
17. Bonus Expeditionary Force
19. liquidate
20. forlorn

## VOCABULARY BUILDING

*Listed below are some words used in this chapter. Look up each word in your dictionary.*

1. coalition
2. equipoise
3. austere
4. gregarious
5. hack (n.)
6. behest
7. askance
8. dour
9. vindication
10. frugality
11. oblige
12. barnstorm
13. perplexing
14. herald
15. disseminate
16. panacea
17. prototype
18. affability

## EXERCISES FOR UNDERSTANDING

*When you have completed reading the chapter, answer each of the following questions. If you have difficulty, go back and reread the section of the chapter related to the question.*

### Multiple-Choice Questions

*Select the letter of the response that best completes the statement.*

1. During the 1920s, progressive reformers
   A. had no influence in national government.
   B. dominated Congress.
   C. held the White House.
   D. controlled the Supreme Court.

2. Secretary of the Treasury Andrew Mellon
   A. raised individual income taxes to pay off the debt from World War I.
   B. opposed a high tariff.
   C. cut taxes on the wealthy.
   D. all of the above

3. The Teapot Dome scandal involved
   A. kickbacks to the president.
   B. oil leases in Wyoming.
   C. Harding's extramarital affairs.
   D. tariffs on products from the Orient, especially tea.

4. Mass production in the automobile industry was the creation of
   A. Henry Ford.
   B. Walter E. Flanders.
   C. F. W. Taylor.

D. all of the above (each contributed in part)
5. As secretary of commerce, Herbert Hoover promoted
   A. keen competition among corporations.
   B. standardization of products (tires, bricks, etc.).
   C. a vigorous trustbusting campaign.
   D. federal ownership of the radio and airline industries.
6. "The chief business of America is business," declared
   A. Calvin Coolidge.
   B. Warren Harding.
   C. Herbert Hoover.
   D. Andrew Mellon.
7. The prosperous economy of the 1920s included
   A. a smaller federal government, especially the Commerce Department.
   B. growing labor unions.
   C. unprecedented prosperity for farmers.
   D. the development of mass advertising.
8. Hoover's approach to recovery placed an emphasis on
   A. government construction of housing.
   B. voluntary efforts of the people.
   C. assistance to European trade.
   D. government aid to the unemployed.

## True-False Questions

*Indicate whether each statement is true or false.*

1. Teapot Dome was the major issue in the 1920 election.
2. Franklin D. Roosevelt was defeated in the 1920 election.
3. Senator Robert La Follette of Wisconsin was the Democratic opponent of Coolidge in the 1924 election.
4. The first woman to fly around the world was Amelia Earhart.
5. McNary-Haugenism sought to provide relief to American farmers.
6. Buying stocks on margin helped restrain speculation in the stock market.
7. Excessively high wages for labor in the 1920s helped cause the stock market crash in 1929.
8. The Reconstruction Finance Corporation assisted farmers, homeowners, and labor unions.

## Essay Questions

1. Compare and contrast the elections of 1920 and 1928.
2. Which best describes the 1920s: "normalcy" or "the New Era"? Why?
3. Describe the problems facing farmers and labor in the 1920s. Which group suffered more? Why?
4. What was Hoover's conception of the role of the federal government and how did he apply it in the 1920s?
5. What caused the stock market to crash in 1929?
6. Evaluate the efforts of both Hoover and Congress to revive the American economy in the late 1920s.

## DOCUMENT

### "Keep the Consumer Dissatisfied"

Charles F. Kettering, general director of the research laboratories at General Motors, discussed one of the major purposes of industrial research and its relationship to prosperity in the New Era.

Not long ago one of the great bankers of the country said to me:
"The trouble with you fellows is that you are all the time chang-

ing automobiles and depreciating old cars, and you are doing it at a time when people have three or four payments to make on the cars they already have.

"Yesterday I got an engraved invitation from one of your companies to see a new model. Out of curiosity I went. I darn near bought one. I didn't because you people wouldn't allow me enough money for my old car."

A few weeks later I was again talking with this banker. He appeared to be greatly disgruntled.

"I bought that new model," he barked. "But it was a rotten shame that I had to accept so much depreciation on my old car. You are the fellow who is to blame. You, with all your changes and refinements, made me dissatisfied with the old model."

He paused, then added, mournfully, "And that old car ran like new."

I told him I thought it was worth what he paid—that is, the difference between the old and the new model—to have his mind changed.

He didn't argue over that but he did say something to the general effect that "the only reason for research is to keep your customers reasonably dissatisfied with what they already have."

I might observe, here and now, that he was right.

A few weeks back I was sitting with a group of executives. All were admiring a new model.

"It is absolutely the best automobile that can be made," enthused one. I objected to that statement.

"Let's take this automobile which, you say, is the 'best that can be made' and put it into a glass showcase," I said. "Let's put it in there—seal it so no person can possibly touch it. Just before we seal it in the case let us mark the price in big letters inside the case.

"Let us do that and come back here a year from today. After looking at it and appraising it, we will mark a price on the outside of the glass. It will be a price something less than what we think the car is worth today. Probably $200 less. Then, let's come back once every year for ten years, look through the glass, and mark a new price. At the end of ten years we won't be able to put down enough ciphers to indicate what we think of the car. That is, of course, eliminating its value as junk.

"In those ten years, no one could possibly have touched the car. There could be no lessened value through handling. The paint would be just as good as new; the crank case just as good; the rear axle just as good; and the motor just as good as ever.

"What, then, has happened to this car?

"People's minds will have been changed; improvements will have come in other cars; new styles will have come. What you have here today, a car that you call 'the best that can be made,' will then be useless. So it isn't the best that can be made. It may be the best you have made and, if that is what you meant, I have no quarrel with what you said." . . .

Change, to a research engineer, is improvement. People, though, don't seem to think of it in that manner. When a change is suggested they hold back and say, "What we have is all right—it does the work." Doing the work is important but doing it better is more important.

The human family in industry is always looking for a park bench where it can sit down and rest. But the only park benches I know of are right in front of an undertaker's establishment.

There are no places where anyone can sit and rest in an industrial situation. It is a question of change, change, change, all the time—and it is always going to be that way. It must always be that way for the world only goes along one road, the road to progress. Nations and industries that have become satisfied with themselves and their ways of doing things, don't last. While they are sitting back and admiring themselves other nations and other concerns have forgotten the looking-glasses and have been moving ahead. . . .

The younger generation—and by that I mean the generation that is always coming—knows what it wants and it will get what it wants. This is what makes for change. It brings about improvements in old things and developments in new things.

You can't stop people being born. You can't stop the thing we call progress. You can't stop the thing we call change. But you can get in tune with it. Change is never waste—it is improvement, all down the line. Because I have no further need for my automobile doesn't mean that that automobile is destroyed. It goes to someone who has need for it and, to get it, he disposes of something that is unnecessary to his happiness. And so on to the end where the thing that is actually thrown away is of no further use to anyone. By this method living standards, all around, are raised.

We hear people complaining because of new models in automobiles. If it were not for these new models these same people would be paying more for what they have. Recognition of the fact that progress is inevitable forces us to recognize that we must have improvements in motor cars.

We, as manufacturers, must offer those improvements after they have been found to be capable improvements. The public buys and disposes of what it has. The fact that it is able to dispose of what it has enables us, as producers, to put a lower price tag on the new model. The law of economy in mass production enters here. We are permitted to turn out cars in volume because there is a market for them.

If automobile owners could not dispose of their cars to a lower buying strata they would have to wear out their cars with a consequent tremendous cutting in the yearly demand for automobiles, a certain increase in production costs, and the natural passing along of these costs to the buyer.

If every one were satisfied, no one would buy the new thing because no one would want it. The ore wouldn't be mined; timber wouldn't be cut. Almost immediately hard times would be upon us.

You must accept this reasonable dissatisfaction with what you have and buy the new thing, or accept hard times. You can have your choice.

[From Charles F. Kettering, "Keep the Consumer Dissatisfied," *Nation's Business*, 17, no. 1 (January 1929), 30–31, 79.]

## Questions for Reflection

The textbook quotes a newspaper editorial from the 1920s as saying that the American's "first importance to his country is no longer that of citizen but that of consumer. Consumption is the new necessity." How does GM's Charles Kettering explain the role of industry in promoting consumption?

## ANSWERS TO MULTIPLE-CHOICE AND TRUE-FALSE QUESTIONS

### Multiple-Choice Questions

1-B, 2-C, 3-B, 4-D, 5-B, 6-A, 7-D, 8-B

### True-False Questions

1-F, 2-T, 3-F, 4-F, 5-T, 6-F, 7-F, 8-F

# 27

# FRANKLIN D. ROOSEVELT AND THE NEW DEAL

## CHAPTER OBJECTIVES

*After you complete the reading and study of this chapter you should be able to*

1. Describe the character and appeal of FDR.
2. Describe the sources of New Deal legislation.
3. Explain the New Deal approaches to the problems of recovery in industry and agriculture.
4. Describe the criticisms made of the New Deal by the left and the right.
5. Describe New Deal efforts to deal with unemployment and welfare.
6. Assess the changes in the United States wrought by the New Deal.
7. Understand the outpouring of literature of social significance during the 1930s.

## CHAPTER OUTLINE

I. The election of 1932
   A. The candidates
   B. Roosevelt's background and character
   C. The campaign contrasts
   D. Results of the election

II. The early New Deal
   A. Mood of the inauguration
   B. Willingness to experiment
   C. Action for banks, the economy, and beer
   D. Overview of the Hundred Days
   E. Measures to improve financial institutions
      1. Extension of farm credit
      2. Help for home mortgages
      3. Action to protect banks and security purchases
      4. Abandonment of the gold standard
   F. Relief measures
      1. Civilian Conservation Corps (CCC)
      2. Federal Emergency Relief Administration (FERA)
      3. Civilian Works Administration (CWA)
      4. Works Progress Administration (WPA)

III. Recovery through regulation and planning
   A. Aid for agriculture
      1. Wide variety of options within the Agricultural Adjustment Administration (AAA)
      2. Creation of the Commodity Credit Corporation

3. General effects on farm income and farmers
4. Dust Bowl and migration
   a. Mexican-Americans
   b. Blacks
   c. "Okies"
5. Supreme Court negates the processing tax of AAA
6. Soil Conservation Act: provisions and effects
7. Second AAA
B. Efforts for the recovery of industry
   1. The Public Works Administration (PWA)
   2. The National Recovery Administration (NRA)
      a. Two primary aims
      b. Nature of the NRA operation
      c. Objections to the NRA codes
      d. Enduring impact of the NRA
C. Regional planning: Tennessee Valley Authority (TVA)
   1. Historical basis
   2. Nature of the legislation
   3. Impact of the TVA
   4. Creation of the Rural Electrification Association (REA)

IV. Critics left and right
A. Increased support for FDR in 1934
B. Conservatives launch the American Liberty League
C. Thunder on the left
   1. Huey Long's threat
   2. Francis Townsend's program
   3. Father Coughlin's role
   4. Potential threat of the left
D. Pressure on FDR to restore competition
E. Roadblocks from the Supreme Court

V. The Second New Deal
A. The Wagner Act for workers
B. The Social Security Act
   1. Old age and survivors' insurance
   2. Unemployment insurance
   3. Public assistance programs
   4. Limitations
C. The Wealth Tax Act
D. Right-wing criticisms of the New Deal

VI. Human effects of the New Deal
A. Family life
B. Civil rights
   1. Black cabinet
   2. NAACP action
   C. Conservative reaction
   D. Eleanor Roosevelt
      1. Role in administration
      2. Social service
      3. FDR's representative

VII. The election of 1936
A. Republicans choose progressive Alf Landon
B. Republican strategy
C. The new Roosevelt coalition
D. Results of the election

VIII. Second-term developments
A. The court-packing controversy
   1. FDR's view of the election
   2. Effects of Court rulings
   3. The court-packing plan
   4. Events blunt the plan
   5. Impact of the fight
B. Stirrings among labor
   1. Impetus to unionization
   2. Rise of industrial unions
   3. Intense conflict with management
      a. Techniques used by management
      b. The sitdown strike
      c. CIO victories
      d. Growing power for organized labor
C. Reaction to a new depression
   1. Course of the 1937 slump
   2. Administration's reaction
   3. The battle over policy
      a. Fear of the unbalanced budget
      b. A move from regulation to antitrust action
   4. Roosevelt's call for spending
   5. Reforms of 1937 and 1938
      a. Housing legislation
      b. Assistance for tenant farmers
      c. Fair Labor Standards Act
D. Setbacks to the New Deal
   1. Emergence of an opposition
      a. Defection of the southerners
      b. Victories of the opposition in 1938
   2. Roosevelt's 1938 purge
   3. Results of the 1938 elections
   4. Limited legislation in 1939

IX. Impact of the New Deal
A. Some enduring changes
B. A course between extremes
C. Creation of the "broker state"

X. Literature of the 1930s
  A. Impact of the depression
  B. Novelists of social significance
    1. John Steinbeck
    2. Richard Wright
  C. The Southern Renaissance
  1. Effect of Mencken's critique
  2. Novelists
    a. Thomas Wolfe
    b. William Faulkner
  D. Rediscovery of American culture

## KEY ITEMS OF CHRONOLOGY

Roosevelt's administrations — 1933–April 1945
The Hundred Days — March 4–June 16, 1933
Second New Deal initiatives — 1935
Court-packing plan presented — 1937

## TERMS TO MASTER

*Listed below are some important terms or people with which you should be familiar after you complete the study of this chapter. Explain the significance of each name or term.*

1. The Hundred Days
2. brain trust
3. Securities and Exchange Commission
4. Civilian Conservation Corps
5. Agricultural Adjustment Administration
6. Dust Bowl
7. "Okies"
8. *United States v. Butler*
9. Soil Conservation Act
10. Public Works Administration
11. Tennessee Valley Authority
12. Huey Long
13. *Schechter Poultry Corp. v. United States*
14. Wagner Act
15. Social Security Act
16. court-packing plan
17. CIO
18. John L. Lewis
19. Fair Labor Standards Act
20. broker state
21. modernism
22. Southern Renaissance
23. William Faulkner

## VOCABULARY BUILDING

*Listed below are some words used in this chapter. Look up each word in your dictionary.*

1. crass
2. requisite
3. pedestrian (adj.)
4. distraught
5. fiscal
6. foreclosure
7. analogue
8. prime (v.)
9. vitality
10. nostrum
11. consummate
12. tantalize
13. halitosis
14. discretionary
15. maudlin
16. stoical
17. liaison
18. malevolent
19. veneration
20. convoluted

## EXERCISES FOR UNDERSTANDING

*When you have completed reading the chapter, answer each of the following questions. If you have difficulty, go back and reread the section of the chapter related to the question.*

## Multiple-Choice Questions

*Select the letter of the response that best completes the statement.*

1. In 1933 the New Deal immediately attacked problems in
   A. race relations.
   B. banking and finance.
   C. labor.
   D. diplomacy with Germany.

2. The Agricultural Adjustment Act paid farmers if they
   A. gave food to the needy.
   B. cut production.
   C. grew more food and less cotton and tobacco.
   D. voted for Democrats.

3. Black farmers suffered especially during the depression because they
   A. owned small farms.
   B. had voted for Republicans.
   C. were mostly landless tenants.
   D. lived primarily in the South.

4. The National Industrial Recovery Act provided for
   A. $3.3 billion in spending through the PWA.
   B. codes of fair practice for industries.
   C. the right of workers to form unions.
   D. all of the above

5. The New Deal's "cornerstone" and "supreme achievement," according to FDR, was
   A. Social Security.
   B. the Wagner Labor Relations Act.
   C. the Tennessee Valley Authority.
   D. the PWA and WPA.

6. Eleanor Roosevelt helped her husband most by
   A. remaining discreetly noncontroversial.
   B. maintaining ties to blacks and labor.
   C. pulling him toward more conservative policies.
   D. going on diplomatic missions to Asia and Africa.

7. The Supreme Court–packing plan was defeated in part because of
   A. Democratic losses in 1936.
   B. its violation of the Constitution.
   C. a change in the Court's direction in rulings on key measures.
   D. all of the above.

8. Perhaps the most skilled creator of a modernist literary style was
   A. William Faulkner.
   B. Richard Wright.
   C. Thomas Wolfe.
   D. John Steinbeck.

## True-False Questions

*Indicate whether each statement is true or false.*

1. In his 1932 campaign, FDR spelled out in detail his plans for fighting the depression.
2. Before becoming president, Franklin D. Roosevelt had run unsuccessfully for vice-president.
3. The AAA of 1933 tried to help farmers by getting them to reduce production.
4. The Wagner Act regulated the nation's stock markets.
5. The Social Security tax did "soak the rich."
6. The GOP candidate in 1936 was a longtime opponent of the entire New Deal.
7. The Fair Labor Standards Act of 1938 outlawed child labor.
8. Perhaps the most enduring voting change brought by FDR was the shift of the farm vote to the Democratic party.

## A Match of New Deal Agencies

*The New Deal period witnessed the creation of a plethora of new government agencies that became known as the alphabet agencies because they were referred to by their initials. To help you focus on major agencies and to test your grasp of the material, on the following pages, match the description or statement on the right with the agencies or act on the left. Some of the agencies or acts may match with more than one description. Answers are at the end of this chapter.*

| Agency or Act | Description |
|---|---|
| 1. FDIC | a. created a regional rehabilitation of a river basin |
| 2. FERA | b. investigated the concentration of economic power in the United States |
| 3. Economy Act | c. set minimum wages and maximum hours for certain industries in interstate commerce |
| 4. First AAA | d. provided a variety of methods for increasing farm income |
| 5. Civilian Conservation Corps | e. provided insurance for bank deposits |
| 6. PWA | f. provided $3.3 billion for jobs on major building projects |
| 7. TVA | g. established a stopgap plan for aiding the unemployed from 1933 to 1935 |
| 8. NRA | h. provided loans to rural cooperatives to run electrical lines to remote farms |
| 9. REA | i. established a plan to cut wages of veterans and federal employees |
| 10. Wagner Act | j. provided jobs for young men in the nation's parks |
| 11. Social Security Act | k. regulated the sale of stocks and bonds |
| 12. Wealth Tax Act | l. allowed industries to collaborate to limit production of goods and raise wages |
| 13. SEC | m. provided payments to farmers to conserve soil by not planting crops |
| 14. TNEC | n. created a committee to oversee elections for unions |
| 15. Farm Security Administration | o. established the welfare system for mothers and dependent children |

| Agency or Act | Description |
| --- | --- |
| 16. Soil Conservation Act | p. greatly increased income taxes |
| 17. Fair Labor Standards Act | q. provided a tax on incomes to ensure retirement benefits |
| 18. WPA | r. placed a tax on farm products when first processed for market |
| | s. provided loans to help farm tenants buy their land |
| | t. established a long-term federal program to provide jobs, including in symphony orchestras, and in artistic and theater projects |
| | u. provided aid to the states for work projects as well as a dole |
| | v. built dams to produce and sell electricity |
| | w. a counterpart to NRA, this agency provided jobs on major construction projects |

## Essay Questions

1. Discuss Franklin D. Roosevelt's background and his qualifications to be president.
2. How did the "first" and "second" New Deals differ? How were they similar?
3. Compare and contrast the New Deal's policies toward labor and agriculture.
4. How did the depression and the New Deal affect African Americans?
5. What factors in 1937 and 1938 contributed to a decline of the New Deal?
6. Evaluate the long-term significance of the New Deal.
7. Explain the "tonic effect" that the depression had on writers.

## DOCUMENT

### Excerpts from the Federal Writers' Project Interviews with Depression Victims

Through the efforts of New Deal agencies Americans learned much about themselves in the 1930s. The Federal Writers Project, for instance, published poignant accounts of the lives of people in some southern states. The excerpts below come from those accounts. You may wish to compare them with the accounts in Chapter 20 of industrial workers in Illinois in the 1880s.

## From the Account of a White Brick-Plant Worker and His Washer-Woman Wife

"Hub's hired solid time and has been for two years. He works every day from six in the morning till six at night in Mr. Hunter's brick plant across the tracks. Some days more'n that—twenty-four hours on a stretch. That's over-time, but it don't mean no extra pay. It's forty dollars a month straight, no matter what."

Rena Murray—small, stooped, hollow-chested—put her whole ninety pounds behind the heavy flatiron. Collar and cuffs came from under the heat, stiff and slick. She lifted the shirt from the board for final inspection.

"Hub fires the boiler most of the time. Then when they're drying bricks, he has to run the fan for twenty-four hours. They couldn't make out in that kiln unless Hub was there.

"He ought to git more for the work he puts out. Forty dollars a month just ain't enough for us to live on. Me and Hub and the three children. We have to pay four dollars out every month for this shack. Mr. Hunter makes the hands live close by the plant. And he gits ahold of that four dollars for rent before we ever see a cent of Hub's wages. This shack ain't worth four dollars a month, neither. Mr. Hunter won't do nothing toward fixing it up. If a window pane's broke, we do the putting in. Leak done ruint the paper and it's up to us to see to new paper."

Rena stooped to the tub of sprinkled clothes. She shook out a rolled-up bundle and slipped another shirt over the narrow end of the home-made ironing board. She settled the board again between the center table and the lard bucket set in a backless kitchen chair.

"I take in washing or do what I can to help out."

"We ain't been to church for years. I was taught working on Sunday was wrong. Folks that holds out against working on Sunday don't have to hire others to work for 'em if they don't show up. Hub had to pay a dollar and a quarter yesterday to git a man to turn the fan so's he could see after his sister. She's about to die. Dirty shame for a man to have to pay to go see his own die. I sure wish he could find hisself a better job."

"What he aims to do is to turn over every stone he can to git back on the WPA. We got along a lot better on the WPA. We had our check regular and had good warm clothes for the girls. And they give Hub clothes, too, because his work kept him in the open. I didn't git none but I could manage all right when the others was gitting all they did. Whenever one of us would git down, the WPA would send a doctor and medicine. They give us food, too. Things that are supposed to be healthy for eating such as prunes and raisins. We can't buy 'em now."

"Burial insurance is a good thing. I wish I had a policy on me and every one of the children. That's just wishing. It pinches us plumb to death to keep Hub's going. We was always behind in dues till he got put on solid time. I couldn't git no insurance noways on account of my bad health. I've had the pneumonia since we've been here. Down three months. There wasn't a Hunter had feeling enough to set foot in this shack. Mrs. Hunter has spoke to me times since, but Mr. Hunter don't trouble about speaking to them that slaves for him. My mammy taught me a dog was good enough to be nice to."

## From the Account of a Young Shoe-Factory Worker

"My work is hard all right. It's hard on me because I ain't but only seventeen and ain't got my full growth yet. It's work down in the steam room which they call it that because it's always full of steam which sometimes when you go in it you can't hardly see. You steam leather down there and that steam soaks you clean to the skin. It makes me keep a cold most of the time because when I go out doors I'm sopping wet. Another thing that's hard about it is having so much standing up to do. My hours is from seven o'clock in the morning till four in the evening. And it's stand on my feet the whole time. When noon time comes and I'm off an hour, why I just find me somewheres to set and I sure set there. You couldn't pay me to stand up during lunch time.

"I'm on piecework now and I can't seem to get my production up to where I make just a whole lot. You get paid by the production hour and it takes fifty pair of shoes to make that hour. You get forty-two cents for the hour. Highest I ever made in one week was eleven dollars and the lowest was seven dollars and forty-two cents. I usually hit in between and make eight or nine dollars.

"Now and then somebody will say, 'We ought to have us a union here of some sort.' That kind of talk just makes me mad all over. Mr. Pugh is a Christian man. He brought his factory here to give us some work which we didn't have any before. We do pretty well, I think, to just stay away from that kind of talk. All but the sore-heads and trouble-makers is satisfied and glad to have work.

"I don't blame Mr. Pugh a bit the way he feels about the unions. The plant manager knows Mr. Pugh mighty well and he told my foreman what Mr. Pugh said. Mr. Pugh said, 'If the union ever comes in here and I have to operate my plant under a union, why I'll just close the plant down and move it away from Hancock so quick it'll make your head swim.' That's his word on it and I don't blame him none. I'd hate to see a union try here. No plant and no jobs for anybody. They just operate these unions out of Wall Street, anyhow, trying to ruin people like Mr. Pugh. . . .

"My money has to go a long way. I've got to pay eight dollars a month rent and I have to buy coal and stove wood. I got to buy clothes for the family and something to eat for them. Then twice a month there's that five dollar ambulance bill which it's to take my brother that's got the T.B. to the City Hospital in Memphis where they take and drain his lungs. Sure charge you for an ambulance, don't they? Now, some people say if you just take one trip in an ambulance, the undertaker won't ask a cent for it. Figures he'll get your custom if you pass on. But they sure charge me for my brother.

"Well, I'm always glad when it's quitting time. I like to work there, but you can't help getting tired. I go on home. I walk four blocks and I'm there. Usually I have to wait a while for supper so I just set at the window. I like to watch and see if maybe something will come along the street and I can watch it. Sometimes there's a new funny paper there and I will look it over—specially if it's Tarzan. That's the best thing in a funny paper, the Tarzan part. Nobody ever gets it over old Tarzan, do they? Most times, though, I like to just set there and watch."

"I work steady but I'm most always financially in need of money. It takes a lot to keep a family going. My little sister needs glasses but they cost too much. All of my family has weak eyes but we can't afford to wear glasses.

"So I haven't the money for running around. I wouldn't if I had the money, either. The Bible is against running around and playing cards and seeing the moving pictures. People should study their Bible more and we'd have more Christian men like Mr. Pugh and more jobs. So me and a young lady I know of go to church and Sunday School instead of running around. My family belongs to the Baptist Church, but this certain young lady is a Nazarene and that's where we go.

"You know, when you're blue and down at the mouth and don't see any use anyhow, a good sermon just lifts you up. You haven't got a thing to lose by living a Christian life. Take Mr. Pugh. He lives it and look where he is now. And if you don't make out that way, if you're poor all your life, then you get a high place in the Kingdom. Just do the best you know how and the Lord will take care of you either here or hereafter. It sure is a comfort."

## From the Account of a Young Man in Charge of a WPA Supply Room

"The way I look at it is this. This is a rich country. I figger it ain't going to hurt the government to feed and clothe them that needs it. Half of 'em can't get work, or just ain't fixed to handle work if they get it. I imagine this country's worth near on to ten billion dollars. We've got the money. Plenty of it. No sense in the big fellows kicking about a little handout to the poor. Matter's not if some ain't deserving.

"I'll admit there's some don't deserve a nickel of the government's money. Lot of them that comes here, why I'd sooner give them a kick in the pants than shove 'em out supplies. But you got to take the good with the bad. Or bad with the good, whichever way you've a mind to put it. Most that comes here are poor and can't help it. Needs help. Needs it just same I need this job. Always going to be more poor folks than them that ain't poor. Now take me. I've always been poor and I guess I always will be. I ain't saying that's the government's fault. It's just a downright truth, that's all.

"There's a lot of things I'd like different in the world. But I can't say I got so much to complain of. If I'd had more education like as not I'd be getting more pay. Maybe, I wouldn't. Not getting no schooling is my own fault. Poor or rich, humans is faulty one way or the next. Time I got to the seventh grade I got the making of money in my head. Wages looked to be about the best thing in the world. Well, I had a run of good jobs. Made fair money for a year or two driving trucks. Took a turn at auto fixing, too, around a filling station. Just first one thing and another. Jobs was easy to get then. That's before women got set on going to work. That's what caused all this depression business. I'm not saying that the women don't need jobs now. They does. But they got themselves to thank for the fix the world's in. They started out taking jobs from men when there wasn't no sense in them working. Them men lost out on good jobs and dropped right down and took ours. Just wasn't no jobs left for poor folks.

"Folks that ain't never been poor just don't know nothin' a-tall about doing on nothing. I get so all-fired full of laugh when some of these women from the higher ups comes down to the Welfare Department. Nice ladies, but it ain't a salt spoon of sense about poor folks in their heads. Pretty little thing come last week to tell the women come here about cooking. Before she started spieling, she seen them cans of salmon I took from the big case and put on that shelf back there. That give her a start. She aimed to tell them how to make up a pot dish from salmon. We ain't really got no salmon here. Just a cheap grade of canned mackerel. She sailed in. 'Brush the baking dish with melted butter,' says she. If she hadn't been so pretty and so young, I'd liked to asked right off—'Where they going to get the butter? Ain't two in the room's got butter for their bread. You'll have to shift to a skillet for the cooking. That's about the best they got for greasing up.' Of course I didn't say no such to her. She was just plumb wore out time she got that salmon out of her head and into the cook stove. When she come to tail part of the talk giving them leave to ask her questions, she looked to me about ready to fall off the box I'd drug out for her to speak from. It's a blessing the Lord made it easy for some. A blessing. And I'm glad He done it."

"Asides from groceries and rent and clothes there's ten dollars a week wages. I figger our spending, all told, about twenty dollars a month. Things we got to have that ain't give us is bought on the installment plan. Cost more that way. But what you going to do when things got to be got and there's no spot cash to hand! We's pulling long through debt right well. Just fifteen dollars owing on the furniture and about twenty-five on the washing machine. Lord, that washing machine's worth ever cent we paid for it. I told Ella if I ever seen another thing that'd be as big help to her I'd buy it if I had to bust a bank. It don't take her half the time used to to get all them younguns' clothes did and the house things and such. Ella keep everthing from the kids to the kivers clean as a pin. House the same. We keep our kids close to home. Don't let them run round with just any trash. I got the last one of ours insured for burial—except sister. I'll get her fixed time she's year old. I pay twenty cents a week on me and Ella. Ten cents for the two oldest boys, five cents for the others.

"Thing that worries me most about a large family is the feeding of them right. I know ours don't have what they's supposed to. Not if half's right I hear them ladies who come here to talk says. We can't manage the milk we should for them. If we get Grade A they ain't enough for more than a cup around. I guess that cheap canned milk's good enough for cooking. We uses what they give us. Them things concocted for the place of butter ain't as cheap as you'd think. I ain't strong like I used to be. And with all this talk I hear floating round I wonder if its the things I ain't had to eat that'd done it."

## From the Account of a CCC Boy

"I ain't never been much to school. Jist went to the second grade, that's all, excepting what I learned here in the CCC. I could have gone, I guess, but for some reason didn't keer nothing about it. Jist didn't want to go. I would have went if I wanted to. They didn't make me not go. We jist didn't none of us go. I got one brother that went to the second grade, too, and my sister she went to the first. Then she quit. We jist wasn't a family that like school.

"I quit that old second grade when I was fourteen. I left home and went to work. Been on my own ever since. I went down here to Woolard and went to work on a farm. The man he was sick and not able to work and had to have somebody to help him. That's why I got to work so long, and even got the job at all. Got twenty dollars a month."

I asked, "Would you go on to school and finish now if you had the chance?"

"Don't know whether I could or not. I would really like to learn." He flushed and scowled. "The boys they make fun of us when we can't read the funnies nor nothing. I look at pictures in books, and things like that in the recreation hall, so they won't laugh at me. I wish I had gone on to school now and would go as far as I could if I git the chance. Guess I couldn't git much learning now though, could I? I'm too old most to learn now."

I asked if he wanted to stay with the CCC.

"Yes'm, as long as I kin, because I git plenty to eat here. I didn't always at home, not the same kind of stuff, anyhow. Guess we had plenty, such as it was, at home, but it jist wasn't good like this, nor enough of it for the kind it was. I git to go more, git to see more. I'm learning too. I watch the others, and then, I have more clothes and can keep cleaner too."

"Do I go to church?"

"Well, no'm. Not now. But while in the C's I do. The chaplain preaches to us two times a month, and I like to hear him. He makes tears come in my eyes, too. I quit drinking all on account of him. I'm a good boy now. I don't go to church at town much because I'm afraid they'll laugh at me. My mother she's a Baptist, but I jist go to any of them. I always give some money when I have it to give.

"Down home it's different. I've rambled all over that place and they ain't got no churches down there. I been there two years and ain't ever seen no church yet. Some of my little brothers ain't never seen no church yet."

[From *These Are Our Lives* (1939), as told to and written by members of the Federal Writers' Project of the W.P.A. (New York: W. W. Norton & Co., 1975), pp. 224–228, 231–235, 366–368, 412–414]

## Questions for Reflection

Compare the wages and expenses of these workers. Which one seems to be better situated financially? What role does religion play in the lives of these people? How do they feel about their "bosses" and others in positions superior to them? Whom do they blame for their financial difficulties? What was the attitude of the shoe-factory worker toward labor unions? One of the benefits of the New Deal was improved public education on nutrition. What evidence do you find in these accounts of nutritional awareness? What evidence is there that the advice of government social workers to the poor was impractical?

How do these accounts of workers' lives compare with those of the 1880s Illinois workers in Chapter 20?

## ANSWERS TO MULTIPLE-CHOICE, TRUE-FALSE, AND MATCHING QUESTIONS

### Multiple-Choice Questions

1-B, 2-B, 3-C, 4-D, 5-A, 6-B, 7-C, 8-A

### True-False Questions

1-F, 2-T, 3-T, 4-F, 5-F, 6-F, 7-T, 8-F

### Matching Questions

1-e, 2-q,u, 3-i, 4-d,r, 5-j, 6-f,w, 7-a,v, 8-1, 9-h, 10-n, 11-o,q, 12-p, 13-k, 14-b, 15-s, 16-m, 17-c, 18-t

# 28

## FROM ISOLATION TO GLOBAL WAR

## CHAPTER OBJECTIVES

*After you complete the reading and study of this chapter you should be able to*

1. Explain and account for the foreign policy pursued by the United States in the interwar period.
2. Describe the aggressions of Japan, Italy, and Germany in the 1930s.
3. Account for American efforts at neutrality in the face of aggression and assess the effectiveness of neutrality in preventing war.
4. Describe the election of 1940.
5. Explain American support of Britain and Russia prior to the United States's entry into the war.
6. Explain and account for the effectiveness of the attack on Pearl Harbor.

## CHAPTER OUTLINE

I. Postwar isolationism
   A. Evidences of isolationist sentiment
   B. Counteractions of world involvement
   C. Relations with the League
   D. The war-debt tangle
      1. Problems with repayment of debts
      2. Linkage of debts to reparations
      3. Depression and debt cancellation
   E. Efforts toward disarmament
      1. A substitute for League membership
      2. Strained Japanese-American relations
      3. The Washington Armaments Conference
         a. Hughes's initiative
         b. Agreements made at the conference
         c. Effects of the treaties
      4. The movement to outlaw war
         a. Development of the Kellogg-Briand Pact
         b. Effect of the pact
   F. The "Good Neighbor" Policy
      1. Early efforts to improve relations with Latin America
      2. Hoover and the Clark Memorandum
      3. Further improvements under FDR

II. War clouds
   A. Japanese incursion in China
      1. Chinese weaknesses
      2. Japanese occupation of Manchuria
      3. Reactions to occupation
         a. League condemnation
         b. Japan's withdrawal from the League
   B. Mussolini's rise to power
   C. Hitler's rise to power

    D. American recognition of the Soviet Union
    E. Aggression in Asia and Europe
       1. Italian invasion of Ethiopia, 1935
       2. Hitler's occupation of the Rhineland, 1936
       3. Spanish Civil War, 1936
       4. Japanese invasion of China, 1937
       5. Hitler's *Anschluss* with Austria, 1938
       6. The Munich Agreement, 1938
       7. War begun over Poland, 1939
III. American efforts for neutrality
    A. The Nye Committee investigations
    B. Congressional effort to avoid another world war
    C. The first Neutrality Act, 1935
       1. Sale of arms to belligerents forbidden
       2. Travel on belligerents' ships discouraged
    D. Reaction to the invasion of Ethiopia
    E. The second Neutrality Act: loans to belligerents forbidden
    F. Extension of the Neutrality Act to cover civil wars
    G. Further neutrality provisions
    H. Reactions to Japanese action in China
       1. Lack of use of neutrality laws
       2. Quarantine speech
    I. Reactions to war in Europe
       1. Change to cash-and-carry arms sales
       2. Extension of war zone
IV. The storm in Europe
    A. Hitler's *Blitzkrieg*
    B. American aid to embattled Britain
       1. Growth of U.S. defense effort
       2. Sales of arms to Britain
    C. Other defense measures
    D. The destroyer-bases deal
    E. Peacetime conscription
    F. Polarization of public opinion
       1. Committee to Defend America
       2. America First Committee
V. The election of 1940
    A. The choice of Willkie
    B. The choice of FDR
    C. Nature of the campaign
    D. Results of the election
VI. The arsenal of democracy
    A. The Lend-Lease program
    B. Further Axis gains
    C. Reaction to the invasion of the Soviet Union
    D. The Atlantic Charter
    E. Conflict with the Germans in the Atlantic
VII. The storm in the Pacific
    A. Japanese aggression in Southeast Asia
    B. Tripartite Pact
    C. Negotiations between Japan and the United States
    D. Warlords gain control in Japan
    E. Attack on Pearl Harbor
       1. Extent of U.S. foreknowledge
       2. Errors in warning
       3. Damage from the attack
       4. Other Japanese aggression in the Pacific
    F. Declaration of war

## KEY ITEMS OF CHRONOLOGY

| | |
|---|---|
| Washington Armaments Conference | 1921–1922 |
| Mussolini takes power in Italy | 1925 |
| Kellogg-Briand Pact | 1928 |
| Japanese invasion of Manchuria | 1931 |
| Hitler takes power in Germany | 1933 |
| London Economic Conference | 1933 |
| Nye Committee | 1934–1937 |
| Italy's invasion of Ethiopia | 1935 |
| Japan's invasion of China | 1937 |
| Quarantine Speech | 1937 |
| World War II begins | September 1, 1939 |

| | |
|---|---|
| First peacetime draft | 1940 |
| Fall of France | June 1940 |
| Lend-Lease program begins | 1941 |
| Germany's invasion of Russia | June 1941 |
| Japanese extend protectorate over Indochina | July 1941 |
| Attack on Pearl Harbor | December 7, 1941 |

## TERMS TO MASTER

*Listed below are some important terms or people with which you should be familiar after you complete the study of this chapter. Explain the significance of each name or term.*

1. World Court
2. Washington Armaments Conference
3. reparations
4. Five-Power Treaty
5. Kellogg-Briand Pact
6. "Good Neighbor" Policy
7. London Naval Conference
8. Cordell Hull
9. Reciprocal Trade Agreements
10. Nye Committee
11. Neutrality Acts
12. cash and carry
13. *Blitzkrieg*
14. America First Committee
15. Wendell Willkie
16. Lend-Lease program
17. Four Freedoms
18. Atlantic Charter

9. tyranny
10. flout
11. potent
12. abstain
13. mandatory
14. intrigue (n.)
15. vacillate
16. attrition
17. conscription
18. dishevel
19. ingenious
20. beneficiary

## VOCABULARY BUILDING

*Listed below are some words used in this chapter. Look up each word in your dictionary.*

1. moratorium
2. default
3. refrain
4. enunciate
5. tacitly
6. expropriation
7. dissension
8. fester

## EXERCISES FOR UNDERSTANDING

*When you have completed reading the chapter, answer each of the following questions. If you have difficulty, go back and reread the section of the chapter related to the question.*

### Multiple-Choice Questions

*Select the letter of the response that best completes the statement.*

1. A great spur to isolationism in the United States in the 1920s was
   A. disarmament after the Washington Conference.
   B. controversy over repayment of war debts.

C. membership in the League of Nations under Harding.
D. the economic depression.

2. The naval armaments race after World War I came in response to
   A. the rise of Hitler.
   B. British expansion in East Asia and the Pacific.
   C. the Harding administration's commitment to a big navy.
   D. the growing power of Japan.

3. The Nine-Power Treaty of 1921 called for
   A. an Open Door to trade in China.
   B. the outlawing of war.
   C. obedience to the League of Nations.
   D. a "Good Neighbor" Policy throughout the world.

4. The Nye Committee investigations seemed to prove that
   A. the United States entered World War I to permit the munitions manufacturers to make greater profits.
   B. the United States should back down from its dispute with Japan over China.
   C. the only way to end the war was with a treaty.
   D. the United States was not responsible for the success of the attack by Japan.

5. The Neutrality Act of 1939
   A. prohibited all trade with belligerents.
   B. allowed trade with only one side in a war.
   C. kept U.S. ships from war zones but approved cash-and-carry trade even for arms.
   D. permitted nonmilitary trade in American ships only.

6. "Your boys are not going to be sent into any foreign wars," said
   A. Wendell Willkie.
   B. Cordell Hull.
   C. Gerald Nye.
   D. Franklin D. Roosevelt.

7. The Atlantic Charter of 1941
   A. declared British-American war aims.
   B. ordered German U-boats out of the Atlantic.
   C. ended U.S. neutrality on the seas and led to conflict with Germany.
   D. reaffirmed the Kellogg-Briand Pact.

8. The Japanese attack on Pearl Harbor
   A. was a complete success.
   B. sank or severely damaged all U.S. aircraft carriers in the Pacific.
   C. killed 25,000 Americans.
   D. missed vital shore installations and oil tanks.

## True-False Questions

*Indicate whether each statement is true or false.*

1. America's allies in World War I had paid all their war debts by 1924.
2. The "Good Neighbor" Policy applied to Latin America.
3. The Clark Memorandum attacked the Japanese invasion of Korea.
4. The United States gave diplomatic recognition to the Soviet Union in 1933.
5. The Neutrality Act of 1935 forbade the sale of arms and munitions to belligerents.
6. Charles A. Lindbergh and Herbert Hoover advocated aid to Britain.
7. In 1941 the Lend-Lease program concentrated on stopping Italian conquests in Eastern Europe.
8. The United States declaration of war in 1941 passed the Congress unanimously.

## Essay Questions

1. Was the United States more isolationist in its foreign policy from 1920 to 1929 or from 1930 to 1939? Explain.
2. Describe American efforts to achieve peace and disarmament during the 1920s.
3. How did United States relations with Latin America change between 1920 and 1941? Did they improve or not?
4. How did the United States and the Allied nations react to Axis aggressions in the 1930s? Why?
5. What were the isolationists' arguments in the 1930s? In what ways were they wise or foolish?
6. Explain the importance of foreign policy issues in the election of 1940.
7. Trace the major events that led to United States involvement in World War II.

## DOCUMENTS

### Document 1. Roosevelt's Quarantine Speech, 1937

In the wake of the rearmament of Germany, the Italian invasion of Ethiopia, the Spanish Civil War, and finally the Japanese invasion of China, Roosevelt visited Chicago, the heart of isolationist sentiment in America, on October 5, 1937, to make what has generally been dubbed his Quarantine Speech. Look carefully in the following excerpts for the promises or pledges that the president sought to exact on the issues of peace and war.

> I am glad to come once again to Chicago and especially to have the opportunity of taking part in the dedication of this important project of civic betterment. . . .
>
> Without a declaration of war and without warning or justification of any kind, civilians, including women and children, are being ruthlessly murdered with bombs from the air. In times of so-called peace ships are being attacked and sunk by submarines without cause or notice. Nations are fomenting and taking sides in civil warfare in nations that have never done them any harm. Nations claiming freedom for themselves deny it to others. . . .
>
> The peace-loving nations must make a concerted effort in opposition to those violations of treaties and those ignorings of humane instincts which today are creating a state of international anarchy and instability from which there is no escape through mere isolation or neutrality. . . .
>
> There is a solidarity and interdependence about the modern world, both technically and morally, which makes it impossible for any nation completely to isolate itself from economic and political upheavals in the rest of the world, specially when such upheavals appear to be spreading and not declining.
>
> It seems to be unfortunately true that the epidemic of world lawlessness is spreading.
>
> When an epidemic of physical disease starts to spread, the community approves and joins in a quarantine of the patients in order to protect the health of the community against the spread of the disease.
>
> War is a contagion, whether it be declared or undeclared. It can engulf states and peoples remote from the original scene of hostilities. . . . We are adopting such measures as will minimize our risk of involvement, but we cannot have complete protection in a world of disorder in which confidence and security have broken down.
>
> If civilization is to survive the principles of the Prince of Peace must be restored. Shattered trust between nations must be revived.
>
> Most important of all, the will for peace on the part of peace-loving nations must express itself to the end that nations that may be tempted to violate their agreements and the rights of others will desist from such a cause. There must be positive endeavors to preserve peace.
>
> America hates war. America hopes for peace. Therefore, America actively engages in the search for peace.
>
> [U.S. Department of State, *Peace and War: United States Foreign Policy, 1931–1941* (Washington, D.C.: U.S. Government Printing Office, 1943), pp. 384–387]

## Document 2. Roosevelt's "Four Freedoms" Speech, 1941

The "Four Freedoms," formulated in Roosevelt's annual message to Congress on January 6, 1941, have come to be accepted as the most succinct statement of the things for which the American people were prepared to fight.

*To the Congress of the United States:*

I address you, the Members of the Seventy-Seventh Congress, at a moment unprecedented in the history of the Union. I use the word "unprecedented," because at no previous time has American security been as seriously threatened from without as it is today. . . .

It is true that prior to 1914 the United States often had been disturbed by events in other Continents. We had even engaged in two wars with European nations and in a number of undeclared wars in the West Indies, in the Mediterranean and in the Pacific for the maintenance of American rights and for the principles of peaceful commerce. In no case, however, had a serious threat been raised against our national safety or our independence.

What I seek to convey is the historic truth that the United States as a nation has at all times maintained opposition to any attempt to lock us in behind an ancient Chinese wall while the procession of civilization went past. Today, thinking of our children and their children, we oppose enforced isolation for ourselves or for any part of the Americas.

Even when the World War broke out in 1914, it seemed to contain only small threat of danger to our own American future. But, as time went on, the American people began to visualize what the downfall of democratic nations might mean to our own democracy.

We need not over-emphasize imperfections in the Peace of Versailles. We need not harp on failure of the democracies to deal with problems of world deconstruction. We should remember that the Peace of 1919 was far less unjust than the kind of "pacification" which began even before Munich, and which is being carried on under the new order of tyranny that seeks to spread over every continent today. The American people have unalterably set their faces against that tyranny.

Every realist knows that the democratic way of life is at this moment being directly assailed in every part of the world—assailed either by arms, or by secret spreading of poisonous propaganda by those who seek to destroy unity and promote discord in nations still at peace. During sixteen months this assault has blotted out the whole pattern of democratic life in an appalling number of independent nations, great and small. The assailants are still on the march, threatening other nations, great and small.

Therefore, as your President, performing my constitutional duty to "give to the Congress information of the state of the Union," I find it necessary to report that the future and the safety of our country and of our democracy are overwhelmingly involved in events far beyond our borders.

Armed defense of democratic existence is now being gallantly waged in four continents. If that defense fails, all the population and all the resources of Europe, Asia, Africa and Australasia will be dominated by the conquerors. The total of those populations and their resources greatly exceeds the sum total of the population and resources of the whole of the Western Hemisphere—many times over.

In times like these it is immature—and incidentally untrue—for anybody to brag that an unprepared America, single-handed, and with one hand tied behind its back, can hold off the whole world.

No realistic American can expect from a dictator's peace international generosity, or return of true independence, or world disarmament, or freedom of expression, or freedom of religion—or even good business. Such a peace would bring no security for us or for our neighbors. "Those, who would give up essential liberty to purchase a little temporary safety, deserve neither liberty nor safety." As a nation we may take pride in the fact that we are soft-hearted; but we cannot afford to be soft-hearted. We must always be wary of those who with sounding brass and a tinkling cymbal preach the "ism" of appeasement. We must especially beware of that small group of selfish men who would clip the wings of the American eagle in order to feather their own nests.

I have recently pointed out how quickly the tempo of modern warfare could bring into our very midst the physical attack which we must expect if the dictator nations win this war.

There is much loose talk of our immunity from immediate and direct invasion from across the seas. Obviously, as long as the British Navy retains its power, no such danger exists. Even if there were no British Navy, it is not probable that any enemy would be stupid enough to attack us by landing troops in the United States from across thousands of miles of ocean, until it had acquired strategic bases from which to operate. But we learn much from the lessons of the past years in Europe—particularly the lesson of Norway, whose essential seaports were captured by treachery and surprise built up over a series of years. The first phase of the invasion of this Hemisphere would not be the landing of regular troops. The necessary strategic points would be occupied by secret agents and their dupes—and great numbers of them are already here, and in Latin America.

As long as the aggressor nations maintain the offensive, they—not we—will choose the time and the place and the method of their attack. That is why the future of all American Republics is today in serious danger. That is why this Annual Message to the Congress is unique in our history. That is why every member of the Executive branch of the government and every member of the Congress face great responsibility—and great accountability.

The need of the moment is that our actions and our policy should be devoted primarily—almost exclusively—to meeting this foreign peril. For all our domestic problems are now a part of the great emergency. Just as our national policy in internal affairs has been based upon a decent respect for the rights and dignity of all our fellowmen within our gates, so our national policy in foreign affairs has been based on a decent respect for the rights and dignity of all nations, large and small. And the justice of morality must and will win in the end.

Our national policy is this.

First, by an impressive expression of the public will and without regard to partisanship, we are committed to all-inclusive national defense.

Second, by an impressive expression of the public will and without regard to partisanship, we are committed to full support of all those resolute peoples, everywhere, who are resisting aggression and are thereby keeping war away from our Hemisphere. By this support, we express our determination that the democratic cause shall prevail; and we strengthen the defense and security of our own nation.

Third, by an impressive expression of the public will and without regard to partisanship, we are committed to the proposition that principles of morality and considerations for our own security will never permit us to acquiesce in a peace dictated by aggressors and sponsored by appeasers. We know that enduring peace cannot be bought at the cost of other people's freedom.

In the recent national election there was no substantial difference between the two great parties in respect to that national policy. No issue was fought out on this line before the American electorate. Today, it is abundantly evident that American citizens everywhere are demanding and supporting speedy and complete action in recognition of obvious danger. Therefore, the immediate need is a swift and driving increase in our armament production. . . .

Our most useful and immediate role is to act as an arsenal for them as well as for ourselves. They do not need man power. They do need billions of dollars worth of the weapons of defense. . . .

Let us say to the democracies: "We Americans are vitally concerned in your defense of freedom. We are putting forth our energies, our resources and our organizing powers to give you the strength to regain and maintain a free world. We shall send you, in ever-increasing numbers, ships, planes, tanks, guns. This is our purpose and our pledge." In fulfillment of this purpose we will not be intimidated by the threats of dictators that they will regard as a breach of international law and as an act of war our aid to the democracies which dare to resist their aggression. Such aid is not an act of war, even if a dictator should unilaterally proclaim it so to be. When the dictators are ready to make war upon us, they will not wait for an act of war on our part. They did not wait for Norway or Belgium or the Netherlands to commit an act of war. Their only interest is in a new one-way international law, which lacks mutuality in its observance, and, therefore, becomes an instrument of oppression.

The happiness of future generations of Americans may well depend upon how effective and how immediate we can make our aid felt. No one can tell the exact character of the emergency situations that we may be called upon to meet. The Nation's hands must not be tied when the Nation's life is in danger. We must all prepare to make the sacrifices that the emergency—as serious as war itself—demands. Whatever stands in the way of speed and efficiency in defense preparations must give way to the national need.

A free nation has the right to expect full cooperation from all groups. A free nation has the right to look to the leaders of business, of labor, and of agriculture to take the lead in stimulating effort, not among other groups but within their own groups. The best way of dealing with the few slackers or trouble makers in our midst is, first, to shame them by patriotic example, and, if that fails, to use the sovereignty of government to save government.

As men do not live by bread alone, they do not fight by armaments alone. Those who man our defenses, and those behind them who build our defenses, must have the stamina and courage which come from an unshakable belief in the manner of life which they are defending. The mighty action which we are calling for cannot be based on a disregard of all things worth fighting for.

The Nation takes great satisfaction and much strength from the things which have been done to make its people conscious of their individual stake in the preservation of democratic life in America. Those things have toughened the fibre of our people, have renewed their faith and strengthened their devotion to the institutions we make ready to protect. Certainly this is no time to stop thinking about the social and economic problems which are the root cause of the social revolution which is today a supreme factor in the world.

There is nothing mysterious about the foundations of a healthy and strong democracy. The basic things expected by our people of their political and economic systems are simple. They are: equality of opportunity for youth and for others; jobs for those who can work; security for those who need it; the ending of special privilege for the few; the preservation of civil liberties for all; the enjoyment of the fruits of scientific progress in a wider and constantly rising standard of living.

These are the simple and basic things that must never be lost sight of in the turmoil and unbelievable complexity of our modern world. The inner and abiding strength of our economic and political systems is dependent upon the degree to which they fulfill these expectations.

Many subjects connected with our social economy call for immediate improvement. As examples: We should bring more citizens under the coverage of old age pensions and unemployment insurance. We should widen the opportunities for adequate medical care. We should plan a better system by which persons deserving or needing gainful employment may obtain it.

I have called for personal sacrifice. I am assured of the willingness of almost all Americans to respond to that call. . . .

In the future days, which we seek to make secure, we look forward to a world founded upon four essential human freedoms.

The first is freedom of speech and expression—everywhere in the world.

The second is freedom of every person to worship God in his own way—everywhere in the world.

The third is freedom from want—which, translated into world terms, means economic understandings which will secure to every nation a healthy peacetime life for its inhabitants—everywhere in the world.

The fourth is freedom from fear—which, translated into world terms, means a worldwide reduction of armaments to such a point and in such a thorough fashion that no nation will be in a position to commit an act of physical aggression against any neighbor—anywhere in the world.

That is no vision of a distant millenium. It is a definite basis for a kind of world attainable in our own time and generation. That kind of world is the very antithesis of the so-called new order of tyranny which the dictators seek to create with the crash of a bomb.

To that new order we oppose the greater conception—the moral order. A good society is able to face schemes of world domination and foreign revolutions alike without fear.

Since the beginning of our American history we have been engaged in change—in a perpetual peaceful revolution—a revolution which goes on steadily, quietly adjusting itself to changing conditions—without the concentration camp or the quick-lime in the ditch. The world order which we seek is the cooperation of free countries, working together in a friendly, civilized society.

This nation has placed its destiny in the hands and heads and hearts of its millions of free men and women; and its faith in freedom under the guidance of God. Freedom means the supremacy of human rights everywhere. Our support goes to those who struggle to gain those rights or keep them. Our strength is in our unity of purpose.

To that high concept there can be no end save victory.

[From *The Public Papers and Addresses of Franklin D. Roosevelt* (New York: Macmillan, 1940), 9:663*ff.*]

## Questions for Reflection

What actions did Roosevelt ask of the United States or other powers in his 1937 Quarantine Speech? What actions *seemed* to be *implied*? Why do you think this speech caused a great outcry of opposition from those groups who did not want the United States to become involved in the affairs of other nations?

What, specifically, did Roosevelt propose that the United States do, in his 1941 speech? Was Roosevelt able to stake out a position between isolation and intervention? How would you assess his leadership in this crisis?

## ANSWERS TO MULTIPLE-CHOICE AND TRUE-FALSE QUESTIONS

### Multiple-Choice Questions

1-B, 2-D, 3-A, 4-A, 5-C, 6-D, 7-A, 8-D

### True-False Questions

1-F, 2-T, 3-F, 4-T, 5-T, 6-F, 7-F, 8-F

# 29

## THE WORLD AT WAR

### CHAPTER OBJECTIVES

*After you complete the reading and study of this chapter you should be able to*

1. Describe the major military strategies in both the European and Pacific theaters.
2. Explain the problems relating to mobilization and financing of the war.
3. Describe the impact of the war on the economy.
4. Assess the impact of the war on women, blacks, Japanese-Americans, and the West.
5. Explain the decisions made at the Yalta Conference.
6. Account for the decision to use the atomic bomb and discuss its consequences.

### CHAPTER OUTLINE

I. America's early battles
   A. Retreat in the Pacific
      1. Collapse along the Pacific
      2. Surrender of the Philippines
      3. Japanese strategy
      4. Battle of the Coral Sea (May 1942)
   B. Midway: a turning point
   C. Early setbacks in the Atlantic
      1. Devastation from German submarines
      2. Strategy of small patrol vessels

II. Mobilization at home
   A. Preparedness and mobilization
   B. Economic conversion to war
      1. War Production Board
      2. Role of the Office of Scientific Research and Development
      3. Effects of wartime spending
   C. Financing the war
      1. Roosevelt's effort to raise taxes
      2. Congressional reaction to taxation
      3. Sale of bonds
   D. Impact of the war on the economy
      1. Personal incomes
      2. Efforts to control prices
      3. Efforts to control wages and farm prices
      4. Seizure of industries
   E. Social effects of the war on women
      1. Women in the civilian work force and the military
      2. Changing attitudes toward sex roles
   F. Social effects of the war on blacks
      1. Problems of the segregated armed forces
      2. Role of blacks in war industries
         a. The March on Washington Movement
         b. Impact of black militancy
      3. Challenges to other forms of discrimination
      4. Militant white counterreaction

G. Native Americans support war
H. Impact of the war on Japanese-Americans
   1. General effect of the war on civil liberties
   2. Internment
I. Development of the West
   1. Urban growth
   2. High-wage jobs
   3. Migration
   4. *Bracero* program
   5. Ethnic tensions
J. Evidences of domestic conservatism
   1. Congressional elections of 1942
   2. Abolition of New Deal agencies
   3. Actions against labor
K. Congressional reaction to the war

III. The war in Europe
A. Initial decisions
   1. Basis for moving against Germany first
   2. Aspects of joint conduct of the war
   3. The formulation of the decision for the North African invasion
B. The North Africa campaign
C. Agreements at Casablanca
D. Sicily and Italy
   1. Invasion of Sicily
   2. Italian surrender
   3. German control of northern Italy
   4. The battle for Rome
E. Strategic bombing of Europe
   1. British and American cooperation
   2. Impact of the bombing
F. Decisions of the Teheran Conference
G. The D-Day invasion
   1. Development and implementation of "Overlord"
   2. German preparations and reaction
   3. Invasion of the French Mediterranean coast
   4. Slowing momentum of the drive on Germany

IV. The war in the Pacific
A. Guadalcanal offensive
B. MacArthur's sweep up the western Pacific
   1. Approval for the MacArthur plan
   2. The technique of "leapfrogging"
C. Nimitz's moves in the Central Pacific
D. The naval battle of Leyte Gulf

V. The election of 1944
A. Republican strategy
B. Democratic vice-presidential choice
C. Campaign and results

VI. Closing on Germany
A. The German counteroffensive
B. Allied moves
C. Berlin and the Russians

VII. The Yalta Conference
A. Nature of the decisions
B. Call for a United Nations
C. Occupation of Germany
D. Decisions about eastern Europe
E. An assessment of the Yalta decisions

VIII. Collapse of the Third Reich
A. Roosevelt's death
B. Collapse of Germany
C. Discovery of the Nazi Holocaust

IX. The grinding war in the Pacific
A. Japanese resistance in the Philippines
B. Occupation of Iwo Jima and Okinawa
C. Impact of these victories on the conduct of the war

X. The atomic bomb
A. Manhattan Project
B. The decision to use the bomb
C. Effect of dropping two bombs
D. Negotiation for surrender

XI. The final ledger of the war
A. Estimates of death and destruction
B. Impact on the United States and the USSR

## KEY ITEMS OF CHRONOLOGY

| | |
|---|---|
| Battle of Midway | June 1942 |
| American troops invade North Africa | November 1942 |
| Casablanca Conference | January 1943 |
| Teheran Conference | November–December 1943 |
| *Smith v. Allwright* | 1944 |

| | |
|---|---|
| D-Day invasion | June 6, 1944 |
| Yalta Conference | February 1945 |
| Roosevelt's death and Truman's accession | April 12, 1945 |
| V-E Day | May 8, 1945 |
| Potsdam Conference | July 1945 |
| Atomic bomb dropped on Hiroshima | August 6, 1945 |
| Japan's surrender | September 2, 1945 |

## TERMS TO MASTER

*Listed below are some important terms or people with which you should be familiar after you complete the study of this chapter. Explain the significance of each name or term*

1. War Production Board
2. Office of Price Administration
3. rationing
4. "Rosie the Riveter"
5. *Smith v. Allwright*
6. War Relocation Camps
7. Smith-Connally Act
8. Winston Churchill
9. second front
10. unconditional surrender
11. General Dwight D. Eisenhower
12. Operation "Overlord"
13. "leapfrogging"
14. General Douglas MacArthur
15. Battle of Leyte Gulf
16. Yalta Conference
17. Nazi Holocaust
18. Hiroshima

12. collaborate
13. pincers
14. dictum
15. strategic
16. elusive
17. genocide
18. labyrinth
19. repository
20. ledger

## VOCABULARY BUILDING

*Listed below are some words used in this chapter. Look up each word in your dictionary.*

1. epochal
2. impregnable
3. foray
4. negligible
5. proximity
6. infusion
7. stevedores
8. resolute
9. decipher
10. internment
11. vexation

## EXERCISES FOR UNDERSTANDING

*When you have completed reading the chapter, answer each of the following questions. If you have difficulty, go back and reread the section of the chapter related to the question.*

### Multiple-Choice Questions

*Select the letter of the response that best completes the statement.*

1. The Battle of Midway was the turning point of the war in the Pacific because that battle
   A. stopped the eastward advance of the Japanese.
   B. destroyed most of what was left of the American fleet after Pearl Harbor.
   C. destroyed the Japanese fleet so that they were unable to pursue naval war after this.
   D. placed the United States Air Force close enough to the mainland of Japan to carry out bombing raids there.

2. Blacks during World War II achieved
   A. an end to segregation in the military.
   B. equal employment opportunities in the government and industry.
   C. a court ruling outlawing white primaries.
   D. social and political equality in the South.
3. Under the *bracero* program,
   A. Mexican farm workers came to the United States.
   B. Mexican-Americans received free clothing.
   C. Mexico agreed to remain neutral in the war.
   D. the federal government provided housing for Mexican-Americans.
4. During the war, the West experienced
   A. depopulation for national security reasons.
   B. fast growth because of defense contracts.
   C. rapid rural growth to supply food for the armed forces.
   D. none of the above.
5. From the start, British and American leaders completely agreed
   A. to defeat Japan first.
   B. to attack Germany only indirectly through Africa.
   C. to strike directly at Germany across the English Channel.
   D. on none of the above.
6. Strategic bombing of Germany in 1943
   A. cut German production by at least 25 percent.
   B. broke German morale.
   C. involved British and American planes.
   D. failed because of a lack of planes.
7. At the end of the war, the Russians took Berlin because
   A. Churchill thought the city was unimportant.
   B. the Allies lacked the troops to take it.
   C. the United States was focused on fighting in the Pacific.
   D. Eisenhower thought taking the city would be too costly.
8. The decisions made at the Yalta Conference did *not* include agreement that
   A. Russia would have three votes in the U.N. General Assembly.
   B. Russia would have an occupation zone in the nonindustrialized area of East Germany as well as in part of Berlin.
   C. free elections would be held in Poland to select a government.
   D. both Russia and the United States would reduce their armaments by half after the war ended.

**True-False Questions**

*Indicate whether each statement is true or false.*

1. In the first half of 1942 German submarines sank several hundred ships just off the U.S. coast.
2. During the war, most working women for the first time were married women.
3. Native Americans served in segregated military units.
4. "Zoot suit" riots involved black servicemen in Europe.
5. The Battle of the Philippine Sea was the largest naval battle in history.
6. The major matter of dispute in the Democratic convention of 1944 was the selection of a vice-presidential nominee.
7. The War Refugee Board was amazingly successful at rescuing Jews from Europe.
8. The Manhattan Project developed the atomic bomb.

**Essay Questions**

1. Compare United States strategies in the Pacific and in Europe.
2. What effects did World War II have on the power of the federal government? Be specific in your response.
3. Explain the major decisions made at Casablanca, Teheran, and Yalta.
4. How did the war affect the respective status of blacks, women, Native Americans, and Japanese-Americans?
5. What innovations, technical and tactical, helped the Allies win the war?
6. Why did the United States use the atomic bomb? What were the effects of dropping the bomb?

## DOCUMENTS

### Document 1. Executive Order 9066 Authorizing the Secretary of War to Prescribe Military Areas

On February 19, 1942, President Roosevelt issued an executive order that would later be used as the authority to remove Japanese-Americans from the West Coast to areas in the interior of the nation. Another executive order one month later (no. 9102) established the War Relocation Authority to carry out the removal program.

>Whereas the successful prosecution of the war requires every possible protection against espionage and against sabotage to national-defense material, national-defense premises, and national-defense utilities. . . .
>
>Now, therefore, by virtue of the authority vested in me as President of the United States, and Commander in Chief of the Army and Navy, I hereby authorize and direct the Secretary of War, and the Military Commanders whom he may from time to time designate, whenever he or any designated commander deems such action necessary or desirable, to prescribe military areas in such places and of such extent as he or the appropriate Military Commander may determine, from which any or all persons may be excluded, and with respect to which, the right of any person to enter, remain in, or leave shall be subject to whatever restrictions the Secretary of War or the appropriate Military Commander may impose in his discretion. The Secretary of War is hereby authorized to provide for residents of any such area who are excluded therefrom, such transportation, food, shelter, and other accommodations as may be necessary, in the judgment of the Secretary of War or the said Military Commander, and until other arrangements are made, to accomplish the purpose of this order. . . .
>
>I hereby further authorize and direct the Secretary of War and the said Military Commanders to take such other steps as he or the appropriate Military Commander may deem advisable to enforce compliance with the restrictions applicable to each Military area hereinabove authorized to be designated, including the use of Federal troops and other Federal Agencies with authority to accept assistance of state and local agencies.
>
>I hereby further authorize and direct all Executive Departments, independent establishments and other Federal Agencies, to assist the Secretary of War or the said Military Commanders in carrying out this Executive Order, including the furnishing of medical aid, hospitalization, food, clothing, transportation, use of land, shelter, and other supplies, equipment, utilities, facilities, and services.
>
>[From Federal Register, vol. 7, no. 38 (February 25, 1942), p. 1407.]

In a case challenging the forced relocation of Japanese-Americans during the war, the Supreme Court upheld as constitutional the work of the War Relocation Authority as necessary for military reasons. It followed by two years the Court's endorsement in Hirabayshi v. United States (320 U. S. 81) of a curfew for Japanese-Americans on the West Coast.

The petitioner, an American citizen of Japanese descent, was convicted in a federal district court for remaining in San Leandro, California, a "Military Area," contrary to Civilian Exclusion Order No. 34, of the Commanding General of the Western Command, U.S. Army, which directed that after May 9, 1942, all persons of Japanese ancestry should be excluded from that area. No question was raised as to petitioner's loyalty to the United States. The Circuit Court of Appeals affirmed, and the importance of the constitutional question involved caused us to grant certiorari.

It should be noted, to begin with, that all legal restrictions which curtail the civil rights of a single racial group are immediately suspect. That is not to say that all such restrictions are unconstitutional. It is to say that courts must subject them to the most rigid scrutiny. Pressing public necessity may sometimes justify the existence of such restrictions; racial antagonism never can. . . .

Exclusion Order No. 34, which the petitioner knowingly and admittedly violated, was one of a number of military orders and proclamations, all of which were substantially based upon Executive Order No. 9066, 7 Fed. Reg. 1407. . . .

[W]e are unable to conclude that it was beyond the war power of Congress and the Executive to exclude those of Japanese ancestry from the West Coast war area at the time they did. True, exclusion from the area in which one's home is located is a far greater deprivation than constant confinement to the home from 8 P.M. to 6 A.M. Nothing short of apprehension by the proper military authorities of the gravest imminent danger to the public safety can constitutionally justify either. But exclusion from a threatened area, no less than curfew, has a definite and close relationship to the prevention of espionage and sabotage. The military authorities, charged with the primary responsibility of defending our shores, concluded that curfew provided inadequate protection and ordered exclusion. They did so . . . in accordance with Congressional authority to the military to say who should, and who should not, remain in the threatened areas.

In this case the petitioner challenges the assumptions upon which we rested our conclusions in the *Hirabayashi* case. He also urges that by May 1912, when Order No. 31 was promulgated, all danger of Japanese invasion of the West Coast had disappeared. After careful consideration of these contentions we are compelled to reject them. . . .

[E]xclusion of those of Japanese origin was deemed necessary because of the presence of an unascertained number of disloyal members of the group, most of whom we have no doubt were loyal to this country. It was because we could not reject the finding of the military authorities that it was impossible to bring about an immediate segregation of the disloyal from the loyal that we sustained the validity of the curfew order as applying to the whole group. In the instant case, temporary exclusion of the entire group was rested by the military on the same ground. The judgment that exclusion of the whole group was for the same reason a military imperative answers the contention that the exclusion was in the nature of group punishment based on antagonism to those of Japanese origin. That there were members of the group who retained loyalties to Japan has been confirmed by investigations made subsequent to the exclusion. Approximately five thousand American citizens of Japanese ancestry refused to swear unqualified allegiance to the United States and to renounce allegiance to the Japanese Emperor, and several thousand evacuees requested repatriation to Japan.

We uphold the exclusion order as of the time it was made and when the petitioner violated it. . . . In doing so, we are not unmindful of the hardships imposed by it upon a large group of American citizens. . . . But hardships are part of war, and war is an aggregation of hardships. All citizens alike, both in and out of uniform, feel the impact of war in greater or lesser measure. Citizenship has its responsibilities as well as its privileges, and in time of war the burden is always heavier. Compulsory exclusion of large groups of citizens from their homes, except under circumstances of direst emergency and peril, is inconsistent with our basic governmental institutions. But when under conditions of modern warfare our shores are threatened by hostile forces, the power to protect must be commensurate with the threatened danger. . . .

After May 3, 1942, the date of Exclusion Order No. 34, Korematsu was under compulsion to leave the area not as he would choose but via an Assembly Center. The Assembly Center was conceived as a part of the machinery for group evacuation. The power to exclude includes the power to do it by force if necessary. And any forcible measure must necessarily entail some degree of detention or restraint whatever method of removal is selected. But whichever view is taken, it results in holding that the order under which petitioner was convicted was valid.

It is said that we are dealing here with the case of imprisonment of a citizen in a concentration camp solely because of his ancestry, without evidence or inquiry concerning his loyalty and good disposition towards the United States. Our task would be simple, our duty clear, were this a case involving the imprisonment of a loyal citizen in a concentration camp because of racial prejudice. Regardless of the true nature of the assembly and relocation centers—and we deem it unjustifiable to call them concentration camps with all the ugly connotations that term implies—we are dealing specifically with nothing but an exclusion order. To cast this case into outlines of racial prejudice, without reference to the real military dangers which were presented, merely confuses the issue. Korematsu was not excluded from the Military Area because of hostility to him or his race. He *was* excluded because we are at war with the Japanese Empire, because the properly constituted military authorities feared an invasion of our West Coast and felt constrained to take proper security measures, because they decided that the military urgency of the situation demanded that all citizens of Japanese ancestry be segregated from the West Coast temporarily and finally, because Congress, reposing its confidence in this time of war in our military leaders—as inevitably it must—determined that they should have the power to do just this. There was evidence of disloyalty on the part of some, the military authorities considered that the need for action was great and time was short. We cannot—by availing ourselves of the calm perspective of hindsight—now say that at that time these actions were unjustified.

[From 323 U.S. 214 (1944).]

## Document 3. Public Law 100-383, 1988

More than forty years after the internment of Japanese-Americans during World War II, Congress apologized for the violation of their civil liberties.

SECTION 1. PURPOSES.

The purposes of this Act are to—

(1) acknowledge the fundamental injustice of the evacuation, relocation, and internment of United States citizens and permanent resident aliens of Japanese ancestry during World War II;

(2) apologize on behalf of the people of the United States for the evacuation, relocation, and internment of such citizens and permanent resident aliens;

(3) provide for a public education fund to finance efforts to inform the public about the internment of such individuals so as to prevent the recurrence of any similar event;

(4) make restitution to those individuals of Japanese ancestry who were interned; . . .

(6) discourage the occurrence of similar injustices and violations of civil liberties in the future; and

(7) make more credible and sincere any declaration of concern by the United States over violations of human rights committed by other nations.

SEC. 2. STATEMENT OF THE CONGRESS.

(a) WITH REGARD TO INDIVIDUALS OF JAPANESE ANCESTRY.—The Congress recognizes that, as described by the Commission on Wartime Relocation and Internment of Civilians, a grave injustice was done to both citizens and permanent resident aliens of Japanese ancestry by the evacuation, relocation, and internment of civilians during World War II. As the Commission documents, these actions were carried out without adequate security reasons and without any acts of espionage or sabotage documented by the Commission, and were motivated largely by racial prejudice, wartime hysteria, and a failure of political leadership. The excluded individuals of Japanese ancestry suffered enormous damages, both material and intangible, and there were incalculable losses in education and job training, all of which resulted in significant human suffering for which appropriate compensation has not been made. For these fundamental violations of the basic civil liberties and constitutional rights of these individuals of Japanese ancestry, the Congress apologizes on behalf of the Nation. . . .

[From *U. S. Statutes at Large* 102 (1988): 903–4.]

## Questions for Reflection

How did the federal government justify the relocation of the Japanese-Americans during World War II? Would you have supported the wartime action? Why did the Congress in 1988 apologize for the internment? In the intervening years, how and why had attitudes toward civil liberties and the rights of minorities changed? Would such an action by the government be permitted today?

# ANSWERS TO MULTIPLE-CHOICE AND TRUE-FALSE QUESTIONS

## Multiple-Choice Questions

1-A, 2-C, 3-A, 4-B, 5-C, 6-C, 7-D, 8-D

## True-False Questions

1-T, 2-T, 3-F, 4-F, 5-F, 6-T, 7-F, 8-T

# 30

# THE FAIR DEAL AND CONTAINMENT

## CHAPTER OBJECTIVES

*After you complete the reading and study of this chapter you should be able to*

1. Analyze the problems of demobilization and conversion to peacetime production.
2. Account for Truman's troubles with Congress and assess the measure of accomplishment that he achieved.
3. Explain the policy of containment and trace its development to 1950.
4. Account for Truman's reelection in 1948.
5. Assess the strength of McCarthyism in the United States.
6. Explain the origins of the Korean War and trace its major developments.

## CHAPTER OUTLINE

I. Demobilization under Truman
   A. The Truman style
      1. Truman's background and character
      2. Domestic proposals of 1945
   B. Demobilization
      1. Rapid reduction of armed forces
      2. Escalation of birth rate
      3. Efforts for economic stabilization
   C. Efforts to control inflation
      1. Demands for wage increases
      2. A wave of strikes
      3. Truman's response to strikes
      4. Efforts to control prices
      5. The end of controls
   D. Congressional elections of 1946
II. Record of the Republican Congress
   A. Taft-Hartley Act
   B. Efforts for tax reduction
   C. Governmental reorganization
      1. Features of the National Security Act
      2. Changes in presidential succession
      3. Twenty-second Amendment
III. Development of the Cold War
   A. Creating the United Nations
      1. Background to the U.N.
      2. Scheme of its operations
      3. U.S. ratification of U.N. membership
   B. Differences with the Soviets
      1. Historical debate
      2. Problems relating to eastern Europe
      3. Development of the peace treaties
      4. Proposals to control atomic energy
   C. Development of the containment policy
      1. Kennan's theory
      2. Problems in Iran, Turkey, and Greece
      3. The Truman Doctrine

4. Greek-Turkish Aid
   5. The Marshall Plan
      a. The proposal
      b. European response
   6. Division of Germany
      a. Merger of Allied zones
      b. Berlin Blockade
      c. Berlin Airlift
      d. Creation of West and East Germany
   7. Development of NATO
   8. Establishment of Israel

IV. Truman's domestic politics
   A. Democratic divisions
   B. Truman's game plan
   C. Efforts for civil rights for blacks
   D. The 1948 election
      1. The Republican position
      2. Democratic battle over civil rights
      3. Creation of the Dixiecrats
      4. Wallace's Progressive party
      5. Nature of the campaign
      6. Election results
      7. Assessment of the results
   E. The fate of the Fair Deal

V. The Cold War heats up
   A. Point Four Program
   B. China's fall to communism
      1. History of the movement in China
      2. Assessment of the Communist victory
   C. Soviet atomic bomb
   D. Work on the hydrogen bomb
   E. Decision to maintain peacetime military force

VI. The Korean War
   A. Background to conflict
   B. Response to the invasion
   C. Military developments
      1. Rout of the U.N. forces
      2. Counterattack
      3. The decision to invade the North
      4. Entry of the Chinese Communists
   D. The dismissal of MacArthur
      1. Reasons for the action
      2. Reactions to the firing
   E. Negotiations for peace

VII. Another Red Scare
   A. Evidences of espionage
   B. The Truman loyalty program
   C. The Alger Hiss case
   D. Conviction of spies
   E. McCarthy's witch-hunt
      1. The emergence of Senator McCarthy
      2. Assessment of his tactics
   F. The McCarran Internal Security Act

VIII. Assessing the Cold War


## KEY ITEMS OF CHRONOLOGY

| | |
|---|---|
| FDR dies | April 12, 1945 |
| Taft-Hartley Act | 1947 |
| Truman Doctrine | 1947 |
| Marshall Plan launched | 1947 |
| Berlin Blockade and Berlin Airlift | June 1948–May 1949 |
| Creation of Israel | 1948 |
| Hiss case | 1948–1950 |
| Establishment of NATO | April 1949 |
| China becomes communist | 1949 |
| Senator Joseph McCarthy's speech in Wheeling, West Virginia, citing communists in the State Department | February 1950 |
| Korean War | June 1950–July 1953 |
| MacArthur dismissed | April 1951 |

# THE FAIR DEAL AND CONTAINMENT

## TERMS TO MASTER

*Listed below are some important terms or people with which you should be familiar after you complete the study of this chapter. Explain the significance of each name or term.*

1. Servicemen's Readjustment Act
2. Henry A. Wallace
3. Taft-Hartley Act
4. National Security Act, 1947
5. CIA
6. Twenty-second Amendment
7. United Nations
8. "iron curtain"
9. George F. Kennan
10. containment
11. Truman Doctrine
12. Cold War
13. Marshall Plan
14. Berlin Blockade
15. NATO
16. Dixiecrats
17. Fair Deal
18. Douglas MacArthur
19. Alger Hiss
20. Joseph R. McCarthy
21. McCarran Act

## VOCABULARY BUILDING

*Listed below are some words used in this chapter. Look up each word in your dictionary.*

1. haberdasher
2. unrelenting
3. feisty
4. crony
5. mediocrity
6. credence
7. raucous
8. compliant
9. paranoid
10. brandish
11. charnel
12. rostrum
13. intractable
14. ferry (v.)
15. syndrome
16. appeasement
17. glean
18. "red herring"
19. flank
20. aversion

## EXERCISES FOR UNDERSTANDING

*When you have completed reading the chapter, answer each of the following questions. If you have difficulty, go back and reread the section of the chapter related to the question.*

### Multiple-Choice Questions

*Select the letter of the response that best completes the statement.*

1. After World War II, the economy avoided severe dislocations due to demobilization because
   A. few soldiers and sailors were released before 1947.
   B. wage and price controls continued until 1950.
   C. unions agreed not to strike or demand higher wages.
   D. pent-up demand for consumer goods spurred production.

2. The Taft-Hartley Act of 1947 dealt with
   A. labor unions.
   B. benefits for former soldiers.
   C. wage and price controls.
   D. aid to rebuild postwar Europe.

3. Bipartisan cooperation characterized relations between Congress and Truman on
   A. national security.
   B. right-to-work laws.
   C. taxes.
   D. education and welfare.

4. Postwar disagreements between the United States and the Soviet Union especially concerned

A. the formation of the United Nations.
B. governments in eastern Europe.
C. the reconstruction of Japan.
D. the Nuremberg trials.

5. The Marshall Plan was designed to
   A. help western European nations rebuild their armies.
   B. subvert communist nations into the capitalist camp.
   C. lend money to western European nations.
   D. help all European nations, including communist ones, to rebuild their war-torn economies.

6. An important new issue in the 1948 presidential election was
   A. civil rights.
   B. organized labor.
   C. agricultural policy.
   D. the regulation of business.

7. Alger Hiss was convicted of
   A. belonging to the Communist party.
   B. passing atomic secrets to the Soviets.
   C. lying under oath.
   D. nothing—he was acquitted.

8. The leader of United States forces in Korea was
   A. Joseph McCarthy.
   B. Dean Acheson.
   C. Douglas MacArthur.
   D. Dwight Eisenhower.

**True-False Questions**

*Indicate whether each statement is true or false.*

1. Congress passed the Marshall Plan over Truman's veto.
2. In 1946, the Republicans won control of Congress.
3. The National Security Act of 1947 created the Central Intelligence Agency.
4. Henry Wallace was a major architect of the containment policy.
5. The new state of Israel was created by formal action of the U.N. General Assembly.
6. Civil rights divided the Democrats in 1948.
7. The communists gained control of China, the Soviets exploded an atomic device, and the Korean War started—all in 1949.
8. The North Korean attack on South Korea in 1950 had the support of the Soviet Union.

**Essay Questions**

1. Harry Truman has often been rated a great president. Do you agree? Why or why not?
2. Account for the onset of the Cold War.
3. Compare and contrast the aid provided under the Truman Doctrine and under the Marshall Plan.
4. What were Harry Truman's major political problems in his first term as president and how did he deal with them?
5. Was America's entry into the Korean War a success? Explain.
6. Why did Truman fire MacArthur? Was his action justified? What reactions did it bring?
7. What was the Second Red Scare all about? Was it necessary? What did it accomplish?

## READINGS

### Reading 1. Arthur Schlesinger Explains the Origins of the Cold War

The origin of the Cold War is one of today's complex and controversial historiographical problems. The issues involve which side was responsible for the hostility that developed after World War II between the United States and the Soviet Union. In the article excerpted here, Arthur M. Schlesinger, Jr., a prominent historian and adviser to President Kennedy, takes a position somewhat more centrist than that of the revisionists who place the blame for the Cold War on the United States. Writing in 1967 just after he had broken with the Johnson administration over the Vietnam War, Schlesinger here attempts to show just how complex the development of the Cold War was.

The orthodox American view, as originally set forth by the American government and as reaffirmed until recently by most American scholars, has been that the Cold War was the brave and essential response of free men to communist aggression. Some have gone back well before the Second World War to lay open the sources of Russian expansionism. Geopoliticians traced the Cold War to imperial Russian strategic ambitions which in the nineteenth century led to the Crimean War, to Russian penetration of the Balkans and the Middle East and to Russian pressure on Britain's "lifeline" to India. Ideologists traced it to the Communist Manifesto of 1848 ("the violent overthrow of the bourgeoisie lays the foundation for the sway of the proletariat"). Thoughtful observers (a phrase meant to exclude those who speak in Dullese [John Foster Dulles, secretary of state under Eisenhower] about the unlimited evil of godless, atheistic, militant communism) concluded that classical Russian imperialism and Pan-Slavism, compounded after 1917 by Leninist messianism, confronted the West at the end of the Second World War with an inexorable drive for domination.

The revisionist thesis is very different. In its extreme form, it is that, after the death of Franklin Roosevelt and the end of the Second World War, the United States deliberately abandoned the wartime policy of collaboration and, exhilarated by the possession of the atomic bomb, undertook a course of aggression of its own designed to expel all Russian influence from Eastern Europe and to establish democratic-capitalist states on the very border of the Soviet Union. As the revisionists see it, this radically new American policy—or rather this resumption by Truman of the pre-Roosevelt policy of insensate anti-communism—left Moscow no alternative but to take measures in defense of its own borders. The result was the Cold War. . . .

. . . Any honest reappraisal of the origins of the Cold War requires the imaginative leap—which should in any case be as instinctive for the historian as it is prudent for the statesman—into the adversary's viewpoint. We must strive to see how, given Soviet perspectives, the Russians might conceivably have misread our signals, as we must reconsider how intelligently we read theirs.

Nor can the historian forget the conditions under which decisions are made, especially in a time like the Second World War. These were tired, overworked, aging men: in 1945, Churchill was 71 years old, Stalin had governed his country for 17 exacting years, Roosevelt his for 12 years nearly as exacting. . . . All—even Stalin, behind his screen of ideology—had become addicts of improvisation, relying on authority and virtuosity to conceal the fact that they were constantly surprised by developments. . . . None showed great tactical consistency, or cared much about it; all employed a certain ambiguity to preserve their power to decide big issues; and it is hard to know how to interpret anything any one of them said on any specific occasion. . . .

Peacemaking after the Second World War was not so much a tapestry as it was a hopelessly raveled and knotted mess of yarn. Yet, for purposes of clarity, it is essential to follow certain threads. One theme indispensable to an understanding of the Cold War is the contrast between two clashing views of world order: the "universalist" view, by which all nations shared a common interest in all the affairs of the world, and the "sphere-of-influence" view, by which each great power would be assured by the other great powers of an acknowledged predominance in its own area of special interest. The universalist view assumed that national security would be guaranteed by an international organization. The sphere-of-interest view assumed that national security would be guaranteed by the balance of power. While in practice these views have by no means been incompatible (indeed, our shaky peace has been based on a combination of the two), in the abstract they involved sharp contradictions.

The tradition of American thought in these matters was universalist. . . .

The Kremlin, on the other hand, thought *only* of spheres of interest; above all, the Russians were determined to protect their frontiers, and especially their border to the west, crossed so often and so bloodily in the dark course of their history. . . .

It is now pertinent to inquire why the United States rejected the idea of stabilizing the world by division into spheres of influence and insisted on an East European strategy. . . .

The first reason is that they regarded this solution as containing within itself the seeds of a third world war. The balance-of-power idea seemed inherently unstable. . . .

. . . the second objection: that the sphere-of-influence approach would, in the words of the State Department in 1945, "militate against the establishment and effective functioning of a broader system of general security in which all countries will have their part." The United Nations, in short, was seen as the alternative to the balance of power. . . .

Third, the universalists feared that the sphere-of-interest approach would be what Hull termed "a haven for the isolationists," who would advocate America's participation in Western Hemisphere affairs on condition that it did not participate in European or Asian affairs. . . .

Fourth, the sphere-of-interest solution meant the betrayal of the principles for which the Second World War was being fought—the Atlantic Charter, the Four Freedoms, the Declaration of the United Nations. . . .

Fifth, the sphere-of-influence solution would create difficult domestic problems in American politics. Roosevelt was aware of the six million or more Polish votes in the 1944 election. . . .

Sixth, if the Russians were allowed to overrun Eastern Europe without argument, would that satisfy them? . . .

But the great omission of the revisionists—and also the fundamental explanation of the speed with which the Cold War escalated—lies precisely in the fact that the Soviet Union was not a traditional national state. The Soviet Union was a phenomenon very different from America or Britain: it was a totalitarian state, endowed with an all-explanatory, all-consuming ideology, committed to the infallibility of government and party, still in a somewhat messianic mood, equating dissent with treason, and ruled by a dictator who, for all his quite extraordinary abilities, had his paranoid moments.

Marxism-Leninism gave the Russian leaders a view of the world according to which all societies were inexorably destined to proceed along appointed roads by appointed stages until they achieved the classless nirvana. . . .

A revisionist fallacy has been to treat Stalin as just another Realpolitik statesman, as Second World War revisionists see Hitler as just another Stresemann or Bismarck. But the record makes it clear that in the end nothing could satisfy Stalin's paranoia. His own associates failed. Why does anyone suppose that any conceivable American policy would have succeeded?

The difference between America and Russia in 1945 was that some Americans fundamentally believed that, over a long run, a modus vivendi with Russia was possible; while the Russians, so far as one can tell, believed in no more than a short-run modus vivendi with the United States.

In retrospect, if it is impossible to see the Cold War as a case of American aggression and Russian response, it is also hard to see it as a pure case of Russian aggression and American response. . . .

The Cold War could have been avoided only if the Soviet Union had not been possessed by convictions both of the infallibility of the communist word and of the inevitability of a communist world. These convictions turned an impasse between national states into a religious war, a tragedy of ability into one of necessity. One might wish that America had preserved the poise and proportion of the first years of the Cold War and had not succumbed to is own forms of self-righteousness. But the most rational American policies could hardly have averted the Cold War. Only if Russia began to recede from its messianic mission and to accept, in fact if not yet in principle, the permanence of the world of diversity, only then did the hope flicker that this long, dreary, costly contest may at last be taking forms less dramatic, less obsessive and less dangerous to the future kind.

[Arthur Schlesinger, Jr., "Origins of the Cold War," *Foreign Affairs* 46 (October 1967): 22–52]

## Reading 2. Barton Bernstein Presents a Revisionist View

Barton Bernstein has been one of the leading revisionists in the controversy over the origins of the Cold War. The excerpt below will introduce the reader to the essentials of that view.

Despite some dissents, most American scholars have reached a general consensus on the origins of the Cold War. As confirmed internationalists who believe that Russia constituted a threat to America and its European allies after World War II, they have endorsed their nation's acceptance of its obligations as a world power in the forties and its desire to establish a world order of peace and prosperity. Convinced that only American efforts prevented the Soviet Union from expanding past Eastern Europe, they have generally praised the containment policies of the Truman Doctrine, the Marshall Plan, and NATO as evidence of America's acceptance of world responsibility. While chiding or condemning those on the right who opposed international involvement (or had even urged preventive war), they have also been deeply critical of those on the left who have believed that the Cold War could have been avoided, or that the United States shared substantial responsibility for the Cold War.

Despite the widespread acceptance of this interpretation, there has long been substantial evidence (and more recently a body of scholarship) which suggests that American policy was neither so innocent nor so nonideological; that American leaders sought to promote their conceptions of national interest and their values even at the conscious risk of provoking Russia's fears about her security. In 1945 these leaders apparently believed that American power would be adequate for the task of reshaping much of the world according to America's needs and standards.

By overextending policy and power and refusing to accept Soviet interests, American policy-makers contributed to the Cold War. There was little understanding of any need to restrain American political efforts and desires. Though it cannot be proved that the United States could have achieved a *modus vivendi* with the Soviet Union in these years there is evidence that Russian policies were reasonably cautious and conservative, and that there was at least a basis for accommodation. But this possibility slowly slipped away as President Harry S. Truman reversed Roosevelt's tactics of accommodation. As American demands for democratic governments in Eastern Europe became more vigorous, as the new administration delayed in providing economic assistance to Russia and in seeking international control of atomic energy, policy-makers met with increasing Soviet suspicion and antagonism. Concluding that Soviet-American cooperation was impossible, they came to believe that the Soviet state could be halted only by force or the threat of force. . . .

. . . It is clear that Truman was either incapable or unwilling to reexamine his earlier assumption (or decision) of using the bomb. Under the tutelage of Byrnes and Stimson, Truman had come to assume by July that the bomb should be used, and perhaps he was incapable of reconsidering this strategy because he found no compelling reason not to use the bomb. Or he may have consciously rejected the options because he wanted to use the bomb. Perhaps he was vindictive and wished to retaliate for Pearl Harbor and other atrocities. (In justifying the use of the bomb against the Japanese, he wrote a few days after Nagasaki, "The only language they seem to understand is the one we have been using to bombard them. When you have to deal with a beast you have to treat him as a beast.") Or, most likely, Truman agreed with Byrnes that using the bomb would advance other American policies: It would end the war before the Russians could gain a hold in Manchuria, it would permit the United States to exclude Russia from the occupation government of Japan, and it would make the Soviets more manageable in Eastern Europe. It would enable the United States to shape the peace according to its own standards.

At minimum, then, the use of the bomb reveals the moral insensitivity of the President—whether he used it because the moral implications did not compel a reexamination of assumptions, or because he sought retribution, or because he sought to keep Russia out of Manchuria and the occupation government of Japan, and to make her more manageable in Eastern Europe. In 1945 American foreign policy was not innocent, nor was it unconcerned about Russian power, nor did it assume that the United States lacked the power to impose its will on the Russian state, nor was it characterized by high moral purpose or consistent dedication to humanitarian principles.

While the Soviet Union would not generally permit in Eastern Europe conditions that conformed to Western ideals, Stalin was pursuing a cautious policy and seeking accommodation with the West. He was willing to allow capitalism but was suspicious of American efforts at economic penetration which could lead to political dominance. Though by the autumn of 1945 the governments in Russia's general area of influence were subservient in foreign policy, they varied in form and in degree of independence—democracy in Czechoslovakia (the only country in this area with a democratic tradition), free elections and the overthrow of the Communist party in Hungary, a Communist-formed coalition government in Bulgaria, a broadly based but Communist-dominated government in Poland, and a Soviet-imposed government in Rumania (the most anti-Russian of these nations). In all of these countries Communists controlled the ministries of interior (the police) and were able to suppress anti-Soviet groups, including anti-communist democrats.

Those who have attributed to Russia a policy of inexorable expansion have often neglected this immediate postwar period, or they have interpreted it simply as a necessary preliminary (a cunning strategy to allay American suspicions until the American Army demobilized and left the continent) to the consolidation and extension of power in east-central Europe. From this perspective, however, much of Stalin's behavior becomes strangely contradictory and potentially self-defeating. If he had planned to create puppets rather than an area of "friendly governments," why (as Isaac Deutscher asks) did Stalin "so stubbornly refuse to make any concessions to the Poles over their eastern frontiers"? Certainly, also, his demand for reparations from Hungary, Rumania, and Bulgaria would have been unnecessary if he had planned to take over these countries. (America's insistence upon using a loan to Russia to achieve political goals, and nearly twenty-month delay after Russia first submitted a specific proposal for assistance, led Harriman to suggest in November that the loan policy "may have contributed to their [Russian] avaricious policies in the countries occupied or liberated by the Red Army.")

Russian sources are closed, so it is not possible to prove that Soviet intentions were conservative; nor for the same reason is it possible for those who adhered to the thesis of inexorable Soviet expansion to prove their theory. But the available evidence better supports the thesis that these years should be viewed not as a cunning preliminary to the harshness of 1947 and afterward, but as an attempt to establish a *modus vivendi* with the West and to protect "socialism in one country." This interpretation explains more adequately why the Russians delayed nearly three years before ending dissent and hardening policies in the countries behind their own military lines. It would also explain why the Communist parties in France and Italy were cooperating with the coalition governments until these parties were forced out of the coalitions in 1947. . . .

If the Russian policy was conservative and sought accommodation (as now seems likely), then its failure must be explained by looking beyond Russian actions. Historians must reexamine this period and reconsider American policies. Were they directed toward compromise? Can they be judged as having sought adjustment? Or did they demand acquiescence to the American world view, thus thwarting real negotiations?

There is considerable evidence that American actions clearly changed after Roosevelt's death. Slowly abandoning the tactics of accommodation, they became even more vigorous after Hiroshima. The insistence upon rolling back Soviet influence in Eastern Europe, the reluctance to grant a loan for Russian reconstruction, the inability to reach an agreement on Germany, the maintenance of the nuclear monopoly—all of these could have contributed to the sense of Russian insecurity. The point, then, is that in 1945 and 1946 there may still have been possibilities for negotiations and settlements, for accommodations and adjustments, if the United States had been willing to recognize Soviet fears, to accept Soviet power in her areas of influence, and to ease anxieties.

[Barton J. Bernstein, "American Foreign Policy and the Origins of the Cold War," in *Politics and Policies of the Truman Administration*, edited by Barton J. Bernstein (Chicago: Quadrangle Books, 1970), pp. 15–49]

## Questions for Reflection

After reading both excerpts and answering the questions that follow, attempt to write in a few paragraphs your own view of the origins of the Cold War.

What is the orthodox view of the origins of the Cold War? The revisionist view? What special considerations should be taken into account in attempting to explain the Cold War? What important theme does Schlesinger want the reader to consider in explaining the development of Cold War events? What does he think the revisionists have omitted in their analysis of the Cold War?

How does Bernstein's initial description of the consensus view of Cold War origins compare with Schlesinger's view above? Needless use of the atomic bomb is one of the central themes of revisionist history. How does Bernstein deal with this matter? How does he argue that the United States acted incorrectly in Eastern Europe? How do we know Russia's motives after World War II? What limitation does that place on historians?

## ANSWERS TO MULTIPLE-CHOICE AND TRUE-FALSE QUESTIONS

**Multiple-Choice Questions**

1-D, 2-A, 3-A, 4-B, 5-D, 6-A, 7-C, 8-C

**True-False Questions**

1-F, 2-T, 3-T, 4-F, 5-F, 6-T, 7-F, 8-T

# 31

## THROUGH THE PICTURE WINDOW: SOCIETY AND CULTURE, 1945–1960

**CHAPTER OBJECTIVES**

*After you complete the reading and study of this chapter you should be able to*

1. Account for the emergence of a consumer culture in the prosperous postwar era.
2. Describe the growth of suburban America after World War II.
3. Illustrate the widespread conformity in American culture in the 1950s.
4. Understand the ideas of the major critics of conformity.
5. Explain the artistic and literary dissent beginning in the 1950s.

**CHAPTER OUTLINE**

I. Postwar economy
   A. Growth and prosperity
      1. Military spending
      2. International trade dominance
      3. Technological innovation
      4. consumer demand
      5. GI Bill of Rights
         a. Enacted in 1944
         b. Impact on education
      6. "Baby boom"
   B. Consumer culture
      1. Television
      2. Marketing and packaging
      3. Credit cards
      4. Shopping malls
   C. Growth of suburbs
      1. Rural-to-urban migration
      2. Levittowns
      3. Automobiles and roads
      4. "White flight"
   D. Great black migration
      1. Southern sources
      2. Urban North and Midwest
      3. Social effects
II. Postwar conformity
   A. Corporate life
      1. Large corporations
      2. Managerial personality
   B. Women and cult of domesticity
   C. Religion
      1. Growth in church membership
         a. Religious revival
         b. Patriotism
         c. Marketing of religion
      2. Reverend Norman Vincent Peale and "positive thinking"
      3. Neo-orthodoxy
         a. Critical of religiosity
         b. Reinhold Niebuhr
III. Social critics of conformity
   A. John Kenneth Galbraith's *Affluent Society*

B. John Keats's *Crack in the Picture Window*
C. David Riesman and *The Lonely Crowd*
IV. Alienation in the arts
   A. Drama
      1. Oppressiveness of mass culture
      2. Arthur Miller's *Death of a Salesman*
      3. Tennessee Williams and Edward Albee
   B. The novel
      1. The individual's struggle for survival
      2. J. D. Salinger's *Catcher in the Rye*
      3. *From Here to Eternity* by James Jones
      4. Saul Bellow, Ralph Ellison, Joseph Heller, Norman Mailer, Joyce Carol Oates, et al.
   C. Painting
      1. Edward Hopper and desolate loneliness
      2. Abstract expressionism
         a. Violent and chaotic modern society
         b. Jackson Pollock
         c. William de Kooning, Mark Rothko, et al.
   D. The Beats
      1. Liberation of self-expression
      2. Greenwich Village background
      3. William Burrough's *Naked Lunch*
      4. *Howl* by Allen Ginsberg
      5. Jack Kerouac's *On the Road*
      6. Influences

## KEY ITEMS OF CHRONOLOGY

| | |
|---|---|
| Dr. Benjamin Spock, *Common Sense Book of Baby and Child Care* | 1946 |
| The first Levittown in New York | 1947 |
| Arthur Miller, *Death of a Salesman* | 1949 |
| David Riesman, *The Lonely Crowd* | 1950 |
| J. D. Salinger, *The Catcher in the Rye* | 1951 |
| Ralph Ellison, *Invisible Man* | 1952 |
| "one Nation under God" added to the Pledge of Allegiance | 1954 |
| Allen Ginsberg, *Howl* | 1956 |
| Jack Kerouac, *On the Road* | 1957 |
| John Kenneth Galbraith, *The Affluent Society* | 1958 |
| Vance Packard, *The Waste Makers* | 1960 |

## TERMS TO MASTER

*Listed below are some important terms or people with which you should be familiar after you complete the study of this chapter. Explain the significance of each name or term*

1. baby-boom generation
2. suburbs
3. William Levitt
4. "white flight"
5. white collar
6. cult of domesticity
7. "in God we trust"
8. Norman Vincent Peale
9. neo-orthodoxy
10. Reinhold Niebuhr
11. "other-directed"
12. *Death of a Salesman*
13. Holden Caulfield
14. abstract expressionism
15. Jackson Pollock
16. The Beats

## VOCABULARY BUILDING

*Listed below are some words used in this chapter. Look up each word in your dictionary.*

1. deprivation
2. recession
3. perpetual
4. catapult
5. catalyst
6. parietal
7. differentiate
8. hedonistic
9. dispersion
10. teeming
11. veritable
12. castigate
13. harangue
14. impresario
15. religiosity
16. desolate
17. melancholy
18. vibrant
19. mundane
20. penchant

## EXERCISES FOR UNDERSTANDING

*When you have completed reading the chapter, answer each of the following questions. If you have difficulty, go back and reread the section of the chapter related to the question.*

### Multiple-Choice Questions

*Select the letter of the response that best completes the statement.*

1. One major effect of the GI Bill of Rights was
   A. an increase in black migration from the South.
   B. the democratization of higher education.
   C. an increase in military enlistments.
   D. integration of higher education.

2. The fastest growing periodical of the 1950s was
   A. *Playboy.*
   B. *House Beautiful.*
   C. *Christian Century.*
   D. *TV Guide.*

3. After World War II, black Americans
   A. found equality in higher education.
   B. left the rural South for the urban North.
   C. migrated primarily to the West.
   D. moved from northern ghettos to the rural West.

4. The religious revival of the 1950s was spurred by
   A. the Cold War.
   B. television.
   C. a mobile population's need for community.
   D. all of the above.

5. A critic of "undue complacency and conformity" was
   A. Reinhold Niebuhr.
   B. Norman Vincent Peale.
   C. William Levitt.
   D. Willie Loman.

6. John Keats's *Crack in the Picture Window* was a stinging critique of
   A. the quality of housing in the suburbs.
   B. television.
   C. modern art.
   D. suburban life.

7. A leading abstract expressionist painter was
   A. Gregory Corso.
   B. Ralph Ellison.
   C. Jackson Pollock.
   D. Reinhold Niebuhr.

8. The Beats included
   A. Arthur Miller, Edward Albee, and Tennessee Williams.
   B. William de Kooning, Mark Rothko, and Robert Motherwell.
   C. William Burroughs, Allen Ginsburg, and Jack Kerouac.
   D. none of the above.

### True-False Questions

*Indicate whether each statement is true or false.*

1. By 1960, nine out of ten American homes had a television.
2. Consumer debt declined in the prosperous 1950s.
3. The baby boom began in the late 1950s.
4. "In God We Trust" was put on all American currency starting in 1955.

5. Arthur Miller wrote *The Lonely Crowd*.
6. The Beats originated in Greenwich Village in New York City.
7. The author of *The Catcher in the Rye* was J. D. Salinger.
8. Allen Ginsberg's autobiography was *On the Road*.

## Essay Questions

1. What factors contributed to the economic growth and prosperity of the postwar period?
2. Who was William Levitt and why was his work important?
3. Describe some of the drawbacks of suburban living in the 1950s.
4. Among Christians in the 1950s, how did "positive thinking" differ from neo-orthodoxy?
5. Compare the nonfiction of David Riesman and John Keats with the fiction of Arthur Miller and J. D. Salinger. What do they all tell us about the 1950s?
6. How would Jack Kerouac and Willy Loman respond to Levittown?

## DOCUMENT

**Betty Friedan Describes the Attitude of the "Bored Housewife"**

As the text shows, the ideal American woman in the 1950s was the housewife-mother. In the following excerpt from her influential work *The Feminine Mystique* (1963), Betty Friedan analyzes this "ideal" and explores how it came about.

In the early 1960's *McCall's* has been the fastest growing of the women's magazines. The image of woman that emerges from this big, pretty magazine is young and frivolous, almost childlike; fluffy and feminine; passive; gaily content in a world of bedroom and kitchen, sex, babies, and home. The magazine surely does not leave out sex; the only passion, the only pursuit, the only goal a woman is permitted is the pursuit of a man. It is crammed full of food, clothing, cosmetics, furniture, and the physical bodies of young women, but where is the world of thought and ideas, the life of the mind and spirit? In the magazine image, women do no work except housework and work to keep their bodies beautiful and to get and keep a man.

This was the image of the American woman in the year Castro led a revolution in Cuba and men were trained to travel into outer space; the year that the African continent brought forth new nations, and a plane whose speed is greater than the speed of sound broke up a Summit Conference; the year artists picketed a great museum in protest against the hegemony of abstract art; physicists explored the concept of anti-matter; astronomers, because of new radio telescopes, had to alter their concepts of the expanding universe; biologists made a breakthrough in the fundamental chemistry of life; and Negro youth in Southern schools forced the United States, for the first time since the Civil War, to face a moment of democratic truth. But this magazine, published for over 5,000,000 American women, almost all of whom have been through high school and nearly half to college, contained almost no mention of the world beyond the home. In the second half of the twentieth century in America, woman's world was confined to her own body and beauty, the charming of man, the bearing of babies, and the physical care and serving of husband, children, and home. And this was no anomaly of a single issue of a single women's magazine.

I sat one night at a meeting of magazine writers, mostly men, who work for all kinds of magazines, including women's magazines. . . . [We] spent an hour listening to Thurgood Marshall on the inside story of the desegregation battle, and its possible effect on the presidential election. "Too bad I can't run that story," one editor said. "But you just can't link it to woman's world."

As I listened to them, a German phrase echoed in my mind—"*Kinder, Kuche, Kirche,*" the slogan by which the Nazis decreed that women must once again be confined to their biological role. But this was not Nazi Germany. This was America. The whole world lies open to American women. Why, then, does the image deny the world? Why does it limit women to "one position, one role, one occupation"? Not long ago, women dreamed and fought for equality, their own place in the world. What happened to their dreams; when did women decide to give up the world and go back home?

I sat for many days in the New York Public Library, going back through bound volumes of American women's magazines for the last twenty years. I found a change in the image of the American woman, and in the boundaries of the woman's world, as sharp and puzzling as the changes revealed in the cores of ocean sediment.

In 1939, the heroines of women's magazine stories were not always young, but in a certain sense they were younger than their fictional counterparts today. They were young in the same way that the American hero has always been young: they were New Women, creating with a gay determined spirit a new identity for women—a life of their own. There was an aura about them of becoming, of moving into a future that was going to be different from the past. The majority of heroines in the four major women's magazines (then *Ladies' Home Journal, McCall's, Good Housekeeping, Woman's Home Companion*) were career women—happily, proudly, adventurously, attractively career women—who loved and were loved by men. And the spirit, courage, independence, determination—the strength of character they showed in their work as nurses, teachers, artists, actresses, copywriters, saleswomen—were part of their charm. There was a definite aura that their individuality was something to be admired, not unattractive to men, that men were drawn to them as much for their spirit and character as for their looks.

These were the mass women's magazines—in their heyday. The stories were conventional: girl-meets-boy or girl-gets-boy. But very often this was not the major theme of the story. These heroines were usually marching toward some goal or vision of their own, struggling with some problem of work or the world, when they found their man. And this New Woman, less fluffily feminine, so independent and determined to find a new life of her own, was the heroine of a different kind of love story. She was less aggressive in pursuit of a man. Her passionate involvement with the world, her own sense of herself as an individual, her self-reliance, gave a different flavor to her relationship with the man.

These stories may not have been great literature. But the identity of their heroines seemed to say something about the housewives who, then as now, read the women's magazines. These magazines were not written for career women. The New Woman heroines were the ideal of yesterday's housewives; they reflected the dreams, mirrored the yearning for identity and the sense of possibility that existed for women then. And if women could not have these dreams for themselves, they wanted their daughters to have them. They wanted their daughters to be more than housewives, to go out in the world that had been denied them.

As for not earning any money, the argument goes, let the housewife compute the cost of her services. Women can save more money by their managerial talents inside the home than they can bring into it by outside work. As for woman's spirit being broken by the boredom of household tasks, maybe the genius of some women has been thwarted, but "a world full of feminine genius, but poor in children, would come rapidly to an end. . . . Great men have great mothers."

The feminine mystique says that the highest value and the only commitment for women is the fulfillment of their own femininity. It says that the great mistake of Western culture, through most of its history, has been the undervaluation of this femininity. It says this femininity is so mysterious and intuitive and close to the creation and origin of life that man-made science may never be able to understand it. But however special and different, it is in no way inferior to the nature of man; it may even in certain respects be superior. The mistake, says the mystique, the root of women's troubles in the past is that women envied men, women tried to be like men, instead of accepting their own nature, which can find fulfillment only in sexual passivity, male domination, and nurturing maternal love.

But the new image this mystique gives to American women is the old image: "Occupation: housewife." The new mystique makes the housewife-mothers, who never had a chance to be anything else, the model for all women; it presupposes that history has reached a final and glorious end in the here and now, as far as women are concerned. Beneath the sophisticated trappings, it simply makes certain concrete, finite, domestic aspects of feminine existence—as it was lived by women whose lives were confined, by necessity, to cooking, cleaning, washing, bearing children—into a religion, a pattern by which all women must now live or deny their femininity.

Fulfillment as a woman had only one definition for American women after 1949—the housewife-mother. As swiftly as in a dream, the image of the American woman as a changing, growing individual in a changing world was shattered. Her solo flight to find her own identity was forgotten in the rush for the security of togetherness. Her limitless world shrunk to the cozy walls of home.

The end of the road, in an almost literal sense, is the disappearance of the heroine altogether, as a separate self and the subject of her own story. The end of the road is togetherness, where the woman has no independent self to hide even in guilt; she exists only for and through her husband and children.

Coined by the publishers of *McCall's* in 1954, the concept "togetherness" was seized upon avidly as a movement of spiritual significance by advertisers, ministers, newspaper editors. For a time, it was elevated into virtually a national purpose. But very quickly there was sharp social criticism, and bitter jokes about "togetherness" as a substitute for larger human goals—for men. Women were taken to task for making their husbands do housework, instead of letting them pioneer in the nation and the world. Why, it was asked, should men with the capacities of statesmen, anthropologists, physicists, poets, have to wash dishes and diaper babies on weekday evenings or Saturday mornings when they might use those extra hours to fulfill larger commitments to their society?

But forbidden to join man in the world, can women be people? Forbidden independence, they finally are swallowed in an image of such passive dependence that they want men to make the decisions, even in the home. The frantic illusion that togetherness can impart a spiritual content to the dullness of domestic routine, the need for a religious movement to make up for the lack of identity, betrays the measure of women's loss and the emptiness of the image. Could making men share the housework compensate women for their loss of the world? Could vacuuming the living-room floor together give the housewife some mysterious new purpose in life?

In 1956, at the peak of togetherness, the bored editors of *McCall's* ran a little article called "The Mother Who Ran Away." To their amazement, it brought the highest readership of any article they had ever run. "It was our moment of truth," said a former editor. "We suddenly realized that all those women at home with their three and a half children were miserably unhappy."

But by then the new image of American woman, "Occupation: housewife," had hardened into a mystique, unquestioned and permitting no questions. . . .

By the time I started writing for women's magazines, in the fifties, it was simply taken for granted by editors, and accepted as an immutable fact of life by writers, that women were not interested in politics, life outside the United States, national issues, art, science, ideas, adventure, education, or even their own communities, except where they could be sold through their emotions as wives and mothers.

Politics, for women, became Mamie's clothes and the Nixons' home life. Out of conscience, a sense of duty, the *Ladies' Home Journal* might run a series like "Political Pilgrim's Progress," showing women trying to improve their children's schools and playgrounds. But even approaching politics through mother love did not really interest women, it was thought in the trade. Everyone knew those readership percentages. An editor of *Redbook* ingeniously tried to bring the bomb down to the feminine level by showing the emotions of a wife whose husband sailed into a contaminated area.

"Women can't take an idea, an issue, pure," men who edited the mass women's magazines agreed. "It had to be translated in terms they can understand as women." This was so well understood by those who wrote for women's magazines that a natural childbirth expert submitted an article to a leading woman's magazine called "How to Have a Baby in a Atom Bomb Shelter." "The article was not well written," an editor told me, "or we might have bought it." According to the mystique, women, in their mysterious femininity, might be interested in the concrete biological details of having a baby in a bomb shelter, but never in the abstract idea of the bomb's power to destroy the human race.

Such a belief, of course, becomes a self-fulfilling prophecy. In 1960, a perceptive social psychologist showed me some sad statistics which seemed to prove unmistakably that American women under thirty-five are not interested in politics. "They may have the vote, but they don't dream about running for office," he told me. "If you write a political piece, they won't read it. You have to translate it into issues they can understand—romance, pregnancy, nursing, home furnishings, clothes. Run an article on the economy, or the race question, civil rights, and you'd think that women had never heard of them."

This is the real mystery: why did so many American women, with the ability and education to discover and create, go back home again, to look for "something more" in housework and rearing children? For, paradoxically, in the same fifteen years in which the spirited New Woman was replaced by the Happy Housewife, the boundaries of the human world have widened, the pace of world change has quickened, and the very nature of human reality has become increasingly free from biological and material necessity.

[From Betty Friedan, *The Feminine Mystique* (New York: W. W. Norton & Co., 1974; originally published 1963), pp. 36, 37, 38, 40, 42, 43–44, 47–48, 50–51, 67]

## Questions for Reflection

What effects do the images depicted in magazines (and on television) have on readers (and viewers)? Discuss this with specific regard to the images of women in the 1950s.

What does Friedan see as "the feminine mystique," and what does she think of it? How appropriate is "the feminine mystique" as a guideline for women today?

## ANSWERS TO MULTIPLE-CHOICE AND TRUE-FALSE QUESTIONS

### Multiple-Choice Questions

1-B, 2-D, 3-B, 4-D, 5-A, 6-D, 7-C, 8-C

### True-False Questions

1-T, 2-F, 3-F, 4-T, 5-F, 6-T, 7-T, 8-F

# 32

# CONFLICT AND DEADLOCK: THE EISENHOWER YEARS

## CHAPTER OBJECTIVES

*After you complete the reading and study of this chapter you should be able to*

1. Describe Eisenhower's style and his approach to the nation's problems.
2. Assess the nature of modern Republicanism in relation to New Deal liberalism, focusing especially on Eisenhower's stance on key domestic legislation.
3. Assess the early performance of Dulles's diplomacy, especially as compared to the policy of containment.
4. Explain the origins of the Indochina War and assess Eisenhower's response to it.
5. Describe the developments in civil rights in the Eisenhower era and assess his responses to them.
6. Explain the Suez Crisis and the Hungarian revolt, their interrelations and their consequences.
7. Assess the impact of Sputnik.

## CHAPTER OUTLINE

I. Rise of Eisenhower
   A. Election of 1952
      1. Appeal of Ike
      2. Adlai Stevenson
   B. Ike's background and personality
      1. Army career
      2. Warmth and unpretentiousness
II. The early Eisenhower administration
   A. Appointments
   B. Dynamic conservatism
      1. Some New Deal programs cut
         a. Reconstruction Finance Corporation
         b. Wage and price controls
      2. Some New Deal programs extended
         a. Social security
         b. Minimum wage
         c. Health care
         d. Housing
   C. Public works
      1. St. Lawrence Seaway
      2. Interstate highways
   D. Armistice in Korea
      1. Ike's bold stand
      2. Reasons for settlement
   E. End to McCarthyism
      1. McCarthy's tactics
      2. McCarthy and the army
      3. Senate condemnation
   F. Internal security worries
   G. Dulles and foreign policy
      1. Dulles's background
      2. Idea of liberation

3. Covert action and Allen Dulles
4. Massive retaliation
5. Brinksmanship
    H. Problems in Indochina
        1. Background to war
            a. Nationalism in Asia
            b. French control
            c. Ho Chi Minh and independence
        2. First Indochina war
            a. Outbreak of fighting
            b. American aid
            c. Ike's domino theory
        3. Geneva Accords
            a. French defeat
            b. Provisions of the agreement
        4. Creation of SEATO
        5. Government of Diem
            a. Need for reform
            b. Opposition suppressed
III. Stirrings in civil rights
    A. Ike's stance on civil rights
    B. *Brown v. Board of Education*
        1. Court's decision
        2. Reactions
            a. Eisenhower's reluctance
            b. Token compliance
            c. Massive resistance
    C. Montgomery bus boycott
        1. Cause for action
        2. Role of Martin Luther King, Jr.
        3. Strategy of nonviolence
        4. Results
    D. Civil rights legislation
    E. Little Rock
IV. Election of 1956
    A. Eisenhower's health
    B. Stevenson defeated again
V. A season of troubles
    A. The Suez crisis
        1. Eisenhower's Middle East policy
        2. Rise of Nasser in Egypt
        3. Offer and withdrawal of loan
        4. Nasser's seizure of Suez
        5. Israeli invasion
        6. Resolution of crisis
    B. The Hungarian revolt
    C. Sputnik
        1. The Russian feat
        2. American reactions
            a. U.S. space effort
            b. Deployment of missiles
            c. Creation of NASA
            d. National Defense Education Act
    D. Corruption in administration
    E. Other foreign problems
        1. Eisenhower doctrine
        2. Marines to Lebanon
        3. The Berlin problem
        4. The U-2 affair
            a. Spy plane downed
            b. Collapse of summit
        5. Castro's Cuba
            a. Castro's takeover
            b. American responses
VI. Assessing the Eisenhower years
    A. Accomplishments
    B. Farewell address

## KEY ITEMS OF CHRONOLOGY

| | |
|---|---|
| Fall of Dien Bien Phu | May 1954 |
| *Brown v. Board of Education* | May 1954 |
| Geneva Accords signed | July 1954 |
| SEATO created | September 1954 |
| McCarthy condemned by the Senate | December 1954 |
| Montgomery bus boycott | December 1955–December 1956 |
| Suez crisis (and Hungarian revolt) | October 1956 |
| Little Rock High School crisis | September 1957 |
| Sputnik launched | October 1957 |
| U-2 incident | May 1960 |

## TERMS TO MASTER

*Listed below are some important terms or people with which you should be familiar after you complete the study of this chapter. Explain the significance of each name or term.*

1. Adlai Stevenson
2. "dynamic conservatism"
3. St. Lawrence Seaway
4. interstate highway system
5. Earl Warren
6. "liberation"
7. "massive retaliation"
8. Ho Chi Minh
9. Dien Bien Phu
10. Geneva Accords
11. SEATO
12. *Brown v. Board of Education*
13. Martin Luther King, Jr.
14. Suez crisis
15. Sputnik
16. U-2 incident

## VOCABULARY BUILDING

*Listed below are some words used in this chapter. Look up each word in your dictionary.*

1. liability
2. stalemate
3. wheelhorse
4. unpretentious
5. apathetic
6. novice
7. aloof
8. rapier
9. skulking
10. despotism
11. affinity
12. bulwark
13. tenacious
14. unilateral
15. interlude
16. sporadic
17. ostensibly
18. synchronize
19. capitulation
20. acronym

## EXERCISES FOR UNDERSTANDING

*When you have completed reading the chapter, answer each of the following questions. If you have difficulty, go back and reread the section of the chapter related to the question.*

### Multiple-Choice Questions

*Select the letter of the response that best completes the statement.*

1. In the 1952 campaign, Eisenhower promised to
   A. destroy Joseph McCarthy.
   B. end the social security system.
   C. go to Korea.
   D. put Adlai Stevenson in his cabinet.

2. In regard to internal security, President Eisenhower
   A. restricted Truman's loyalty program.
   B. deferred to Senator McCarthy.
   C. expanded investigations to include security risks.
   D. thought no problem existed.

3. Eisenhower once said the "biggest damn-fool mistake I ever made" was
   A. retiring from the army and entering politics.
   B. appointing Earl Warren to the Supreme Court.
   C. not attacking China with atomic weapons.
   D. using federal troops in Little Rock, Arkansas.

4. The Geneva Accords involving Southeast Asia
   A. were signed by the United States.
   B. neutralized Vietnam.
   C. divided Laos and Cambodia at the 38th parallel.
   D. called for elections to unify Vietnam.

5. In *Brown v. Board of Education*, the Supreme Court ruled that
   A. racial segregation was constitutional.
   B. "separate but equal" public education was unconstitutional.
   C. all children under the age of eighteen had to attend school.
   D. Kansas must provide free education for Indian children.

6. Dwight Eisenhower was the first Republican presidential candidate in the twentieth century to
   A. be elected twice.
   B. carry a Deep South state.
   C. receive a plurality of the popular vote.
   D. win every state.
7. In the Suez crisis of 1956, the United States was on the same side as
   A. the Soviet Union.
   B. France and Great Britain.
   C. Israel.
   D. Hungary.
8. Eisenhower's Farewell Address dealt with
   A. the need for greater military spending.
   B. the dangers of a military-industrial complex.
   C. how to solve problems of civil rights.
   D. the need for a better highway system.

**True-False Questions**

*Indicate whether each statement is true or false.*

1. The Eisenhower administration threatened to use nuclear weapons in Korea.
2. The Eisenhower administration was especially strong in its denunciation of U.S. policy commitments made at Yalta.
3. Under Secretary of State Dulles, American policy radically changed from the containment followed by Truman and Acheson.
4. SEATO was exactly like NATO except in Southeast Asia.
5. Eisenhower thought that laws could quickly and easily provide equal rights for blacks.
6. To integrate the public schools of Little Rock, President Eisenhower sent in federal paratroopers.
7. The NDEA was a United States response to the launching of Sputnik.
8. The crisis in Cuba caused the collapse of the Eisenhower-Khrushchev summit in 1960.

**Essay Questions**

1. How did Ike's administrative style, philosophy, and programs differ from those of the New Deal?
2. What factors contributed to the fall of Senator McCarthy?
3. Who was John Foster Dulles and what was his role in the Eisenhower administration?
4. Assess America's involvement in Indochina during the Eisenhower administration.
5. What role did the federal government play in the early years of the civil rights movement? Was the government essential to the start of the movement?
6. Account for the United States position in both the Suez crisis and the Hungarian revolt of 1956.
7. How successful was Eisenhower as a president? Explain.

## DOCUMENT

### Eisenhower's Farewell Address, January 17, 1961

Eisenhower's farewell address, below, includes his famous warning about the growing influence of "the military-industrial complex."

> *My fellow Americans:*
> Three days from now, after half a century in the service of our country, I shall lay down the responsibilities of office as, in traditional and solemn ceremony, the authority of the Presidency is vested in my successor. . . .

We now stand ten years past the midpoint of a century that has witnessed four major wars among great nations. Three of them involved our own country. Despite these holocausts America is today the strongest, the most influential and most productive nation in the world. Understandably proud of this pre-eminence we yet realize that America's leadership and prestige depend, not merely upon our unmatched material progress, riches and military strength, but on how we use our power in the interests of world peace and human betterment.

Throughout America's adventure in free government, our basic purposes have been to keep the peace; to foster progress in human achievement, and to enhance liberty, dignity and integrity among people and among nations. To strive for less would be unworthy of a free and religious people. Any failure traceable to arrogance, or our lack of comprehension or readiness to sacrifice would inflict upon us grievous hurt both at home and abroad.

Progress toward these noble goals is persistently threatened by the conflict now engulfing the world. It commands our whole attention, absorbs our very beings. We face a hostile ideology—global in scope, atheistic in character, ruthless in purpose, and insidious in method. Unhappily the danger it poses promises to be of indefinite duration. To meet it successfully, there is called for, not so much the emotional and transitory sacrifices of crisis, but rather those which enable us to carry forward steadily, surely, and without complaint the burdens of a prolonged and complex struggle—with liberty the stake. Only thus shall we remain, despite every provocation, on our charted course toward permanent peace and human betterment. . . .

A vital element in keeping the peace is our military establishment. Our arms must be mighty, ready for instant action, so that no potential aggressor may be tempted to risk his own destruction.

Our military organization today bears little relation to that known by any of my predecessors in peacetime, or indeed by the fighting men of World War II or Korea.

Until the latest of our world conflicts, the United States had no armaments industry. American makers of plowshares could, with time and as required, make swords as well. But now we can no longer risk emergency improvisation of national defense; we have been compelled to create a permanent armaments industry of vast proportions. Added to this, three and a half million men and women are directly engaged in the defense establishment. We annually spend on military security more than the net income of all United States corporations.

This conjunction of an immense military establishment and a large arms industry is new in the American experience. The total influence—economic, political, even spiritual—is felt in every city, every statehouse, every office of the federal government. We recognize the imperative need for this development. Yet we must not fail to comprehend its grave implications. Our toil, resources, and livelihood are all involved; so is the very structure of our society.

In the councils of government, we must guard against the acquisition of unwarranted influence, whether sought or unsought, by the military-industrial complex. The potential for the disastrous rise of misplaced power exists and will persist.

We must never let the weight of this combination endanger our liberties or democratic processes. We should take nothing for granted. Only an alert and knowledgeable citizenry can compel the proper meshing of the huge industrial and military machinery of defense with our peaceful methods and goals, so that security and liberty may prosper together.

Akin to, and largely responsible for the sweeping changes in our industrial-military posture, has been the technological revolution during recent decades.

In this revolution, research has become central; it also becomes more formalized, complex, and costly. A steadily increasing share is conducted for, by, or at the direction of, the federal government....

The prospect of domination of the nation's scholars by federal employment, project allocations, and the power of money is ever present—and is gravely to be regarded.

Yet, in holding scientific research and discovery in respect, as we should, we must also be alert to the equal and opposite danger that public policy could itself become the captive of a scientific-technological elite.

It is the task of statesmanship to mold, to balance, and to integrate these and other forces, new and old, within the principles of our democratic system—ever aiming toward the supreme goals of our free society.

Another factor in maintaining balance involves the element of time. As we peer into society's future, we—you and I, and our government—must avoid the impulse to live only for today, plundering, for our own ease and convenience, the precious resources of tomorrow. We cannot mortgage the material assets of our grandchildren without risking the loss also of their political and spiritual heritage. We want democracy to survive for all generations to come, not to become the insolvent phantom of tomorrow.

Down the long lane of the history yet to be written America knows that this world of ours, ever growing smaller, must avoid becoming a community of dreadful fear and hate, and be, instead, a proud confederation of mutual trust and respect.

Such a confederation must be one of equals. The weakest must come to the conference table with the same confidence as do we, protected as we are by our moral, economic, and military strength. That table, though scarred by many past frustrations, cannot be abandoned for the certain agony of the battlefield.

Disarmament, with mutual honor and confidence, is a continuing imperative. Together we must learn how to compose differences, not with arms, but with intellect and decent purpose. Because this need is so sharp and apparent I confess that I lay down my official responsibilities in this field with a definite sense of disappointment. As one who has witnessed the horror and the lingering sadness of war—as one who knows that another war could utterly destroy this civilization which has been so slowly and painfully built over thousands of years—I wish I could say tonight that a lasting peace is in sight.

Happily, I can say that war has been avoided. Steady progress toward our ultimate goal has been made. But, so much remains to be done. As a private citizen, I shall never cease to do what little I can to help the world advance along that road....

[From *Public Papers of the Presidents: Dwight D. Eisenhower,* 1960–1961 (Washington, D. C.: U. S. Government Printing Office, 1961), no. 421, pp. 1035–1040]

## Questions for Reflection

Describe the conflict that Eisenhower saw as "now engulfing the world." Why did Eisenhower consider it significant that the United States for the first time had a permanent armaments industry? What dangers did he think the "military-industrial complex" posed? Explain whether or not you agree with Eisenhower's analysis.

## ANSWERS TO MULTIPLE-CHOICE AND TRUE-FALSE QUESTIONS

### Multiple-Choice Questions

1-C, 2-C, 3-B, 4-D, 5-B, 6-B, 7-A, 8-B

### True-False Questions

1-T, 2-F, 3-F, 4-F, 5-F, 6-T, 7-T, 8-F

# 33

# NEW FRONTIERS: KENNEDY AND JOHNSON

## CHAPTER OBJECTIVES

*After you complete the reading and study of this chapter you should be able to*

1. Describe Kennedy's style and compare it to the style of his predecessor and his successor.
2. Assess Kennedy's domestic legislative achievements.
3. Assess the Kennedy record in foreign affairs.
4. Describe and account for LBJ's legislative accomplishments.
5. Explain why the Vietnam War became a quagmire for the United States and why LBJ changed his policy there in 1968.
6. Trace the transformation of the civil rights movement into the black power movement.

## CHAPTER OUTLINE

I. The 1960 election
   A. Nixon's experience
   B. Kennedy's background
   C. Campaign
      1. Televised debates
      2. Results

II. The New Frontier
   A. Start of the administration
      1. Appointments
      2. Inaugural address
   B. Legislative achievements
      1. Urban renewal, minimum wage, social security
      2. Alliance for Progress
      3. Peace Corps
      4. Trade Expansion Act
   C. Civil rights
      1. Kennedy's commitment
      2. Martin Luther King, Jr.
      3. Students and sit-ins
      4. CORE freedom rides
      5. Crisis at University of Mississippi
      6. Birmingham
      7. Wallace and the University of Alabama
      8. March on Washington
   D. Warren Court
      1. School prayer
      2. Rights of defendants

III. Kennedy and foreign affairs
   A. Early setbacks
      1. Bay of Pigs disaster
      2. Vienna summit
      3. Berlin

B. Cuban missile crisis
  1. Causes of crisis
  2. Kennedy's action
  3. Resolution of crisis
  4. Aftereffects
C. Vietnam
  1. Neutrality for Laos
  2. Problems with Diem
  3. Kennedy's reluctance to escalate
  4. Overthrow of Diem

IV. Assassination of President Kennedy
  A. Lee Harvey Oswald
  B. Warren Commission
  C. Continuing controversy

V. Lyndon Johnson and the Great Society
  A. Lyndon Johnson
    1. Personality
    2. Background
      a. Texas
      b. Congress
  B. War on poverty
    1. *The Other America*
    2. 1964 tax cut
    3. Economic Opportunity Act
  C. Election in 1964
    1. Goldwater—choice not echo
    2. LBJ appeals to consensus
    3. Johnson landslide
  D. Landmark legislation
    1. Health insurance
    2. Aid to education
    3. Appalachian redevelopment
    4. Housing and urban development
    5. Immigration Act of 1965
      a. End to national quotas
      b. Influx from Asia and Latin America
  E. Shortcomings of Great Society

VI. From civil rights to black power
  A. Civil Rights Act of 1964
  B. Voting Rights Act of 1965
    1. The Selma march
    2. Provisions of the act
  C. Development of black power
    1. Race riots of 1965 and 1966
    2. Plight of urban blacks
    3. Call for black power
      a. Stokely Carmichael
      b. Black Panther party
      c. Malcolm X
    4. Assessment of black power
      a. Limited appeal
      b. Spurs pride in racial heritage
      c. Prompts new stage in civil rights movement
      d. Backlash

VII. The tragedy of Vietnam
  A. Dimensions of war
    1. Troop commitments
    2. Cost of fighting
  B. Escalation
    1. Gulf of Tonkin Resolution
    2. Bombing and combat troops in 1965
  C. Context for policy
    1. Containment theory
    2. Not an accident
    3. Erosion of support for war
    4. Unity of North Vietnamese
  D. Turning point of the war
    1. Tet offensive
    2. Presidential primaries
    3. LBJ decides not to run

VIII. The crescendo of the sixties
  A. Assassinations in 1968
    1. Martin Luther King, Jr.
    2. Robert F. Kennedy
  B. Election of 1968
    1. Chicago and Miami
    2. George Wallace
    3. Election of Nixon

## KEY ITEMS OF CHRONOLOGY

| | |
|---|---|
| Kennedy administration | 1961–63 |
| Bay of Pigs invasion | April 1961 |
| Freedom rides | May 1961 |
| Cuban missile crisis | October 1963 |
| Overthrow of Ngo Dinh Diem | November 1963 |
| Kennedy assassination | November 22, 1963 |
| Civil Rights Act (public accommodations) | July 1964 |
| Gulf of Tonkin Resolution | August 1964 |

Voting Rights Act — 1965
Tet offensive — January–February 1968
Assassinations of King and Robert Kennedy — 1968

## TERMS TO MASTER

*Listed below are some important terms or people with which you should be familiar after you complete the study of this chapter. Explain the significance of each name or term.*

1. New Frontier
2. Peace Corps
3. Martin Luther King, Jr.
4. SNCC
5. Freedom rides
6. Bay of Pigs invasion
7. Berlin Wall
8. Cuban missile crisis
9. Nuclear Test Ban Treaty
10. Ngo Dinh Diem
11. Great Society
12. *The Other America*
13. Medicare and Medicaid
14. Barry Goldwater
15. Watts riot
16. black power
17. Malcolm X
18. Gulf of Tonkin Resolution
19. Vietcong
20. Tet offensive
21. Eugene McCarthy
22. Robert Kennedy

12. bellicose
13. languish
14. parochial
15. visa
16. stipulate
17. nihilistic
18. hyperbole
19. defoliant
20. quagmire

## EXERCISES FOR UNDERSTANDING

*When you have completed the reading of the chapter, answer each of the following questions. If you have difficulty, go back and reread the section of the chapter related to the question.*

### Multiple-Choice Questions

*Select the letter of the response that best completes the statement.*

1. By 1960 John F. Kennedy had
   A. a long and distinguished political career.
   B. a great reputation as an able legislator.
   C. charm, good looks, wit, and wealth.
   D. all of the above

2. The correct order for events in the civil rights movement is
   A. Montgomery bus boycott, Greensboro sit-ins, freedom rides, and black power.

## VOCABULARY BUILDING

1. trauma
2. introvert
3. intransigence
4. acquiescence
5. martyr
6. paradox
7. guise
8. obstreperous
9. censure
10. impervious
11. feasible

B. freedom rides, Greensboro sit-ins, assassination of King, and Voting Rights Act.
C. Greensboro sit-ins, Montgomery bus boycott, assassination of Malcolm X, and freedom rides.
D. Montgomery bus boycott, black power, Voting Rights Act, and Greensboro sit-ins.

3. In the Cuban missile crisis, President Kennedy ordered
   A. surgical air strikes of Cuba.
   B. a quarantine of Cuba.
   C. the Bay of Pigs invasion.
   D. removal of U.S. missiles from Turkey.

4. By the end of 1963, the United States had sent to Vietnam
   A. only 2,000 military advisers.
   B. more than 15,000 military advisers.
   C. 25,000 fighting troops.
   D. over 100,000 fighting troops.

5. Before becoming vice-president, Lyndon Johnson had been
   A. senate majority leader.
   B. Secretary of State.
   C. governor of Texas.
   D. speaker of the House of Representatives.

6. The Immigration Act of 1965
   A. was the most controversial part of the Great Society.
   B. favored immigrants from western Europe and Britain.
   C. ended national quotas.
   D. discriminated against relatives of citizens.

7. Discrimination in hotels and restaurants was outlawed by
   A. the Supreme Court's *Brown* decision in 1954.
   B. Martin Luther King's "I Have a Dream" speech.
   C. presidential order of Kennedy.
   D. the Civil Rights Act of 1964.

8. Johnson sought to deescalate the Vietnam War because

A. the Tet offensive showed that the U.S. could not win.
B. political challengers showed the high level of public opposition to the war.
C. key national leaders called on him to end the war.
D. of all of the above.

**True-False Questions**

*Indicate whether each statement is true or false.*

1. Nixon's 1960 campaign benefited from his televised debate with Kennedy.
2. In 1962 John Kennedy send United States troops to Mississippi but not to Cuba.
3. Kennedy supported neutrality for Laos.
4. The effects of the 1964 tax cut helped finance the War on Poverty.
5. Lyndon Johnson opposed the Civil Rights Act of 1957.
6. Black power led to greater attention to the plight of the inner-city poor.
7. The first American combat troops went to Vietnam in 1966.
8. The Tet offensive had a great effect on American public opinion.

**Essay Questions**

1. Compare the personalities and backgrounds of Kennedy and Johnson. How did they affect each man's presidency?
2. Assess the successes and failures of JFK's foreign policy.
3. Compare and contrast the achievements of the New Frontier and the Great Society.
4. Trace the changes in United States policy in Vietnam from 1961 to 1968.
5. What was black power, was its origin, and what effect did it have?
6. Account for the election of Richard Nixon in 1968.

# DOCUMENT

## Johnson's Speech on Vietnam, 1965

The speech that follows, given at Johns Hopkins University on April 7, 1965, contains President Johnson's rationale for a critical buildup of American forces in South Vietnam. That year, 1965, proved to be a fateful year for American involvement in Vietnam.

... Over this war, and all Asia, is the deepening shadow of Communist China. The rulers in Hanoi are urged on by Peking. This is a regime which has destroyed freedom in Tibet, attacked India, and been condemned by the United Nations for aggression in Korea. It is a nation which is helping the forces of violence in almost every continent. The contest in Vietnam is part of a wider pattern of aggressive purpose.

Why are these realities our concern? Why are we in South Vietnam? We are there because we have a promise to keep. Since 1954 every American President has offered support to the people of South Vietnam. We have helped to build, and we have helped to defend. Thus, over many years, we have made a national pledge to help South Vietnam defend its independence. And I intend to keep our promise.

To dishonor that pledge, to abandon this small and brave nation to its enemy, and to the terror that must follow, would be an unforgivable wrong.

We are also there to strengthen world order. Around the globe, from Berlin to Thailand, are people whose well-being rests, in part, on the belief that they can count on us if they are attacked. To leave Vietnam to its fate would shake the confidence of all these people in the value of American commitment, the value of America's word. The result would be increased unrest and instability, and even wider war.

We are also there because there are great stakes in the balance. Let no one think for a moment that retreat from Vietnam would bring an end to conflict. The battle would be renewed in one country and then another. The central lesson of our time is that the appetite of aggression is never satisfied. To withdraw from one battlefield means only to prepare for the next. We must say in Southeast Asia, as we did in Europe, in the words of the Bible: "Hitherto shalt thou come, but no further."

There are those who say that all our effort there will be futile, that China's power is such it is bound to dominate all Southeast Asia. But there is no end to that argument until all the nations of Asia are swallowed up.

There are those who wonder why we have a responsibility there. We have it for the same reason we have a responsibility for the defense of freedom in Europe. World War II was fought in both Europe and Asia, and when it ended we found ourselves with continued responsibility for the defense of freedom.

Our objective is the independence of South Vietnam, and its freedom from attack. We want nothing for ourselves, only that the people of South Vietnam be allowed to guide their own country in their own way.

We will do everything necessary to reach that objective. And we will do only what is absolutely necessary.

In recent months, attacks on South Vietnam were stepped up. Thus it became necessary to increase our response and to make attacks by air. This is not a change of purpose. It is a change in what we believe that purpose requires.

We do this in order to slow down aggression.

We do this to increase the confidence of the brave people of South Vietnam who have bravely borne this brutal battle for so many years and with so many casualties.

And we do this to convince the leaders of North Vietnam, and all who seek to share their conquest, of a very simple fact:

We will not be defeated.

We will not grow tired.

We will not withdraw, either openly or under the cloak of a meaningless agreement. . . .

Once this is clear, then it should also be clear that the only path for reasonable men is the path of peaceful settlement.

Such peace demands an independent South Vietnam securely guaranteed and able to shape its own relationships to all others, free from outside interference, tied to no alliance, a military base for no other country.

These are the essentials of any final settlement.

We will never be second in the search for such a peaceful settlement in Vietnam.

There may be many ways to this kind of peace: in discussion or negotiation with the governments concerned; in large groups or in small ones; in the reaffirmation of old agreements or their strengthening with new ones.

We have stated this position over and over again fifty times and more, to friend and foe alike. And we remain ready, with this purpose, for unconditional discussions.

And until that bright and necessary day of peace we will try to keep conflict from spreading. We have no desire to see thousands die in battle, Asians or Americans. We have no desire to devastate that which the people of North Vietnam have built with toil and sacrifice. We will use our power with restraint and with all the wisdom we can command. But we will use it. . . .

We will always oppose the effort of one nation to conquer another nation.

We will do this because our own security is at stake.

But there is more to it than that. For our generation has a dream. It is a very old dream. But we have the power and now we have the opportunity to make it come true.

For centuries, nations have struggled among each other. But we dream of a world where disputes are settled by law and reason. And we will try to make it so.

For most of history men have hated and killed one another in battle. But we dream of an end to war. And we will try to make it so.

For all existence most men have lived in poverty, threatened by hunger. But we dream of a world where all are fed and charged with hope. And we will help to make it so.

The ordinary men and women of North Vietnam and South Vietnam—of China and India—of Russia and America—are brave people. They are filled with the same proportions of hate and fear, of love and hope. Most of them want the same things for themselves and their families. Most of them do not want their sons ever to die in battle, or see the homes of others destroyed. . . .

Every night before I turn out the lights to sleep, I ask myself this question: Have I done everything that I can do to unite this country? Have I done everything I can to help unite the world, to try to bring peace and hope to all the peoples of the world? Have I done enough?

Ask yourselves that question in your homes and in this hall tonight. Have we done all we could? Have we done enough? . . .

[*Department of State Bulletin*, April 26, 1965 (Washington, D. C.: U. S. Government Printing Office, 1940– )]

## Questions for Reflection

Compare Lyndon Johnson's address to Franklin Roosevelt's "Four Freedoms" speech of January 1941 in Chapter 28. To what extent were they concerned about the same kinds of threats? Was Johnson correct in drawing parallels between events in Vietnam and events in Europe before World War II? What similarities and differences do you see? What is your view of the policy Johnson outlines here?

## ANSWERS TO MULTIPLE-CHOICE AND TRUE-FALSE QUESTIONS

### Multiple-Choice Questions

1-C, 2-A, 3-B, 4-B, 5-A, 6-C, 7-D, 8-D

### True-False Questions

1-F, 2-T, 3-T, 4-T, 5-F, 6-T, 7-F, 8-T

# 34

## REBELLION AND REACTION IN THE SEVENTIES

### CHAPTER OBJECTIVES

*After you complete the reading and study of this chapter you should be able to*

1. Account for the rise and decline of New Left protests.
2. Describe the counterculture and its impact.
3. Trace the reform movements for women, Hispanics, Indians, and gays.
4. Explain Nixon's aims in Vietnam.
5. Assess the impact of the Vietnam War on American society, military morale, and later foreign policy.
6. Explain Nixon's goals in domestic policy and account for his limited accomplishments.
7. Explain the problems plaguing the United States economy in the 1970s, and describe the various cures Nixon tried.
8. Describe Nixon's foreign policy triumphs in China and the Soviet Union, and explain their significance.
9. Discuss the Watergate cover-up and account for the difficulty in unraveling it.
10. Describe the brief presidency of Gerald Ford.
11. Assess the Carter administration's successes and failures.

### CHAPTER OUTLINE

I. Youth revolt
   A. Baby boomers as young adults
   B. Sit-ins and end of apathy

II. New Left
   A. Students for a Democratic Society
      1. Port Huron Statement
      2. Participatory democracy
   B. Free Speech movement
      1. Berkeley
      2. Quality of campus life
   C. Antiwar protests
   D. Growing militance
   E. 1968
      1. Columbia University uprising
      2. Democratic convention in Chicago
      3. Fracturing of SDS

III. Counterculture
   A. Descendants of the Beats
   B. Contrast with New Left
   C. Drugs, communes, hedonism
   D. Rock music
      1. Woodstock
      2. Altamont

IV. Feminism
   A. Betty Friedan's *Feminine Mystique*

    B. National Organization of Women
    C. Federal actions
        1. Affirmative action
        2. *Roe v. Wade*
        3. Equal Rights Amendment's failure
    D. Divisions and reactions
V. Minorities
    A. Hispanic rights
        1. Effects of World War II
        2. Activism in 1950s and 1960s
        3. Use of term *Chicano*
        4. United Farm Workers
            a. César Chávez
            b. Migrant workers
            c. Grape strike and boycott
        5. Growth of population
        6. Electoral successes
    B. American Indians
        1. Emergence of Indian rights
        2. American Indian Movement
        3. Legal actions
VI. Gay rights
    A. Stonewall Inn raid
    B. Gay Liberation Front
    C. Gay rights movement
    D. AIDS
VII. "Silent majority"
VIII. Nixon and Vietnam
    A. The policy of gradual withdrawal
    B. Movement on three fronts
        1. Insistence on Communist withdrawal from South Vietnam
        2. Efforts to undercut unrest in the United States
            a. Troop reductions
            b. Lottery and volunteer army
        3. Expanded air war
    C. Occasions for public outcry against the war
        1. My Lai massacre
        2. Cambodian "incursion"
            a. Campus riots
            b. Public reaction
        3. *Pentagon Papers*
            a. Method of disclosure
            b. Revelations of the papers
            c. Supreme Court ruling
    D. American withdrawal
        1. Kissinger's efforts before the 1972 election
        2. The Christmas bombings
        3. Final acceptance of peace
        4. U.S. withdrawal in March 1973
    E. Ultimate victory of the North: March–April 1975
    F. Assessment of the war
        1. Communist control
        2. Failure to transfer democracy
        3. Erosion of respect for the military
        4. Drastic division of the American people
        5. Impact on future foreign policy
IX. Nixon and Middle America
    A. A reflection of Middle American values
    B. Domestic affairs
        1. Continuance of civil rights progress
            a. Voting Rights Act continued over a veto
            b. Courts uphold integration
                i. In Mississippi
                ii. School busing
                iii. Limitation on busing
                iv. The Bakke decision
        2. Revenue sharing
        3. Other domestic legislation
    C. The economic malaise
        1. The causes of "stagflation"
        2. Nixon's efforts to improve the economy
            a. Reducing the federal deficit
            b. Reducing the money supply
            c. Wage and price controls
X. Nixon's foreign triumphs
    A. Rapprochement with China
    B. Détente with the Soviet Union
        1. The visit to Moscow
        2. The SALT agreement
    C. Kissinger's shuttle diplomacy in the Middle East
XI. The election of 1972
    A. Removal of the Wallace threat
    B. The McGovern candidacy
    C. Results of the election
XII. Watergate
    A. Unraveling the cover-up
        1. Judge Sirica's role
        2. Nixon's personal role
        3. April resignations
        4. Discovery of the tapes
        5. The Saturday Night Massacre

                6. The Court decides against the president
                7. Articles of impeachment
                8. The resignation
            B. The aftermath of Watergate
                1. Ford's selection
                2. The Nixon pardon
                3. Resiliency of American institutions
                4. War Powers Act
                5. Campaign financing legislation
                6. Freedom of Information Act
XIII. An Unelected President
        A. Ford administration
            1. Drift at the end of Nixon administration
            2. Battle with the economy
            3. Diplomatic accomplishments
        B. Election of 1976
            1. Ford's nomination
            2. Rise of Jimmy Carter
            3. Carter's victory
XIV. Carter presidency
        A. Early domestic moves
            1. Appointments
            2. Amnesty for draft dodgers
            3. Environmental legislation
            4. Energy crisis
            5. Crisis of confidence
        B. Foreign policy initiatives
            1. Human rights
            2. Panama Canal treaties
            3. Camp David Agreement
        C. Troubles
            1. Stagflation
            2. SALT II Treaty
            3. Soviet invasion of Afghanistan
        D. Iranian crisis
            1. Background
            2. Efforts to aid hostages
            3. End of 444-day crisis

## KEY ITEMS OF CHRONOLOGY

| | |
|---|---|
| Port Huron Statement | 1962 |
| Betty Friedan's *Feminine Mystique* | 1963 |
| NOW founded | 1966 |
| My Lai massacre | 1968 |
| Stonewall Inn riot | 1969 |
| Woodstock music festival | 1969 |
| Cambodian "incursion" | April 1970 |
| *Swann v. Charlotte-Mecklenburg Board of Education* | 1971 |
| *Pentagon Papers* published | June 1971 |
| *Roe v. Wade* | 1972 |
| Nixon's visit to China | February 1972 |
| SALT agreement signed | May 1972 |
| Watergate break-in occurs | June 1972 |
| Last American troops leave Vietnam | March 1973 |
| War Powers Act | 1973 |
| Nixon's resignation | Aug. 9, 1974 |
| South Vietnam falls to the North | April 1975 |
| *Bakke v. Board of Regents of California* | 1978 |

## TERMS TO MASTER

*Listed below are some important terms or people with which you should be familiar after you complete the study of this chapter. Explain the significance of each name or term.*

1. New Left
2. SDS
3. participatory democracy
4. Free Speech movement
5. Weathermen
6. counterculture
7. Betty Friedan
8. NOW
9. Equal Rights Amendment
10. Chicano
11. AIDS
12. *Pentagon Papers*
13. *Swann v. Charlotte-Mecklenburg Board of Education*
14. *Bakke v. Board of Regents of California*
15. revenue sharing
16. Spiro Agnew
17. OPEC
18. SALT
19. George McGovern
20. Watergate
21. Saturday Night Massacre
22. Henry Kissinger
23. War Powers Act

## VOCABULARY BUILDING

*Listed below are some words used in this chapter. Look up each word in your dictionary.*

1. hierarchical
2. precipitate
3. manifesto
4. ransack
5. disaffected
6. utopian
7. bastion
8. connotation
9. recalcitrant
10. fracas
11. fractious
12. chauvinist
13. incursion
14. contingency
15. poignant
16. ignoble
17. eunuch
18. effete
19. impudent
20. malaise

## EXERCISES FOR UNDERSTANDING

*When you have completed reading the chapter, answer each of the following questions. If you have difficulty, go back and reread the section of the chapter related to the question.*

## Multiple-Choice Questions

*Select the letter of the response that best completes the statement.*

1. The leaders of the New Left included
   A. Tom Hayden and Mark Rudd.
   B. Abbie Hoffman and César Chávez.
   C. Richard Daley and Spiro Agnew.
   D. Timothy Leary and Richie Havens.

2. Betty Friedan launched the women's movement with claims that women
   A. were too educated to dabble in politics.
   B. deserved equality with men in all areas.
   C. should be permitted to serve in the armed forces.
   D. were bored with housework and child care.

3. César Chávez had his most notable success in
   A. protesting against immigration laws.
   B. leading a boycott of grapes.
   C. organizing lettuce workers.
   D. running for the U.S. Congress.

4. The Stonewall Inn riot of 1969 involved
   A. free speech on college campuses.
   B. the Vietnam war.
   C. gay rights.
   D. none of the above.

5. Nixon sought to lessen criticism of the Vietnam War by
   A. slowly reducing the number of American troops there.
   B. creating a lottery to determine who would be drafted.
   C. using more air strikes rather than ground warfare.
   D. all of the above methods.

6. The greatest protests against Nixon's Vietnam policy came after
   A. the Cambodian incursion.

B. he pardoned Lt. William Calley.
C. the start of the draft lottery.
D. the publication of *The Pentagon Papers*.

7. The Nixon administration's civil rights policies included
   A. endorsement of the Voting Rights Act.
   B. opposition to school busing.
   C. support for school integration.
   D. sending troops to support integration of Boston schools.

8. Carter's most significant accomplishment in foreign policy was
   A. retaining complete control over the Panama Canal.
   B. an agreement with OPEC on oil prices.
   C. opposition to Soviet invasion of Afghanistan.
   D. a treaty between Israel and Egypt.

## True-False Questions

*Indicate whether each statement is true or false.*

1. Participatory democracy was one of the ideals of the counterculture.
2. Betty Friedan wrote *The Feminine Mystique*.
3. The Stonewall Inn riot was a key event in the Chicano rights movement.
4. Nixon used wage and price controls to stem inflation.
5. The War Powers Act requires a president to withdraw troops sent abroad after sixty days unless Congress specifically authorizes a longer stay.
6. Gerald Ford called the fight against inflation "the moral equivalent of war."
7. Carter stressed a foreign policy of pragmatism rather than supporting a policy based on fixed principle.
8. The shah's secret police masterminded the seizure of Americans in Teheran in 1979.

## Essay Questions

1. Did the New Left or the counterculture have the greater impact on American society? Explain.
2. How the civil rights movement affect women, Chicanos, homosexuals, and Indians?
3. What was Nixon's Vietnam policy and was it successful?
4. Discuss the impact of the Vietnam War on American society.
5. How did Nixon try to appeal to the "silent majority" with his domestic policies? Did he succeed?
6. How important were Nixon's diplomatic achievements with China and Russia? Could a Democrat have achieved the same gains? Explain.
7. Explain the Watergate controversy and Nixon's involvement in it.
8. Jimmy Carter has often been viewed as an unsuccessful president. Was his failure caused by his personal shortcomings or by the times in which he served?

## DOCUMENTS

### Document 1. The Charges against Nixon

When the House Judiciary Committee completed its investigation and voted the impeachment of Nixon in July 1974, three articles obtained a majority vote of the committee. Those three articles are excerpted here.

> Article I. In his conduct of the office of President of the United States, Richard M. Nixon, in violation of his constitutional oath faithfully to execute the office of President of the United States and, to the best of his ability, preserve, protect, and defend the Constitution

of the United States, and in violation of his constitutional duty to take care that the laws be faithfully executed, has prevented, obstructed, and impeded the administration of justice, . . . Richard M. Nixon, using the powers of his high office, engaged personally and through his subordinates and agents, in a course of conduct or plan designed to delay, impede, and obstruct the investigation of such unlawful entry; to cover up, conceal and protect those responsible; and to conceal the existence and scope of other unlawful covert activities. . . .

Article II. . . . Richard M. Nixon . . . has repeatedly engaged in conduct violating the constitutional rights of citizens, impairing the due and proper administration of justice and the conduct of lawful inquiries, or contravening the laws governing agencies of the executive branch and the purpose of these agencies. . . .

Article III. Richard M. Nixon, contrary to his oath faithfully to execute the office of President of the United States . . . has failed without lawful cause or excuse to produce papers and things as directed by duly authorized subpoenas issued by the Committee on the Judiciary of the House of Representatives on April 11, 1974, May 15, 1974, May 30, 1974, and June 24, 1974, and willfully disobeying such subpoenas. . . . In refusing to produce these papers and things, Richard M. Nixon, substituting his judgment as to what materials were necessary for the inquiry, interposed the powers of the Presidency against the lawful subpoenas of the House of Representatives, thereby assuming to himself functions and judgments necessary to the exercise of the sole power of impeachment vested by the Constitution in the House of Representatives.

[U.S. Congress, House of Representatives, *Report of the Committee on the Judiciary,* 93rd Cong., 2d sess., 1974.]

## Document 2. Senator Sam Ervin Explains the Meaning and Consequences of Watergate

Prior to the report quoted above, the Ervin Committee of the Senate had throughout the summer of 1973 treated the American public to weeks of televised hearings at which various Watergate conspirators had testified about the labyrinthine developments of the Watergate affair. In June 1974, shortly before the House Judiciary Committee moved to impeach Nixon, the Ervin Committee made its report. Accompanying the report was a statement from Senator Ervin in which he tried to summarize the Watergate episode in a few paragraphs. Because the report was made prior to the House committee's decision to move toward impeachment of the president, Ervin began his report with a disclaimer to indicate that he was not trying to pass judgment on the president's guilt in the matter. His report is a succinct statement of the Watergate affair and a comment on its implications for the future.

I am not undertaking to usurp and exercise the power of impeachment, which the Constitution confers upon the House of Representatives alone. As a consequence, nothing I say should be construed as an expression of an opinion in respect to the question of whether or not President Nixon is impeachable in connection with the Watergate or any other matter. . . .

I shall also refrain from making any comment on the question of whether or not the President has performed in an acceptable manner his paramount constitutional obligation "to take care that the laws be faithfully executed."

Watergate was not invented by enemies of the Nixon administration or even by the news media. On the contrary, Watergate was perpetrated upon America by White House and political aides, whom President Nixon himself had entrusted with the management of his campaign for reelection to the Presidency, a campaign which was divorced to a marked degree from the campaigns of other Republicans who sought election to public office in 1972. I note at this point without elaboration that these White House and political aides were virtually without experience in either Government or politics apart from their association with President Nixon.

5. Watergate was without precedent in the political annals of America in respect to the scope and intensity of its unethical and illegal actions. To be sure, there had been previous milder political scandals in American history. That fact does not excuse Watergate. Murder and stealing have occurred in every generation since Earth began, but that fact has not made murder meritorious or larceny legal.

## What Was Watergate?

Watergate was a conglomerate of various illegal and unethical activities in which various officers and employees of the Nixon reelection committee and various White House aides of President Nixon participated in varying ways and degrees to accomplish these successive objectives:

1. To destroy, insofar as the Presidential election of 1972 was concerned, the integrity of the process by which the President of the United States is nominated and elected.

2. To hide from law enforcement officers, prosecutors, grand jurors, courts, the news media, and the American people the identities and wrongdoing of those officers and employees of the Nixon reelection committees, and those White House aides who had undertaken to destroy the integrity of the process by which the President of the United States is nominated and elected.

To accomplish the first of these objectives. . . .

1. They exacted enormous contributions—usually in cash—from corporate executives by impliedly implanting in their minds the impressions that the making of the contributions was necessary to insure that the corporations would receive governmental favors, or avoid governmental disfavors, while President Nixon remained in the White House. A substantial portion of the contributions were made out of corporate funds in violation of a law enacted by Congress a generation ago.

2. They hid substantial parts of these contributions in cash in safes and safe deposits to conceal their sources and the identities of those who had made them.

3. They disbursed substantial portions of these hidden contributions in a surreptitious manner to finance the bugging and the burglary of the offices of the Democratic National Committee in the Watergate complex in Washington. . . .

4. They deemed the departments and agencies of the Federal Government to be the political playthings of the Nixon administration rather than impartial instruments for serving the people, and undertook to induce them to channel Federal contracts, grants, and

loans to areas, groups, or individuals so as to promote the reelection of the President rather than to further the welfare of the people.

5. They branded as enemies of the President individuals and members of the news media who dissented from the President's policies and opposed his reelection, and conspired to urge the Department of Justice, the Federal Bureau of Investigation, the Internal Revenue Service, and the Federal Communications Commission to pervert the use of their legal powers to harass them for so doing.

6. They borrowed from the Central Intelligence Agency disguises which E. Howard Hunt used in political espionage operations, and photographic equipment which White House employees known as the "Plumbers" and their hired confederates used in connection with burglarizing the office of a psychiatrist which they believed contained information concerning Daniel Ellsberg which the White House was anxious to secure.

7. They assigned to E. Howard Hunt, who was at the time a White House consultant occupying an office in the Executive Office Building, the gruesome task of falsifying State Department documents which they contemplated using in their altered state to discredit the Democratic Party by defaming the memory of former President John Fitzgerald Kennedy, who as the hapless victim of an assassin's bullet had been sleeping in the tongueless silence of the dreamless dust for 9 years.

8. They used campaign funds to hire saboteurs to forge and disseminate false and scurrilous libels of honorable men running for the Democratic Presidential nomination in Democratic Party primaries.

During the darkness of the early morning of June 17, 1972, James W. McCord, the security chief of the John Mitchell committee, and four residents of Miami, Fla., were arrested by Washington police while they were burglarizing the offices of the Democratic National Committee in the Watergate complex to obtain political intelligence....

The arrest of McCord and the four residents of Miami created consternation in the Nixon reelection committees and the White House.... various White House aides undertook to conceal from law enforcement officers, prosecutors, grand jurors, courts, the news media, and the American people the identities and activities of those officers and employees of the Nixon reelection committee and those White House aides who had participated in any way in the Watergate affair....

1. They destroyed the records of the Nixon reelection committee antedating the bugging and the burglary.

2. They induced the Acting Director of the FBI, who was a Nixon appointee, to destroy the State Department documents which E. Howard Hunt had been falsifying.

3. They obtained from the Acting Director of the FBI copies of the scores of interviews conducted by the FBI agents in connection with their investigation of the bugging and the burglary, and were enabled thereby to coach their confederates to give false and misleading statements to the FBI.

4. They sought to persuade the FBI to refrain from investigating the sources of the campaign funds which were used to finance the bugging and the burglary.

5. They intimidated employees of the Nixon reelection committees and employees of the White House by having their lawyers present when these employees were being questioned by agents of the FBI, and thus deterred these employees from making full disclosures to the FBI.

6. They lied to agents of the FBI, prosecutors, and grand jurors who undertook to investigate the bugging and the burglary, and to Judge Sirica and the petit jurors who tried the seven original Watergate defendants in January, 1973.

7. They persuaded the Department of Justice and the prosecutors to take out-of-court statements from Maurice Stans, President Nixon's chief campaign fundraiser, and Charles Colson, Egil Krogh, and David Young, White House aides, and Charles Colson's secretary, instead of requiring them to testify before the grand jury investigating the bugging and the burglary in conformity with established procedures governing such matters, and thus denied the grand jurors the opportunity to question them.

8. They persuaded the Department of Justice and the prosecutors to refrain from asking Donald Segretti, their chief hired saboteur, any questions involving Herbert W. Kalmbach, the President's personal attorney, who was known by them to have paid Segretti for dirty tricks he perpetrated upon honorable men seeking the Democratic Presidential nomination. . . .

9. They made cash payments totaling hundreds of thousands of dollars out of campaign funds in surreptitious ways to the seven original Watergate defendants as hush money to buy their silence. . . .

10. They gave assurances to some of the original seven defendants that they would receive Presidential clemency after serving short portions of their sentences if they refrained from divulging the identities and activities of the officers and employees of the Nixon reelection committees and the White House aides who had participated in the Watergate affair.

11. They made arrangements by which the attorneys who represented the seven original Watergate defendants received their fees in cash from moneys which had been collected to finance President Nixon's reelection campaign.

12. They induced the Department of Justice and the prosecutors of the seven original Watergate defendants to assure the news media and the general public that there was no evidence that any persons other than the seven original Watergate defendants were implicated in any way in the Watergate-related crimes.

13. They inspired massive efforts on the part of segments of the news media friendly to the administration to persuade the American people that most of the members of the Select Committee named by the Senate to investigate the Watergate were biased and irresponsible men motivated solely by desires to exploit the matters they investigated for personal or partisan advantage. . . .

One shudders to think that the Watergate conspiracies might have been effectively concealed and their most dramatic episode might have been dismissed as a "third-rate" burglary conceived and committed solely by the seven original Watergate defendants had it not been for the courage and penetrating understanding of Judge Sirica, the thoroughness of the investigative reporting of Carl Bernstein, Bob Woodward, and the other representatives of the free press, the labors of the Senate Select Committee and its excellent staff, and the dedication and diligence of Special Prosecutors Archibald Cox and Leon Jarworski and their associates.

## Why Was Watergate?

Unlike the men who were responsible for Teapot Dome, the Presidential aides who perpetrated Watergate were not seduced by the love of money, which is sometimes thought to be the root of all evil. On the contrary, they were instigated by a lust for political power, which is at least as corrupting as political power itself. . . .

They knew that the power they enjoyed would be lost and the policies to which they adhered would be frustrated if the President should be defeated.

As a consequence of these things, they believed the President's re-election to be a most worthy objective, and succumbed to an age-old temptation. They resorted to evil means to promote what they conceived to be a good end.

Their lust for political power blinded them to ethical considerations and legal requirements; to Aristotle's aphorism that the good of man must be the end of politics; and to Grover Cleveland's conviction that a public office is a public trust.

They had forgotten, if they ever knew, that the Constitution is designed to be a law for rulers and people alike at all times and under all circumstances; and that no doctrine involving more pernicious consequences to the commonweal has ever been invented by the wit of man than the notion that any of its provisions can be suspended by the President for any reason whatsoever.

On the contrary, they apparently believed that the President is above the Constitution, and has the autocratic power to suspend its provisions if he decides in his own unreviewable judgment that his action in so doing promotes his own political interests or the welfare of the Nation. . . .

## The Antidote for Future Watergates

Is there an antidote which will prevent future Watergates? If so, what is it? . . .

Candor compels the confession . . . that law alone will not suffice to prevent future Watergates. . . .

Law is not self-executing. Unfortunately, at times its execution rests in the hands of those who are faithless to it. And even when its enforcement is committed to those who revere it, law merely deters some human beings from offending, and punishes other human beings for offending. It does not make men good. This task can be performed only by ethics or religion or morality. . . .

When all is said, the only sure antidote for future Watergates is understanding of fundamental principles and intellectual and moral integrity in the men and women who achieve or are entrusted with governmental political power.

[U.S. Congress, Senate, Select Committee on Presidential Campaign Activities, *Final Report*, 93rd Cong., 2d sess., 1974, pp. 1097–1103]

## Questions for Reflection

The United States Constitution in Article II, Section 4, states that the president "shall be removed from office on impeachment for, and on conviction of, treason, bribery, or other high crimes and misdemeanors." Do you consider the crimes of which Nixon was accused impeachable offenses? Why or why not?

Why was Ervin so careful to disavow any indictment of the president in his report? Based on the charges of the House Rules Committee in Document 1, which of the actions attributed to others by Ervin might have been charged to the president also?

Who benefited from the Watergate crimes? Were monetary considerations at the heart of the Watergate crimes? Is a president who is dutifully exercising his responsibilities "above the Constitution" with the power to suspend its provisions when he needs to do so? Explain.

What and/or who does Ervin credit with bringing the Watergate conspirators to justice? What does the case suggest about the need for an independent judiciary and a free press? How do you react to Ervin's prescription for preventing future Watergates?

## ANSWERS TO MULTIPLE-CHOICE AND TRUE-FALSE QUESTIONS

### Multiple-Choice Questions

1-A, 2-D, 3-B, 4-C, 5-D, 6-A, 7-B, 8-D

### True-False Questions

1-F, 2-T, 3-F, 4-T, 5-T, 6-F, 7-T, 8-F

# 35

## A NEW GILDED AGE

## CHAPTER OBJECTIVES

1. Explain the popular appeal of Ronald Reagan.
2. Evaluate Ronald Reagan's economic policies.
3. Understand why commentators perceived the Reagan-Bush years as self-interested and greedy.
4. Discuss the U.S. role in Central America in the 1980s.
5. Assess the Iran-Contra affair.
6. Explain the economic difficulties of the Reagan-Bush era.
7. Describe the decline of communism in Europe in the late 1980s.
8. Discuss the causes and events of the Gulf War.

## CHAPTER OUTLINE

I. Election of Reagan
   A. California background
      1. Hollywood actor
      2. Spokesman for GE
      3. Liberal to conservative
      4. Conservative governor
   B. Political rise of Reagan
      1. Demographic changes
         a. Older population
         b. Growth of Sunbelt
      2. Religious revival
         a. Fundamentalism
         b. "Moral Majority"
         c. Traditional values
      3. Backlash against feminism
         a. Phyllis Schlafly and anti-ERA movement
         b. Anti-abortion movement
   C. Election of 1980
      1. Carter's decline
      2. Reagan's promises
      3. Reagan's victory
      4. Voter apathy
      5. Democrats' declining appeal
II. Reagan's first term
   A. Reaganomics
      1. "Government is the problem"
      2. Tax cuts
      3. Budget deficits
      4. Expenditures slashed
      5. 1982 tax increase
   B. Conflicts of interest
   C. Effects of social policies
      1. Labor unions
      2. Feminism
      3. Minorities
   D. Foreign affairs in the 1980s
      1. Reagan's anti-communism
      2. Military buildup
      3. Emphasis on Central America
         a. El Salvador

           b. Nicaragua
              i. Sandinistas
              ii. Contras
        4. Middle East
           a. Iran-Iraq war
           b. Lebanon, PLO, Israel
        5. Grenada
   III. Reagan's second term
      A. Election of 1984
         1. Economic recovery
         2. Mondale and taxes
         3. Landslide and its dangers
      B. Tax reform of 1986
      C. Arms control
         1. Obstacle of Strategic Defense Initiative ("Star Wars")
         2. Meetings with Gorbachev
      D. Decline in Reagan's popularity
         1. 1986 elections
         2. Revelations of "Irangate"
      E. Iran-Contra scandal
         1. Arms for hostages
         2. Profits to Contras
         3. North, Poindexter, McFarlane, Casey
         4. Congressional investigation
         5. Tower Commission
         6. Special prosecutor and indictments
      F. Troubles in Latin America
         1. Nicaraguan Contras
         2. Electoral defeat in El Salvador
         3. General Manuel Noriega in Panama
      G. Economic difficulties
         1. Soaring debt
         2. Stock market collapse
         3. Fear of recession
      H. INF agreement
      I. Reagan legacy
   IV. The Bush years
      A. 1988 election
         1. Michael Dukakis
         2. George Bush
         3. Mudslinging
         4. Results
      B. Tone of the Bush administration
      C. Domestic policies
         1. Economic problems
            a. Savings and loan crisis
            b. Budget deficits
            c. Tax increases and spending cuts
         2. Social issues
            a. AIDS
            b. Flag burning
            c. War on drug abuse
            d. The "underclass"
      D. Foreign affairs after the Cold War
         1. Democratic movements
            a. China
            b. Eastern Europe
            c. Soviet Union
            d. Mongolia
            e. Chile
            f. South Africa
         2. Dissolution of the Soviet Union
            a. August 18, 1991, cabal
            b. Rise of Yeltsin
            c. Independent republics
            d. Communist party dissolved
            e. Reduction of nuclear weapons
         3. Panama
            a. Manuel Noriega and drugs
            b. U.S. invasion
            c. Surrender of Noriega
      E. The Gulf War
         1. Iraq-Kuwait tension
         2. Iraq invasion of Kuwait
         3. U.N. resolutions 661 and 678
         4. Desert Shield
         5. Congressional debate
         6. Desert Storm
         7. Cease-fire
         8. Civil war
         9. American public reaction

## KEY ITEMS OF CHRONOLOGY

| | |
|---|---|
| Reagan presidency | 1981–1989 |
| Economic Recovery Tax Act | August 1981 |
| Attack on U.S. Marines in Beirut | October 1983 |
| Invasion of Grenada | October 1983 |

| | |
|---|---|
| Explosion of the *Challenger* | January 1986 |
| Tax Reform Act | September 1986 |
| Stock market plunge | October 1987 |
| INF Treaty | December 1987 |
| Tiananmen Square demonstrations | June 1989 |
| Fall of the Berlin Wall | November 1989 |
| Iraq invades Kuwait | August 1990 |
| Operation Desert Storm | January–February 1991 |
| Parts of former Soviet Union become Commonwealth of Independent States | December 1991 |

## TERMS TO MASTER

*Listed below are some important terms or people with which you should be familiar after you complete the study of this chapter. Identify each name or term.*

1. "Moral Majority"
2. stagflation
3. Reaganomics
4. "boll weevils"
5. contras
6. sleaze factor
7. Walter Mondale
8. Strategic Defense Initiative
9. Iran-Contra affair
10. Lieutenant-Colonel Oliver North
11. Tower Commission
12. AIDS
13. yuppies
14. Resolution Trust Corporation
15. *perestroika*
16. *glasnost*
17. Mikhail Gorbachev
18. Boris Yeltsin
19. Manuel Noriega
20. Saddam Hussein
21. Desert Shield
22. Desert Storm

## VOCABULARY BUILDING

*Listed below are some words used in this chapter. Look in the dictionary for the meaning of each.*

1. stagnate
2. enamored
3. provincial
4. pagan
5. fissure
6. galvanize
7. allure
8. strident
9. castigate
10. modicum
11. impede
12. countervailing
13. chide
14. winnow
15. gaggle
16. desecrate
17. interdiction
18. apartheid
19. careen
20. cabal

## EXERCISES FOR UNDERSTANDING

*When you have completed the reading of the chapter, answer each of the following questions. If you have difficulty, go back and reread the section of the chapter related to the question.*

### Multiple-Choice Questions

*Select the letter of the response that best completes the statement.*

1. President Reagan's economic achievements included
   A. balancing the federal budget.
   B. reducing the number of Americans living below the poverty level.
   C. raising taxes by $100 million in 1982.
   D. cutting defense expenditures.

2. By 1983, President Reagan had
   A. doubled the federal debt.
   B. endorsed the Equal Rights Amendment.
   C. yielded to the air traffic controllers' union.
   D. all of the above.

3. The Iran-Contra affair involved
   A. selling arms for hostages in Iran.
   B. Lieutenant-Colonel Oliver North.
   C. secretly supporting rebels in Nicaragua.
   D. all of the above.

4. The savings and loan crisis was caused by
   A. excessive regulation by the government.
   B. high-risk investments other than residential real estate.
   C. low inflation and falling interest rates.
   D. the stock market crash.

5. In 1987, Reagan signed a treaty with Gorbachev
   A. restricting biological and chemical warfare.
   B. eliminating intermediate-range nuclear weapons.
   C. ending the controversy over Afghanistan.
   D. settling the dispute between Israel and Lebanon.

6. In fighting Iraq in "Desert Storm," the Bush administration
   A. had the support of the United Nations in resolution 678.
   B. used 400,000 American troops.
   C. was assisted by forces from more than twenty other nations.
   D. all of the above.

7. "The Cold War is behind us now. Let us not wrangle over who won it," said
   A. Ronald Reagan.
   B. Ross Perot.
   C. George Bush.
   D. Mikhail Gorbachev.

8. In 1989
   A. communist rule ended in most of Eastern Europe.
   B. the Berlin Wall came down.
   C. Soviet troops withdrew from Afghanistan.
   D. all of the above.

**True-False Questions**

*Indicate whether each statement is true or false.*

1. One leader of the backlash against feminism was Phyllis Schlafly.
2. In Nicaragua the Reagan administration supported the Contras.
3. On October 19, 1987, the Dow Jones Industrial Average soared in response to the successful invasion of Grenada.
4. The income of the lowest 10 percent of American families stayed the same between 1977 and 1987.
5. The Iran-Contra affair involved using Sandinistas to fight Saddam Hussein.
6. In the White House, President Bush replaced Truman's picture with one of Coolidge.
7. The U.S. invaded Panama in 1989 to help Manuel Noriega.
8. The Bush White House was known as the "Teflon Presidency."

**Essay Questions**

1. What actions did Reagan and Bush take in Central America?
2. What was "Reaganomics"? Describe its successes and failures.
3. Explain why some people consider the Reagan-Bush administrations a time of greed and corruption throughout American life.
4. Why was the Iran-Contra affair significant?
5. Where did democratic movements emerge after the end of the Cold War? Assess their significance.
6. Describe the background of the Gulf War of 1990–1991.
7. Explain why some social scientists draw comparisons between the 1950s and the 1980s in America.
8. What were the successes and shortcomings of the Bush administration?

# DOCUMENTS

## Document 1. The Moral Majority from a Liberal Christian Point of View

The following excerpt from the *Christian Century* describes several fundamentalist Christian organizations, including the Moral Majority, from a more liberal or mainline Christian perspective.

They [Fundamentalist Christian organizations] share a number of core propositions. The first is that sin and its symptoms are dangerously real in this country. America is suffering from moral decay which, if not stopped, will result in the fall of the country and the rise of atheistic dictatorships. The signs of decay are everywhere: abortion on demand, equal rights for homosexuals, pornography, feminism and drugs, to name but a few. These symptoms, they contend, stem from the philosophy of secular humanism, which holds that God is dead, that people must establish their own moral order, and that individual pleasure is the highest goal.

Furthermore, say these fundamentalist Christians, internal decline is causing the U.S. to lose its position in the world. This nation is a chosen instrument of God, and it carries the major responsibility of implementing God's will in the world....

There is a strong conviction that America's prosperity has resulted from its Christian character: faithfulness to God brings material rewards, and "righteousness exalts a nation."...

Next, these interests see the world divided into two main camps. One is the U.S. and its allies—including Israel as God's biblically chosen people—and the other is the godless force of communism, which satanically seeks the total overthrow of the United States. The constant struggle against communism requires the U.S. to maintain its military strength at all times.

Distinct ideas about the role of government in society are also put forward. Reflecting their conservative views, leaders of these right-wing coalitions believe that God ordained government to protect a nation through strong defense and to enforce fundamental laws, but they do not think that the government should regulate the economy, intervene in the parental responsibility for educating children, or help people who can help themselves. They decry the tremendous growth of federal agencies and the incredible increase in the scope of government control that began during the New Deal administration of Franklin Roosevelt....

Finally, these groups believe that Christians have a God-given responsibility to be politically active. In fact, Jerry Falwell has said that the job of a pastor is to save souls, baptize, and get people registered to vote. Failure to register is a sin. If Christians do not act to throw out of office those officials who perpetuate an unchristian, liberal program, the U.S. will crumble and the cause of God's Kingdom will be frustrated....

The core propositions shared by these leaders translate into specific positions on issues, and the groups have made their program abundantly clear. Concerning family issues, they fervently oppose abortion, seek a constitutional amendment to prohibit it and laud the recent Supreme Court decision that government has no obligation to pay for the abortions of women on welfare. They oppose homosexuality and contend that homosexuals should not have the same vocational and housing opportunities that others have. They strongly oppose movements for women's and children's rights. For example, they oppose the Equal Rights Amendment, insisting that it would take mothers out of their homes; they oppose government child-care programs for similar reasons. Concerning education, they are adamant in the belief that parents rather than the government should be in control. They oppose government regulation of private schools, and they would prefer to have the federal government get out of education entirely. They also believe that prayer and Bible reading should be restored in all schools, by law if necessary. They opposed the creation of the new Department of Education on the grounds that it was an attempt to increase government control.

In the area of foreign policy, the groups call for increased military spending to ensure that the U.S. will be militarily superior. They believe that the use of force may be necessary to stop the inevitable communist aggression and that the U.S. must remain loyal to those countries that have sided with it against communism (e.g., Taiwan). . . . we have several serious disagreements with these groups. The first has to do with their explicit link with ideological conservatism and the implicit suggestion that this ideology is more attuned than is liberalism to the principles found in the Bible. The idea that the principles of God's revelation can be neatly subsumed under the rubric of a humanly devised ideology is pretentious. Any full examination of biblical standards will disclose a subtle blend of "conservatism" and "liberalism." The Bible is full of passages mandating a concern for the poor—a focus too often lacking in laissez-faire conservative circles. The Bible does not see government as the satanic evil which the conservatives decry; rather, the government is a divinely ordained instrument.

The point here is not that liberalism is closer to the Bible than conservatism but that we are using the wrong level of analysis when we seek to portray either ideology as more Christian. God's will is not subordinate to ideological predispositions; it supersedes them.

Furthermore, there is evidence that these new groups take an inconsistent view of the role of government. In short, they do not want government intervention when their own freedoms are at stake, but they are willing to use the power of the government to force life-style changes on others. If it is not right to use the government to force one group to tolerate the life style of others, then it is equally wrong to use the government to compel the second group to tolerate the life style of the first. . . .

The issue is not simply the contrasting perspectives of Christians but the claim by these groups that they have the correct, biblical answer and that those who disagree with them are not fit to hold public office because of their immorality. . . . Every group of Christians, not only the conservative ones discussed here, must refrain from the arrogance of presumed omniscience and must adopt an attitude of humility befitting our sinful nature.

Next, the claim that the United States is *the* instrument to accomplish the will of God is suspect. There is no doubt that God could use, and probably is using, this nation for his purposes, but the claim of these groups carries with it a historical and cultural relativism that seeks to interpret God's plan within a framework of flag-waving nationalism. Their claim further excludes God's use of other countries with strong Judeo-Christian foundations or other religious tenets and ignores the possibility that even "godless" nations are instruments which God can use.

Finally, there is a danger in efforts to use ministers in their pulpits to proclaim the politically conservative gospel. Preaching of the Word, not political mobilization or indoctrination, is the central responsibility of pastors. This statement is not meant to deny pastors a political role or to suggest that their sermons must avoid any consideration of political issues or responsibilities, but it must be stressed that political persuasion is not the first obligation of ministers. There is an additional danger: preaching a political gospel may cause or aggravate splits within churches or denominations and thus hinder the effective proclamation of the gospel of salvation in Christ.

[From *Christian Century*, October 8, 1980.]

## Document 2. Politically Conservative Analysis of the Moral Majority

Joseph Sobran, a columnist for the National Review, offers a positive assessment of Jerry Falwell and the fundamentalist movement in the following selection.

Lately there has been a lot of talk, mostly by worried liberals, about "the electronic church." TV preachers are nothing new: Billy Graham, Herbert W. Armstrong, Oral Roberts, Reverend Ike, and of course Bishop Sheen have long made profitable use of the medium. What worries the liberals, I suspect, is that the evangelicals are now learning to use the mass media to attain political goals.

Regularly cited as among the most sinister of the new TV evangelists is Jerry Falwell, whose conservatism makes no apologies. If he demanded the nationalization of giant oil companies, Falwell would be hailed as an activist who brought social conscience to religion. But what Falwell demands is very different. He demands the preservation of the family—against the attack of government and commercial forces. Hence he is deplored as a threat to the separation of church and state.

I have twice tuned in on this sinister being, who it transpires is about as menacing as the corner grocer.

His method is not to harangue, but to marshall witnesses: in the course of an hour he may show you a documentary film, a U.S. senator, a Christian psychologist, and a kind of chorus line of devout parents with their children, all modestly dressed, perfectly groomed, courteously behaved. Soloists and choirs sing hymns. Falwell seems as much a religious Lawrence Welk as a preacher. What you see is the community he heads, the kind of people he represents, not just himself. It's an epitome and maybe a portent.

Falwell is a sign of the times. Traditionally these people may have been more or less conservative in their politics, but they have carefully kept politics and religion separate. They have, reluctantly, changed. Why?

My guess is that now, for the first time, they feel that politics itself has come to impinge on the sacred. Honest graft they can tolerate. War on morality, on the structure of the family itself, is another matter. They would leave politics alone if they felt it was leaving them alone; but they see that it isn't.

Falwell speaks firmly, calmly, with a glint of humor, about the current tendency of government to foster and accelerate bad trends: promiscuity, divorce, homosexuality, and abortion. Despite liberal propaganda on the subject, I have never heard a Catholic clergyman—not in my church, at any rate—speak as forthrightly against abortion as Falwell does. Though I agree with him, I found myself reacting with shock, as to indelicacy, when he discussed the matter in church. It was not his fault but my custom that caused this reaction. (Gay rights? "The Bible says God created Adam and Eve, not Adam and Steve.")

[From *National Review,* July 27, 1980.]

## Document 3. Barry Goldwater's Opinion of the Moral Majority and Politics

Barry Goldwater, the conservative Republican senator and the presidential nominee in 1964, offered his own evaluation of the Moral Majority and the New Right in a 1981 discussion with journalists. It was reported in *Time*.

"I don't like what they're doing," he said. "I don't think what they're talking about is conservatism."

Goldwater accused the Moral Majority and its kind of giving conservatism a bad name. "The religious issues of these groups [abortion, school prayer] have little or nothing to do with conservative or liberal politics," he said. "They are diverting us away from the vital issues that our Government needs to address," such as "national security and economic survival." To drag theological questions into public debate, in Goldwater's view, is dangerously un-American. Said he: "One of the great strengths of our political system always has been our tendency to keep religious issues in the background."

Goldwater said he finds the New Right's righteousness especially distasteful, even though he admits he shares many of their moral views. "The uncompromising position of these groups is a divisive element that could tear apart the very spirit of our representative system. I am warning them today: I will fight them every step of the way if they try to dictate their moral convictions to all Americans in the name of conservatism." Said Goldwater: "I'm frankly sick and tired of the political preachers across this country telling me as a citizen that if I want to be a moral person I must believe in A, B, C and D. Just who do they think they are?"

[From *Time,* September 28, 1981.]

## Questions for Reflection

What has been the role of the church and ministers in U.S. politics, and what is it today? How important are moral questions in politics? Why are moral issues more important at some times than others? How successful has the fundamentalist Christian movement been in achieving its goals? What is your opinion of the Moral Majority?

## ANSWERS TO MULTIPLE-CHOICE AND TRUE-FALSE QUESTIONS

### Multiple-Choice Questions

1-C, 2-A, 3-D, 4-B, 5-B, 6-D, 7-D, 8-D

### True-False Questions

1-T, 2-T, 3-F, 4-F, 5-F, 6-F, 7-F, 8-F

# 36

## CULTURAL POLITICS

## CHAPTER OBJECTIVES

1. Assess the role and influence of conservative Christians in recent politics.
2. Understand the demographic changes revealed by the 1990 census.
3. Understand the issues in, and the outcome of, the 1992 election.
4. Describe Bill Clinton's domestic policies and their fates.
5. Explain how Clinton's foreign policies resembled and differed from those of George Bush.
6. Explain the new immigration to the United States and how it has affected American society.

## CHAPTER OUTLINE

I. Cultural conservatism
   A. Basic positions
      1. For decency and propriety
      2. Opposed to affirmative action
   B. Religious right
      1. Moral Majority
      2. Christian Coalition
      3. Republican party
II. United States in 1990
   A. Demographic changes
      1. Aging population
         a. Baby-boom generation
         b. Elderly
      2. Shift to South and West
      3. Metropolitan growth
      4. Working women
      5. Decline of family unit
      6. African-American poverty
   B. New immigrants
      1. Legal and illegal immigrants
      2. Visa lottery
      3. Non-Europeans
      4. Ethnic enclaves
      5. Effects
         1. Cultural pluralism
         2. Nativism and ethnic strife
III. Bush to Clinton
   A. Background to 1992 election
      1. Disruptions in foreign policy
         a. Gulf War
         b. Collapse of the Soviet Union
      2. Economic problems
         a. Unemployment
            i. Increasing joblessness
            ii. Layoffs of White-collar workers
         b. Low investment
         c. Declining standard of living
      3. Nomination of Clarence Thomas
         a. Charges of Anita Hill
         b. Senate hearings
         c. Gender gap
   B. Republican problems

307

        1. Tax increases
        2. Christian Right and divisions
    C. Election of 1992
        1. Background of Bill Clinton
        2. The economy
        3. H. Ross Perot
        4. Results
IV. Clinton administration
    A. Start-up problems
        1. Abortion
        2. Gays in the military
        3. Attorney general nominees
        4. Raid at Waco and militia movement
    B. Domestic initiatives
        1. Economic stimulus package
            a. Republican filibuster
            b. Defeat
        2. Deficit reduction
        3. NAFTA
            a. Perot opposition
            b. GOP support
            c. Passage
        4. Health care
            a. Earlier plans
            b. Clinton's plan
                i. Universal coverage
                ii. Alliances
                iii. Subsidies
            c. Alternative plans
            d. Clinton's plan doomed
        5. Other programs
            a. National service
            b. Family Leave Act
            c. Brady Bill
            d. "Motor-voter law"
            e. "Reinventing government"
            f. Education
            g. Crime bill
    C. Whitewater controversy
    D. Foreign affairs
        1. Low priority
        2. Continuation of Bush's policies
            a. support for Yeltsin
            b. Arab-Israeli negotiations
            c. Intervention in Somalia
        3. Agony over Yugoslavia
        4. Haiti
            a. Return of Aristide
            b. Refugees
            c. U.S. forces
    E. Midterm elections
        1. Republican sweep
        2. Repudiation of Clinton
        3. Newt Gingrich as Speaker
        4. Power of the Christian Coalition
    F. Judicial conservatism
        1. New 5–4 majority
        2. Skepticism about race-based policies
    G. Contract with America
        1. Ten initiatives
        2. Stalemate

## KEY ITEMS OF CHRONOLOGY

| | |
|---|---|
| End of the Soviet Union | December 25, 1991 |
| Clarence Thomas–Anita Hill controversy | 1991 |
| Inauguration of Bill Clinton | January 20, 1993 |
| Family Leave Act | February 1993 |
| Siege of Branch Dividians in Waco, Texas | February–April 1993 |
| Israel-PLO agreement | September 13, 1993 |
| Clinton presents health care plan | September 22, 1993 |
| NAFTA passed by Congress | November 1993 |
| Troops land in Haiti | September 19, 1994 |
| Republican landslide | November 1994 |
| Republicans control Congress | January 1995– |

CULTURAL POLITICS 309

## TERMS TO MASTER

*Listed below are some important terms or people with which you should be familiar after you complete the study of this chapter. Identify each name or term.*

1. Christian Coalition
2. "great compression"
3. Clarence Thomas
4. "Read my lips: no new taxes!"
5. H. Ross Perot
6. Family Leave Act
7. David Koresh
8. NAFTA
9. "motor-voter law"
10. Whitewater scandal
11. Tiananmen Square
12. Somalia
13. Jean-Bertrand Aristide
14. Newton Leroy Gingrich
15. affirmative action
16. Sunbelt
17. Proposition 187
18. *E pluribus unum*
19. cultural pluralism

## VOCABULARY BUILDING

*Listed below are some words used in this chapter. Look in the dictionary for the meaning of each.*

1. coalesce
2. propriety
3. defunct
4. prescient
5. fabricate
6. adhesive
7. strident
8. veneer
9. pander
10. apocalyptic
11. polygamist
12. foment
13. reciprocal
14. indigent
15. paradigm
16. dog (v.)
17. intermediary
18. fractious
19. cuisine
20. savvy

## EXERCISES FOR UNDERSTANDING

*When you have completed the reading of the chapter, answer each of the following questions. If you have difficulty, go back and reread the section of the chapter related to the question.*

### Multiple-Choice Questions

*Select the letter of the response that best completes the statement.*

1. To transform its ideas into public policy, the Christian Coalition supported
    A. the Democrats.
    B. H. Ross Perot.
    C. the Republicans.
    D. Jerry Falwell.

2. Clarence Thomas's confirmation hearings involved
    A. charges of sexual harassment.
    B. allegations about his involvement in Whitewater.
    C. concerns about his radical civil rights work in the 1960s.
    D. all of the above.

3. "Read my lips: no new taxes!" said
    A. George Bush.
    B. Bill Clinton.
    C. Newt Gingrich.
    D. H. Ross Perot.

4. The Branch Davidians were an example of
    A. the Christian Coalition.
    B. the Moral Majority.
    C. the militia movement.
    D. what happened after the enactment of NAFTA.

5. In 1995 President Clinton dispatched 20,000 troops to maintain peace in
    A. Somalia.
    B. Israel.
    C. the former Soviet Union.
    D. Yugoslavia.

6. In the 1990s, the Supreme Court
    A. became more liberal.
    B. endorsed affirmative action programs.

C. questioned race-based policies.
D. outlawed abortions.

7. The 1990 census did *not* show that
   A. the Sunbelt was continuing to grow.
   B. incomes had become significantly more equal.
   C. 40 percent of adult African-American males were illiterate.
   D. the fastest growing age groups were the older ones.

8. The fastest-growing segment of the U.S. population in the 1980s and 1990s was
   A. Hispanic-Americans.
   B. Asian-Americans.
   C. African-Americans.
   D. Native Americans.

**True-False Questions**

*Indicate whether each statement is true or false.*

1. Bill Clinton received the support of cultural conservatives in 1992.
2. The "great compression" involved a shrinking work force.
3. George Bush and the Republicans opposed the North American Free Trade Agreement.
4. Bill Clinton's legislative achievements in his first year included the "motor-voter law."
5. The Clinton administration supported Jean-Bertrand Aristide in Haiti.
6. Republicans gained control of Congress in the 1992 elections.
7. By 1990 a majority of Americans lived in cities of at least one million people.
8. The national motto (*E pluribus unum*) means "one out of many."

**Essay Questions**

1. What factors led to George Bush's defeat in 1992?
2. What effects have conservative Christians had in recent politics?
3. Compare Bill Clinton's foreign policy to that of George Bush.
4. What changes in the American population did the 1990 census reveal? How important were the changes?
5. How can the nation reconcile cultural pluralism and ethnic diversity with a national unity without ethnic conflict?

**DOCUMENT**

**Proposition 187**

In a statewide referendum in November 1994, California voters approved Proposition 187 by a 3 to 2 majority.

> Section 1. Findings and Declaration.
> The People of California find and declare as follows: That they have suffered and are suffering economic hardship caused by the presence of illegal aliens in this State.
> That they have suffered and are suffering personal injury and damage caused by the criminal conduct of illegal aliens in this state.
> That they have a right to the protection of their government from any person or persons entering this country unlawfully.
> Therefore, the People of California declare their intention to provide for cooperation between their agencies of state and local government with the federal government, and to establish a system of required notification by and between such agencies to prevent illegal aliens in

the United States from receiving benefits or public services in the State of California.

Section 2. Manufacture, Distribution or Sale of False Citizenship or Resident Alien Document: Crime and Punishment.

Any person who manufactures, distributes or sells false documents to conceal the true citizenship or resident alien status of another person is guilty of a felony, and shall be punished by imprisonment in the state prison for five years or by a fine of seventy-five thousand dollars ($75,000).

Section 3. Use of False Citizenship or Resident Alien Documents: Crime and Punishment.

Any person who uses false documents to conceal his or her true citizenship or resident alien status is guilty of a felony, and shall be punished by imprisonment in the state prison for five years or by a fine of twenty-five thousand dollars ($25,000). . . .

Section 5. Exclusion of Illegal Aliens from Public School Services. . . .

(b) A person shall not receive any public social services to which he or she may be otherwise entitled until the legal status of that person has been verified as one of the following:

(1) A citizen of the United States.

(2) An alien lawfully admitted as a permanent resident.

(3) An alien lawfully admitted for a temporary period of time. . . .

Section 6. Exclusion of Illegal Aliens from Publicly Funded Health Care. . . .

(b) A person shall not receive any health care services from a publicly funded health care facility, to which he or she is otherwise entitled until the legal status of that person has been verified as one of the following:

(1) A citizen of the United States.

(2) An alien lawfully admitted as a permanent resident.

(3) An alien lawfully admitted for a temporary period of time. . . .

Section 7. Exclusion of Illegal Aliens from Public Elementary and Secondary Schools.

(a) No public elementary or secondary school shall admit, or permit the attendance of, any child who is not a citizen of the United States, an alien lawfully admitted as a permanent resident, or a person who is otherwise authorized under federal law to be present in the United States.

(b) Commencing January 1, 1995, each school district shall verify the legal status of each child enrolling in the school district for the first time in order to ensure the enrollment or attendance only of citizens, aliens lawfully admitted as permanent residents, or persons who are otherwise authorized to be present in the United States. . . .

(f) For each child who cannot establish legal status in the United States, each school district shall continue to provide education for a period of ninety days from the date of the notice [of violation of the law]. Such ninety day period shall be utilized to accomplish an orderly transition to a school in the child's country of origin. Each school district shall fully cooperate in this transition effort to ensure that the educational needs of the child are best served for that period of time.

Section 8. Exclusion of Illegal Aliens from Public Postsecondary Educational Institutions.

(a) No public institution of postsecondary education shall admit, enroll, or permit the attendance of any person who is not a citizen of the United States, an alien lawfully admitted as a permanent resident in the United States, or a person who is otherwise authorized under federal law to be present in the United States.

(b) Commencing with the first term or semester that begins after January 1, 1995, and at the commencement of each term or semester thereafter, each public postsecondary educational institution shall verify the status of each person enrolled or in attendance at that institution in order to ensure the enrollment or attendance only of United States citizens, aliens lawfully admitted as permanent residents in the United States, and persons who are otherwise authorized under federal law to be present in the United States. . . .

[From *California State Documents*, 1994.]

## Questions for Reflection

What are the arguments for and against Proposition 187? Why was it proposed in 1994 and not earlier? How does Proposition 187 fit traditional U.S. values? What effects could Proposition 187 have on illegal aliens in California? Is a similar law possible in your state? Would you support or oppose such an initiative?

## ANSWERS TO MULTIPLE-CHOICE AND TRUE-FALSE QUESTIONS

### Multiple-Choice Questions

1-C, 2-A, 3-A, 4-C, 5-D, 6-C, 7-B, 8-B

### True-False Questions

1-F, 2-T, 3-F, 4-T, 5-T, 6-F, 7-T, 8-T